Counselling and Therapy
with Refugees
and Victims of Trauma

Second Edition

Counselling and Therapy with Refugees and Victims of Trauma

Psychological Problems of Victims of War, Torture and Repression

Second Edition

Guus van der Veer

JOHN WILEY & SONS
Chichester · New York · Weinheim · Brisbane · Singapore · Toronto

Other Wiley Editorial Offices

John Wiley & Sons, Inc., 605 Third Avenue, New York, NY 10158–0012, USA

WILEY-VCH Verlag GmbH, Pappelallee 3, D-69469 Weinheim, Germany

Jacaranda Wiley Ltd, 33 Park Road, Milton, Queensland 4064, Australia

John Wiley & Sons (Asia) Pte Ltd, 2 Clementi Loop #02-01, Jin Xing Distripark, Singapore 129809

John Wiley & Sons (Canada) Ltd, 22 Worcester Road, Rexdale, Ontario M9W 1L1, Canada

Library of Congress Cataloging-in-Publication Data

Veer, Guus van der.
    Counselling and therapy with refugees and victims of trauma :
  psychological problems of victims of war, torture, and repression /
  Guus van der Veer. — 2nd ed.
        p.   cm.
    Rev. ed. of: Counselling and therapy with refugees / Guus van der
  Veer. 1992.
    Includes bibliographical references and index.
    ISBN 0–471–98226–1 (cased). — ISBN 0–471–98227–X (pbk.)
    1. Refugees, Political—Mental health. 2. Refugees, Political—
  –Counselling of. 3. Post-traumatic stress disorder—Treatment.
  I. Veer, Guus van der. Counselling and therapy with refugees.
  II. title.
  RC451.4.P57V44 1998
  6166.89'14'08694—dc21   97–45611
                                                             CIP

British Library Cataloguing in Publication Data

A catalogue record for this book is available from the British Library

ISBN 0-471-98226-1
ISBN 0-471-98227-X
Typeset in 10/12pt Meridien from the author's disks by Saxon Graphics Ltd, Derby
Printed and bound in Great Britain by Biddles Ltd, Guildford and King's Lynn
This book is printed on acid-free paper responsibly manufactured from sustainable forestry, in which at least two trees are planted for each one used in paper production

Contents

About the author

Dr Guus van der Veer, a psychologist, works as a transcultural psychothera-pist for the Pharos Foundation for Refugee Health Care in Amsterdam, The Netherlands. As a Mental Health Consultant he presents training courses for counsellors in areas of armed conflict, such as Bosnia, Cambodia and Sri Lanka.

Preface

The number of refugees and displaced persons worldwide has increased drastically in the last few years. As a result the number of people who are confronted with refugees' mental problems has grown. These mental problems may, for example, be manifested during contacts with social workers, therapists, lawyers or government officials.

Many of those who are professionally involved with refugees and victims of trauma are not fully aware of the nature and background of their mental problems, and they usually do not have the time or the opportunity to acquire a deeper understanding. These problems may lead to exasperation and suspicion on the part of officials who are involved both in providing assistance and in exercising control. In the case of professional therapists and social workers and volunteers, this may not only result in irritation but also in feelings of helplessness and disappointment, because their tried and tested methods often do not have the expected outcome. The intensity of these negative sentiments is related to the inability to empathize with refugees and victims of trauma.

Empathy requires expertise and knowledge. In this study the available scientific literature on the psychological consequences of torture, terror, battlefield experience, disappearance of relatives and exile is reviewed. This scientific information has been related to the experiences acquired by psychologists and psychiatrists in the provision of assistance to victims and their relatives. Practical examples are not, however, presented to prove the theory, but rather to illustrate the theoretical concepts and related mode of thought. In these examples personal details have been excluded or altered to prevent identification.

The book is meant to help professionals, particularly those in the mental health sector. But it also provides information which can be of use to government officials, lawyers, interpreters and volunteers who are involved with refugees and other victims of trauma.

In order to make this book accessible to people with little knowledge of psychology, some basic concepts from various psychological theories relevant to the understanding of mental problems in general will be discussed. While these concepts are familiar to most psychologists, they will be explained and related to the specific experiences of refugees on a level that can also be understood by an educated lay audience.

Such frequently occurring terms as refugee, social worker, therapist, client generally refer to both men and women.

Introduction

This study is about refugees and victims of trauma who, as individuals or in small groups, came to live in the West, far from their native country. The term refugee refers to people who have had to leave the country in which they lived because of violence and repression by the authorities, or by violent groups operating under the protection of the authorities, or other militant groups.

Among refugees are people who were politically active and who, as a result of activities ranging from armed struggle against dictatorship to shouting slogans at a demonstration, were persecuted. But also less active people, such as draft dodgers and deserters who refused to participate in what they saw as a cruel and meaningless war, have become refugees. And so have people who were persecuted for other reasons: because they belonged to a certain ethnic group, like the Tamils in Sri Lanka or the Kurds in Turkey, or because they were known to have certain political, religious or cultural tastes; for example monarchists, Baha'is, or fans of Western pop music in Iran. The same can be said about people who were considered deviant in some way, for example because of a homosexual preference. These people have in common that the state in their native country considers them to be dangerous or without rights. In this study, the term refugee also refers to those who had to flee their country because they accidentally became the victim of state repression.

Finally, there are also the relatives who accompanied the refugees as defined above. They have often suffered under the tensions caused by the political activities of their relative or his experience of repression, and have sometimes themselves become victims of reprisals. Therefore they also are considered to be refugees.

The term refugee can refer to people of different ages, with different personal histories and from different ethnic and cultural backgrounds. Not all of them have the same legal status: some have become citizens of the country of exile, others don't have a residence permit and live in fear of being repatriated. Moreover, refugees differ with respect to their ability to cope with traumatic experiences and the capacities they have for dealing with new stressful experiences and adapting to new circumstances in the country of exile.

The abovementioned differences are reflected in the behaviour of refugees in everyday situations, in their attitudes to the professionals and volunteers who try to help them, in the content of the problems for which they seek assistance, in the way they think about the nature of their problems and have tried to cope with them themselves. These differences force us to be very careful when generalizing about refugees and their problems, whether from scientific research, or from clinical experience. Such generalizations can never do justice to the complexity of individual cases, and in making them in this study only a rough sketch is drawn, in order to reduce a very complex reality to less complex abstract statements. This can be done in different ways, depending on the psychological theory one has in mind while attempting to sum up what many refugees have in common.

In this study some generalizations will be presented about refugees and their psychological problems on different levels of analysis and from various theoretical perspectives. It starts on the level of common sense: in Chapter 1 the particular experiences of refugees are discussed, and examples are given of the various subjective meanings these experiences can have for the individual refugee who seeks assistance.

Chapter 2 is about what psychological theories can contribute to understanding the problems of refugees. It contains descriptions based on the conceptual frameworks provided by various theoretical approaches to psychological problems and disturbances that are currently accepted by professionals who provide assistance to refugees, and which present useful points of departure for counselling and therapy.

It is of course impossible to do justice to all the theoretical approaches that might be relevant for understanding the problems of refugees; that would require the writing of a massive encyclopaedic overview of the whole field of psychology and psychiatry. Not many social workers, psychologists and psychiatrists working with refugees would find the time to read it. This study is not meant to be complete, but to provide a didactic approach which introduces a scientific way of thinking about the problems of refugees and shows the practitioner some examples of the many ways in which theoretical knowledge can inspire clinical work: by offering different sets of spectacles through which he can look at the problems of refugees. In Chapter 3, the diagnostic appraisal of the problems of refugees is discussed in relation to the six approaches which have been outlined.

Working with refugees often means that the helping professional or volunteer must overcome language problems and become familiar with, or adapt to, cultural differences. This topic is discussed in Chapter 4. This chapter is meant to sensitize professionals to the problems of working with clients from different cultures. It is not a complete review of all available knowledge on working with specific cultural groups, but deals with issues common to working with people from divergent cultural backgrounds.

After this, the establishment of a therapeutic relationship and the various objectives of the use of psychotherapeutic techniques with refugees are discussed (Chapter 5). Chapter 6 is devoted to therapeutic techniques aimed at dealing with crises and symptoms. Therapeutic techniques aimed at restoring emotional stability are discussed in Chapter 7, along with some remarks about improvisation and guidelines for choosing therapeutic techniques.

The next chapters are devoted to two special groups: victims of sexual violence (Chapter 8) and refugee children and adolescents (Chapter 9). The book is concluded by a chapter on specific issues in working with refugees such as counter-transference and vicarious traumatization (Chapter 10).

CHAPTER 1

The Experiences of Refugees

A First Glance

Refugees have in common that they have suffered from the abuse of power either by the authorities of totalitarian regimes or by armed militant groups. They have often undergone various hardships before and during their flight. Many have been imprisoned, maltreated during arrest or tortured during detention. Some have experienced situations in which death and violence were the order of the day. At a first glance, the following kinds of experiences can be distinguished.

Political Repression

The person who decides to flee does not usually do so on a momentary impulse. His decision is nearly always preceded by an extended period in which he is increasingly exposed to repression by the regime. This repression may include limits to the freedom of speech or education and intimidation by the police, the army or para-military groups of anyone who is criticizing the government or belongs to a particular minority. Such experiences may have caused a great deal of fear and tension which it was difficult to cope with.

Detention

Many refugees have been arrested or abducted by police, military or members of other armed groups in their native country. The experience of detention often included that the refugee was subjected to violence, that he was threatened, was for some time isolated from his family and friends, missed important happenings or ceremonies (e.g. the wedding of a brother, the birth of a child, the death of a parent) and was temporarily unable to take care of his normal responsibilities (such as earning money to support his family, or looking after the children). In many cases, being arrested came as an unexpected shock, and the experiences during detention often made the refugee lose his last illusions about the possibilities for political progress in his country, and about his own capacities to cope with the current political situation.

Torture

Detention sometimes includes torture. The term torture refers to violence directed against the physical and mental integrity of the individual. This involves extended and repeated physical and psychological torment which is aimed at persuading the detainee to provide the authorities with information which will incriminate himself or others, or at intimidating him and his social environment to such an extent that he will renounce further political activity. The aim is also to humiliate the victim and to deprive him of his self-confidence, his sense of identity, his willpower and his affect, thus reducing him to a numbed and helpless being (Santini, 1987).

Torture takes place in a situation in which the victim is helpless and totally at the mercy of his torturers. Generally speaking, torture forms a part of a systematic policy which is directed at intimidating or destabilizing certain communities or ethnic groups. The physical torture undergone by the refugees to whom the author attended involved the conscious and premeditated application of various forms of torment which cause pain and/or physical damage. This was often accompanied by the threat that the physical damage would be permanent. Physical torment included hitting, kicking, burning with cigarettes, cigars, cigarette lighters or other hot objects; stabbing with knives and other sharp objects, the administration of electric shocks; holding the victim's head under water (which was often polluted with urine and faeces); hanging the victim up by the wrists or feet or both at the same time; making him stand, do tiring exercises or adopt uncomfortable positions for long periods; exposing him to cold, heat, strong sun or very intense artificial light; administering chilli pepper to open wounds; failing to treat wounds caused by previous torture; the forced administration of psychotropic drugs by doctors who participated in the torture.

Psychological torture can be defined as the creation of situations or conditions which are meant to evoke emotions which are difficult to cope with. For example, the refugees to whom the author attended mentioned the following forms: imprisonment for an extended period of time without the possibility of contacting family or friends; long-term solitary confinement; sensory deprivation (Daly, 1985); having to listen to the screams of fellow prisoners who were being tortured; deprivation of sleep; having to witness friends, relatives or fellow prisoners being threatened, executed or tortured; being forced to eat excrement, to abuse or execute a fellow prisoner, or to do things which the victim considered 'strange' or immoral; sham executions; sexual violence.

Sexual violence is, of course, also a form of physical torture, but the psychological consequences are at least as drastic as the physical effects. The refugees to whom the author attended mentioned the following varieties: being insulted and humiliated by sexist remarks; being touched in indecent ways; being forced to undress in front of guards; being forced to watch or take part in sexual activities, with guards or with fellow prisoners, either hetero-sexual or homosexual; rape; mutilation of the sexual organs. Sexual torture is often accompanied by the threat that the victim's sexual functioning will be permanently impaired.

Other Kinds of Violence

The other kinds of violence refugees report can, from a psychological perspec-tive, be divided into two kinds. The first involves being subjected to *terror*, which is the systematic use of violence against specific local communities (a village, a neighbourhood), or ethnic groups (Tamils, Kurds). For the victims it is quite clear that they are victims and not perpetrators. They have not per-sonally used violence, or have only used it if they considered it necessary for self-defence. Terror includes the killing of unarmed civilians, public display of the dead and mutilated bodies to serve as a 'warning', abduction of relatives or members of the immediate family of politically active persons (for further examples, see University Teachers for Human Rights, 1989).

The second kind of violence will be referred to as *combat experiences* or *bat-tlefield experiences*. Some refugees were confronted with bloody violence when they were guerrillas or soldiers. These people feel that they have been afflicted by the violence because, for example, they have seen their friends die. Sometimes they feel that they are partly responsible for unjustified violence, or guilty of atrocities. Some refugees with combat experiences have become addicted to drugs which were forced on them by army doctors or command-ing officers.

The Disappearance of Relatives

Some refugees have relatives who disappeared several years ago. In general there are two causes for a relative to disappear: contact with the relative was lost in the confusion of a civil war, or the relative was arrested, detained in an unknown location, and probably killed. The refugees who have a 'missing' rel-ative do not know whether he is still alive or how he might have died. This situation causes many uncertainties.

Research has shown that refugees who have a 'missing' relative have more mental problems than other refugees (Allodi & Rojas, 1985). Years of uncer-tainty as to the fate of the missing person cause inner problems which cannot easily be solved.

Separation and Loss

All refugees have been separated from friends and loved ones. They had to leave familiar surroundings and pets behind and lost many of their material belongings.

Hardships

Refugees have often undergone various hardships before or during their flight. This also applies to those for whom the last leg of the journey was relatively comfortable, for example an aeroplane flight. Many refugees have suffered hunger for an extended period, or have been exposed to extreme temperatures. Others have not had a normal social life for a long time, because they were imprisoned or in hiding. They were separated from family and friends, unable to receive education and in a constant state of fear. By the same token, children and adolescent refugees often have experienced pedagogical neglect.

Exile

Life in exile entails all kinds of adjustment problems. Those seeking political asylum experience a long period of uncertainty in which they are not sure whether or not they will be accepted as refugees. During exile refugees generally continue feeling involved in what is happening in their native country, and if they receive bad news it may affect their psychological well-being. Various feelings, sometimes contradictory, related to the possibility of returning 'home' also play an important role in everyday life (Santini, 1986a) and may generate personal problems.

Traumatization and Uprooting

The terms traumatization and uprooting will be used to summarize the experiences of refugees with repression, torture and other kinds of violence, separation and loss, hardships and exile. Traumatization refers to extreme, painful experiences which are so difficult to cope with that they are likely to result in psychological dysfunction both in the short and in the long term. Uprooting refers to the experience of being forced to leave one's familiar surroundings and to settle in a new and unfamiliar environment for an indefinite period, which brings stress and can cause various long-lasting adjustment problems. Many refugees experience both traumatization and uprooting.

They share the experience of traumatization with other groups, such as war-victims, veterans and some victims of natural disasters and violent crime, and other calamities. They share the experience of uprooting with some emigrants who left their country for economic reasons. Therefore information gathered in studies of such groups may help with understanding the problems of refugees. But in making use of this kind of knowledge it is necessary to keep in mind the fundamental differences between refugees and the other groups.

Refugees and emigrants have in common that they have to adapt to a culture they experience as strange and sometimes hostile, and they may have ambivalent feelings both towards their original cultural background and their present environment. But the mere fact that emigrants had at least some freedom of choice when they left their country, while refugees generally felt forced to leave without much time for preparation, can make a lot of difference. The feeling of having been forced to leave familiar surroundings does not enhance adaptation to a new environment and new customs, whereas the ambition of an emigrant who wants to make it in the West, can certainly be adaptive.

Refugees also differ from people who were traumatized by natural disasters. The process of overcoming a man-made disaster is different because the victim has to come to terms with the fact that human beings caused and organized his suffering. Refugees certainly have something in common with the victims of violent crime. But the fact that the crimes of which they were the victim were justified by the authorities and sometimes by the clergy, and also were not effectively opposed by large groups of their compatriots, makes a psychological difference.

Refugees have sometimes had combat experiences. But the exact content of these experiences may be very different to that which is found in the literature on Vietnam veterans or Israeli soldiers, due to the specific circumstances on the battlefield.

Scientific evidence on, and practical experience with groups of people who have something in common with refugees can draw our attention to interesting details, but it may also blur our vision, and we must be careful in the way we utilize it.

Not All Refugees Seek Help

Most refugees don't need help because of psychological problems (Boekhoorn, 1987). What accounts for the resilience of the majority of refugees? What is the difference between those who request assistance because they are haunted by the memory of traumatic experiences and those who do not? And what is the difference between those who adapt to the situation in exile and those who do not? These are intriguing questions, to which several—speculative—answers can be given.

Differences in Vulnerability

When large groups of people experience comparable traumatic events, there appear to be striking differences in the immediate psychological reactions of individuals. Tyhurst (1951) described three reaction patterns.

1. Disturbed behaviour, such as confused or disoriented reactions, or being paralysed by fear (10–25% of the victims)
2. Stunning and bewilderment (about 75%). The victims' awareness of what is happening is restricted, they are not fully conscious of their emotions, but manifest a physiological fear reaction.

3. Controlled behaviour, aimed at restricting the consequences of the trauma (10–25% of the victims). These victims are able to retain their awareness and react adequately.

These difference are ascribed to differences in vulnerability, related to personality factors such as the capacity to endure fear and control one's behaviour under difficult circumstances. Vulnerability to traumatic experiences seems to be dependent on a large variety of variables (cf. Van der Kolk, 1988). It may be assumed that its distribution follows a normal probability curve (Op den Velde, 1989).

Of course, the use of terms such as sensitivity or vulnerability does not explain which psychological or other mechanisms are responsible for individual differences in reaction to traumatic experiences.

Protective Factors

The fact that people generally show enormous differences in their reaction to stressful events and deprivation has become a popular topic for discussion in developmental psychology. The adaptive reactions of children to stress are thought to be related to *coping skills*, which in their turn are seen as the result of a balance between more or less permanent *stress factors* and *protective factors* (Garmezy, 1985; De Wit, 1987).

The term stress factor (or risk factor) is commonly used to refer to factors such as traumatization in early childhood, marital conflicts between parents, delinquency or mental disorder in one of the parents, and the like. These factors are thought to interfere with normal personality development, and may also make the individual more vulnerable to traumatic experiences. In a retrospective investigation, Davidson *et al.* (1985) have shown that 66% of the people in their sample who were suffering from a mental disorder after a traumatic experience came from a family in which one of the members had a mental disorder.

The term protective factors can refer to individual characteristics observable from early childhood, such as activity, social responsiveness, intelligence and quick recovery from illness, and which can be considered congenital. It may also refer to capabilities like the ability to emotionally distance oneself from traumatic memories, the ability to assimilate the knowledge that one has survived traumatic circumstances and to transform this knowledge into a feeling of inner strength, and the ability to find meaning in one's life (cf. Helmreich, 1992). Another group of protective factors is related to favourable family conditions, such as the availability of at least one competent adult, opportunity for autonomous behaviour, and the absence of disrupting conflicts. A third group consists of conditions outside the family, a supportive school environment, for instance. Some authors subsume both family conditions and protective factors outside the family under the single heading *social support* (Oei, 1987; Parry & Shapiro, 1986). However, some *material* conditions, whether inside or outside the family, may be more protective than others.

Finally, the term protective factor may be used for individual characteristics resulting from a process of personality development where experience and *interaction* with the environment played an important part. Examples are a positive self-image and self-respect; the experience of 'required helpfulness', that is the experience of *competence* as a result of the necessity to help others, Rachman (1979); or, an attitude inviting favourable reactions from the social environment. An illustration of the importance of the latter can be found in a study of the adaptation of young Vietnamese refugees who arrived in The Netherlands as unaccompanied minors (Tuk, 1988). In this study three groups are distinguished: a small group of individuals who had many conflicts with the adults in their environment; a second small group that tended to social isolation; and a majority which adapted well. This majority manifested ambition and a wish to adapt to Dutch culture. Their behaviour could be characterized as polite, modest, industrious and achievement-oriented. Their behaviour seemed to evoke more social support and appreciation from Dutch people than that of the other two groups.

The concept of protective factors could be used to explain individual differences in adult refugees with regard to the after-effects of traumatization and uprooting. It is a promising concept in connection with refugees because protective factors seem to be similar in diverging cultural situations (cf. Werner, 1989).

Delayed Reaction

Some refugees have been adapting adequately for many years, but then suddenly seem to collapse. They manifest a form of delayed reaction to their painful experiences. This may happen when a particular occurrence unexpectedly confronts them with their traumatic past, or echoes the original trauma (cf. Amen, 1985). It may also occur when an accumulation of stressful events like being turned down in a job application, losing a job, retirement, or contracting a physical illness undermines their power of endurance. For example, the arrival of a relative from, or the discussion of plans to return to the native country (cf. Weinstein & Ortic, 1985), pictures of that country on television or in films, news of asylum seekers being expelled, or the rejection of a request for asylum, may contribute to a refugee getting into a condition of psychological crisis.

A.A. had lived in exile for ten years without having any manifest problems. When he came to the therapist, he had been suffering from nightmares and concentration disturbances for six months. Three occurrences seemed to have triggered these symptoms. The nightmares started after he had paid a visit to his native country. He remembered that he had become upset when he passed the prison where he had been detained for several months and tortured.

The visit to his native country, especially the meeting with old friends, had increased his desire to return. But he was afraid to do so, because of the unstable political situation. He had discussed the matter with his wife and children, but they did not want to go back.

He had made the trip immediately after his retirement, and when he returned he had little to do and felt useless.

One could speculate here that A.A. was a rather resilient man, but that retirement had placed him in a new stage of life with new problems, and that, probably partly as a result of his re-experiencing of traumatic experiences and the pressure to continue his life in exile, he was unable to cope with these problems.

Obstacles to Counselling and Therapy

The fact that some refugees do not seek help does not necessarily mean that they do not need help. It is possible that they need help but cannot find it, or that they do not feel attracted to the kind of help mental health institutions usually offer. The mental health care sector is, generally speaking, not yet sufficiently adjusted to providing assistance to different kinds of foreigners and to all those who have experienced extreme violence. Language problems and cultural differences sometimes form a barrier between refugees and health care institutions. Some refugees do seek assistance for somatic complaints, but doctors may not be aware of the possible psychological roots of their complaints. Refugees from certain non-Western cultures sometimes deny their mental problems because these are not readily accepted in their culture, or because they are less well known (Boekhoorn, 1987). And in other cases they do not have words at their disposal to describe their mental problems.

Three Phases of Traumatization

The way in which traumatization and uprooting were discussed may have given the impression that refugees are people who have experienced one or two traumatic events during a limited period in their life and that, to make matters worse, they have also been uprooted from their social and cultural environment, but that they are free and safe today.

However, this picture does not reflect reality, and it would be more adequate to view refugees as people who have been subjected to a process of traumatization (cf. Keilson, 1979) that extended over many years, which reached a climax in certain specific traumatizing events and the subsequent flight into exile, and that still continues in exile. The traumatization process that refugees have to deal with can be characterized as follows:

- *The first phase*: an increase in repression and persecution in their native country. This phase includes the social and political changes preceding the most extreme traumatic experiences in the life of the refugee, his involvement in these changes, and the consequences they have had for his personal life.
- *The second phase*: the period in which the refugee personally became a victim of torture, terror, battlefield experiences, deprivations during escape, or other torment.
- *The third phase*: life in exile, which includes continuing involvement in what is happening back home, the painful after-effects of the traumatic experiences of the preceding phases, the uncertainty and insecurity the refugee inevitably experiences until he receives a residence permit, the never-ending problems of adaptation to a different culture and the recurring experiences of racism and xenophobia. In this third phase new stress may arise when, as a result of political changes, returning to the home country becomes a possibility. This possibility calls up memories of traumatic events, raising old feelings of loss and grief. It also confronts the refugee with an extraordinarily difficult and painful decision. He must choose between giving up the new life he has built in exile, or giving up the illusion of going home (Santini, 1985a).

In what follows these phases will be illustrated with a number of examples. Also a closer look will be taken at the lasting effects of the experiences of refugees which were summed up above, and the special psychological meaning that a particular experience may have for the individual will be stressed.

The First Phase: Increasing Political Repression

In the period preceding the most traumatic events, refugees have often undergone various experiences which, although less directly injurious, were nonetheless painful and had an enduring effect.

A.B. came from an Asian country. As a 23-year-old student, he got mixed up in a tumult while on his way to the university one morning. The tumult had started on a square where two prominent members of the party with which A.B. sympathized were being hanged. A.B. became very emotional when, four years later, he recounted these executions to the therapist. Those who had been executed were not friends of his but he had looked up to them as leaders, and their deaths had signified a turning point in his life. This experience had radically changed his world-view and destroyed his imagined future. 'That day', A.B. said, 'I decided to give up my studies and concentrate on political activities.' A year later he was arrested and tortured.

During the first interview, B.B., a refugee from Africa, told the therapist that he should be preparing for an exam, but that he could not bring himself to study.

He spent the whole day in his room, brooding and worrying. The therapist decided not to delve into the reasons for this worrying, but rather asked B.B. whether he ever went out, to participate in sport, for example. B.B. then told the therapist that fellow students had, on several occasions, invited him to join them in a game of soccer, but that he had refused. He then said that when he was back home he used to like playing soccer with the boys in the neighbourhood. However, he had developed an aversion to one of these boys because, on one occasion, he had stolen their ball. Then one day, about a month before he was arrested and tortured, B.B. went out to the market to buy some fruit. There he saw a poster containing photographs of 'heroes who had died for their country', that is, boys who had died in combat after being forced to join the government army. The boy he disliked was among them.

'That night', B.B. said, 'the boys played soccer as usual. I joined them as I often did. But this time I could not move my legs. I kept thinking of that nasty little boy. Since then I never played any kind of ball game again.'

The Second Phase: Major Traumatic Experiences

It is impossible to give a complete overview of all the kinds of major traumatic experience described to us by refugees, the emotional meaning these experiences had for them and the influence these experiences have on their daily life and behaviour many years later. First a description will be given of some of the lasting effects of detention, specific kinds of torture, the disappearance of relatives and friends, and hardships during escape. Then some emotions will be discussed that may stem equally from detention, torture, combat experience and terror: such as guilt, disgust, mortal fear, bereavement, the feeling of having been deceived, and anger. In some cases, these emotions have become transformed into a general attitude towards life, without the refugee being completely aware of this process. In other cases, these emotions have been repressed, but they suddenly may overwhelm the refugee, even years after the traumatic experiences occurred.

Detention

Some of the complaints of refugees who have been detained become more understandable when one is aware of the circumstances in which they were detained.

C.B., a 25-year-old refugee from the Middle East, often awoke in the middle of the night feeling very scared. This usually happened when he heard the neighbours coming home. He also got scared during the day whenever he heard the sound of keys rattling or footsteps on the stairs. When he entered a block of flats he became so tense that he was unable to visit friends who lived in a flat.

C.B. had been detained in a relatively modern prison, which had been made of concrete. It became clear that he associated blocks of flats with this prison. During his detention, C.B. and his companions were regularly taken from their cells to be tortured. The sound of keys rattling and footsteps on stairs had become associated with the fear that overcame him when the prison guards climbed the stairs of the gallery and rattled their keys while opening the cell doors to take the prisoners to be tortured. He said that hearing these sounds and waiting to see whether he himself would be taken for torture was almost as bad as the torture itself.

C.B. always arrived at the therapist's office at exactly the appointed time, because he did not like to spend time in the waiting-room.

Specific Forms of Torture

Some refugees have only undergone brutal forms of torture, while others also experienced more selectively applied violence. In the latter case, it is often clear that those who carried out the torture deliberately sought out the 'weak spots' in their victim's personality.

D.B., a young refugee from Latin America, told the following story. 'I was beaten for a long time while I was hung to a bar by my hands and feet. I was blind-folded. The guards took turns in beating me. They wanted to see me cry, but I didn't. I lost consciousness. When I awoke they put me in a chair. One guard removed the bandage from my eyes, gave me a cigarette and started talking with a soft and friendly voice. Suddenly he slapped me in the face. Then I started to cry, and I could not stop. I guess it reminded me of a teacher I had in primary school, he used to hit me that way, and I had no defence. From that day on the guards started to slap me in the face whenever they wanted to humiliate me, and I could not help crying. That is why I don't want to come here sometimes. You are friendly and give me tea . . . you know?'

It sometimes happens that the torturer is a relative or acquaintance of the victim. This experience can deliver a tremendous blow to the victim's faith in other people (Santini, 1986b) and thus become an obstacle to the establishment of relationships based on mutual trust later on.

E.B., who spent three years in prison, expressed this as follows. 'The second interrogator was a boy I knew, we had been at primary school together. He sometimes accompanied me home after school, and on a few occasions he stayed for dinner. He recognized me immediately, although we hadn't seen each other for years. I thought he would be a bit gentle with me, and that he would inform my family about my arrest. He did not. He beat me more severely than any other interrogator.' One of E.B.'s most serious problems was that he felt very lonely. He had not learnt to speak the language of the country of exile yet, and he avoided contact with compatriots, because he did not dare to trust any of them.

Sexual torture may in some cases lead to later sexual dysfunction. For instance during sexual activity the refugee may experience flashbacks in which the present partner is perceived as a rapist. Sexual contact may trigger intrusive memories when the partner behaves in a way that even remotely resembles a form of sexual torture.

F.B. had been raped several times by prison guards. Several years later in the country of exile he entered into an intimate relationship. He reported that he was sometimes afraid to have sexual contact, because it might suddenly revive bad memories. This happened on one occasion when his friend touched his nipples— something that had also happened the first time he was raped.

Torture entails by definition that the victim is helpless in the presence of people who abuse their power. For most refugees feelings of powerlessness and anger at the humiliation and pain they have had to undergo are emotions that can easily be relived if they are confronted with people who indeed have power; especially if their appearance and behaviour reminds them in some way of their torturers and interrogators.

G.B. told the therapist that her most important problem was that she had to report to the police every week to get her temporary visa stamped. 'I am so scared that one day I will lose control. Most of the officers behave correctly, but the way they walk in their boots, it's just like the police in my country. One of them always talks in a loud voice, he reminds me of the cop who beat my little brother. You know, they forced me to look when they beat him. Then there's another one who always says: they've forgotten again to kick you out of the country, and then he smiles as if he had just told a funny joke. He knows he is offending me, but what can I do?'

Torture is often combined with interrogation, and for that reason some refugees get very upset or even become almost frozen with fear, in situations in which they feel they are being questioned.

Although one could tell from his face that the abovementioned E.B. desperately sought help, he did not seem to be very cooperative during the first interview. He did not answer the therapist's questions with more than one or two words. The therapist, who knew that E.B. had been tortured, asked him whether the situa-

tion reminded him of the interrogations in prison. E.B. confirmed this and became a bit less tense.

The Disappearance of Relatives or Friends

Not knowing what has happened to a missing person can be a torment for relatives and friends. They sometimes suffer from frightening fantasies about torture and ill treatment.

> *The father of H.B., a boy of 12, disappeared ten years ago. He was probably killed by the government army, but this was never verified, and H.B. and his mother left the country four months later.*
>
> *H.B.'s mother requested assistance for her son, because his school achievements were far below the expected level. H.B. seemed unable to concentrate at school. He often had nightmares about his father being tortured.*

The uncertainty about the fate of a missing person sometimes seems to result in inner conflicts (cf. L'Hoste, 1986; Spolyar, 1974; Benson *et al.*, 1974)

> *H.B.'s mother also suffered from nightmares, of which she could remember nothing, except that she was in a dark, scary place, and that there was something dangerous behind her which she could not identify. The nightmares had become worse two years ago, at about the time she had started going out with a friend. He now wanted to marry her, but she was trying to postpone a decision. In order to marry in the country of exile she would need a certificate from the authorities in her native country to prove that she was unmarried. This could only be obtained if she took legal action to get a divorce from her missing husband, or if she obtained a declaration from these authorities which confirmed that her husband had been killed.*

Some people seem to protect themselves from disturbing thoughts about missing friends or relatives by not speaking about them and removing anything that reminds them of the missing person.

> *I.B., a boy of 13, suffered from concentration problems and nightmares about the death of his missing father. He had never seen a picture of his father because his mother had locked them all away in a suitcase and he never asked her about him because he thought that would make her nervous.*

Hardships Suffered in Refugee Camps or during Escape

Sometimes a clear picture of the hardships and dangers which the refugee had to face during his escape or his stay in a refugee camp makes it easier to understand his behaviour and evaluate the meaning of these events against the background of his personality development. In relation to this topic one should realize that refugee camps or 'reception centres' often are not peaceful and quiet places, and that the living conditions there are often rather unhealthy and primitive. One must also keep in mind that some refugees have the experience of being transferred like parcels from one 'reception centre' to another, without having the opportunity to make a decision about their next destination.

> *Z.B., a refugee from Africa, had lost his parents due to an armed conflict in his country when he was 14. Over a period of two years he had stayed in five different refugee camps. After arrival in Europe, he was transferred from one reception centre to another. Years after, when he was 22, he still had the habit of carrying all his personal papers with him in a big bag: always prepared to move house within 10 minutes. He now rented his own apartment, but did not bother to fix curtains or do anything else to make it a home.*

Guilt

For some refugees, a feeling of guilt is the dominant affect in their life. This may occur if the refugee was forced to divulge information under torture. It may also be related to the fact that he survived detention or other violent experiences while friends, companions or relatives did not.

> *K.B., was a refugee from an African country. She was 16 at the time of her arrest. During detention she had been forced to witness the execution of her brother. She was haunted by the thought that her brother might still be alive if she had told her interrogators everything she knew.*

However, feelings of guilt can have a variety of backgrounds. For instance, some refugees feel guilty because they have been forced, by their torturers or in order to escape, to carry out violent acts themselves, and they feel guilty about this. Others are combat veterans who feel guilty about what they did to the 'enemy' or about the pleasant excitement some of them felt while they were engaged in violent actions (cf. Solursh, 1989). In some cases they are not initially aware of any feelings of guilt; the guilt becomes conscious during therapy (cf. Schwartz, 1984b).

Self-blame can also be interpreted as an effort by the traumatized person to restore a sense of control over his fate and to maintain the illusion that the reoccurrence of traumatic events can be prevented. Or it may be considered as an attempt by the refugee to protect himself against overwhelming affects like helplessness or rage (cf. Roth & Lebowitz, 1988).

Incidentally, feelings of guilt can, of course, also be associated with many other factors which are not directly related to traumatic incidents. There are refugees who feel guilty all day because they are unable to help the friends and relatives they had to leave behind, or because they do not have the energy to continue their political involvement, and so on.

Mortal Fear

One form of psychological torture is bringing the subject into a situation which causes mortal fear. The result is that some refugees worry a lot about death: either their own death or that of still surviving relatives. This preoccupation is often understandable given their experiences.

> *L.B., a girl of 20, fled with her mother from an African country. She often had nightmares in which her mother died, and during the day she could not put the fear of her mother's death out of her mind. Sometimes she woke up thinking that she herself was dead.*
>
> *L.B. had been detained for several months for political reasons. Once she had been forced to undergo a sham execution, in which some of her companions were really executed.*

Mortal fear can of course also have been caused by experiences related to terror or combat. Moreover, it may become disguised as phobic behaviour.

> *M.B. asked assistance, ten years after he had participated as a guerrilla in a liberation war in the Middle East. His complaints were that he became very tense and nervous if he had to use public transport. Therefore he had interrupted most of his recreational activities. He continued working, but all day he was afraid that his colleagues might guess that he was mad. The symptoms had started one day after the war broke out in the Persian Gulf. He had watched the news on television, which had made him very upset.*
>
> *While he was discussing his fears with the therapist, he remembered how once he was sent from the guerrilla base on a mission to a city that was full of soldiers and checkpoints. M.B. had reached the city by bus. He described that he had been alert all the time, especially for people who looked at him with more than casual interest. M.B. said he had not felt any fear at that time, although he was aware all the time that he was in mortal danger.*

Disgust

Torture sometimes involves situations which cause disgust, like sexual abuse, or being confronted with people who are seriously wounded, mauled or dead.

Experiences of terror, for example watching how police abuse defenceless people, being confronted with the results of terrorism, or being forced by intimidation to watch public executions, may also result in feelings of disgust. This disgust may become directed to certain things (e.g. uncooked meat), an individual to whom the refugee has close affective relationship, or oneself.

> *N.B. had been detained in prison for two years, where he was tortured. After his release he was forced to go into military service. One of the nightmares that haunted him was about the battlefield: he saw the mutilated corpses of dead soldiers, and black dogs eating their flesh. When he awoke he felt sick. He said: 'Even when I was awake I smelled those rotten bodies. It is as if it sticks to my body. Sometimes I feel that others can smell it on me.'*

Bereavement

In the cases of some refugees, traumatic experiences are concentrated around the loss of a person with whom they had an affective relationship, such as a partner, close relative, intimate friend or buddy in their prison cell or combat unit. Such specific traumatic experiences seem to result in a series of personal problems in which unassimilated grief, which hinders their entering into new affective relationships, is central.

> *O.B. requested help because of somatic complaints. He related these to the problems he had in making contact with other people. After a few interviews with the therapist it became clear that these problems occurred mainly in situations in which women were present. He was not only shy towards women, but also became very nervous when he saw other boys having a pleasant conversation with a girl. It reminded him of the happy times he had spent with his own girlfriend, who had died as a result of political violence.*

Some refugees have very painful memories of their escape because they were unable to say goodbye to friends and loved ones (cf. Grimberg & Grimberg, 1984). When escape has entailed the sudden rupture of important relationships, the refugee may be very reserved when it comes to establishing new contacts.

> *P.B., a girl of 21, fled with her mother from an Asian country. She was referred because of depressive complaints. During the interviews the therapist noticed that she was unusually strongly oriented towards her mother for her age. She hardly seemed to be interested in associating with her peers. It seemed as if her personality development had been arrested in that respect. This did not seem to be the result of a possessive or overprotective attitude on the part of the mother, and it*

also did not fit in with the picture that she presented of herself as someone who used to have a lot of friends back home.

When P.B.'s escape was discussed, it became apparent that, for reasons of security, she had not told any of her friends that she was leaving. She had not even been able to say goodbye to her fiancé, and had not written to him after her escape for fear of endangering his life.

Some refugees, especially those who have suffered a traumatic loss during adolescence, have the feeling that they do not have any control over their destiny. This observation is in line with Van der Kolk's (1985) description of the feelings of Vietnam veterans who had lost a buddy under traumatic circumstances.

Q.B. was referred because of depressive complaints and extreme passivity, which was becoming annoying for the volunteers who tried to help him. He reacted with complete indifference to any friendly approach. Q.B. himself said that he felt lonely, it seemed to him that people just did not like him. He did not understand why, but he was sure that this would never change.

During the first interview Q.B. told the therapist that he sometimes encountered a black car and that the driver tried to run him over. He was convinced that someone wanted to murder him, and was obsessed by the question why, without thinking of ways of defending himself.

Q.B. had never been arrested or undergone political violence himself. His parents had begged him to leave his country after soldiers had killed his brother, with whom he had a very close relationship. This had happened when the soldiers had come to arrest Q.B.

The Feeling of Having Been Deceived

Many refugees had their most traumatic experiences as a result of their participation in activities, the possible consequences of which they were not fully aware at the time. Some of them were deceived by political leaders who gave the instructions while minimizing the danger, and let them do the dangerous work while they kept out of harm's way.

R.B., who was 13 at the time, had agreed to distribute a political pamphlet. His cousin, who was 25, and the local leader of an oppositional group, had assured him that this was absolutely safe. 'He was the son of my uncle, he was much older than I was, how could I refuse? How could I know he was telling me lies?', R.B. said.

While he was distributing the pamphlets, R.B. was arrested. He was severely tortured and imprisoned for five years. 'My cousin cheated me', R.B. said. 'He left the country after I was arrested, he lives in Europe and he is a rich man now.

When I had escaped, he did not offer any money to get me out of the country. He knows where I live, but he did not even come to ask me how I was doing.'

Anger

Becoming a victim of organized violence implies that the victim is confronted with a lot of aggression. This may cause direct aggressive reactions in the refugee, which usually, at least partly, have to be suppressed because the refugee is defenceless against the perpetrators of the violence. This unexpressed aggression can also become repressed from the conscious of the refugee.

According to psychodynamic theory, it is also possible that the victim or the witness of aggression identifies with the aggressor. The result is that he will show behaviour that seems to be an imitation of the behaviour of the perpetrator, and is prone to experience aggressive impulses.

Be this as it may, working with traumatized refugees means meeting people with a lot of anger inside. This anger may immediately be obvious.

S.B., a refugee from a Middle East country who had gone through a long-lasting ordeal of physical and psychological torture, was referred to a psychotherapist because he could not control his aggression. If he became upset for some reason (for instance after hearing news from his country) he usually became very angry, and hit his housemate. Afterwards he always regretted this and felt very ashamed.

During therapy it became clear that, when he was upset, he experienced anybody that came near to him as a torturer.

In other cases, the aggression seems to be more repressed.

T.B., a refugee from South East Asia, requested assistance because of phobic complaints and hyperventilation. He had left his country after being abducted and severely abused by secret police. Before he left his country, he had lived hidden, in complete isolation, for three months.

It took two years of therapy before the anxiety-related complaints were under control. Then T.B., who impressed as a very gentle, even subassertive person, started to ventilate his anger: he described in which cruel way he wanted to treat the dictator of his country, using exactly those forms of violence he had experienced or witnessed himself. After doing this, he felt rather ashamed and guilty.

The Third Phase: Exile

When living in exile, a refugee often continues to be very much involved in what is happening in his native country, with regard to both the political situation and the weal and woe of family and friends he had to leave behind. The refugee has become physically separated from what was important for him for a long time, but the emotional involvement continues. The news he hears from or about his country can remind him of his own traumatic experiences, fill him with worry, or just be extraordinarily bad.

> *U.B., a refugee from an African country, had witnessed a lot of organized violence, but had never become a direct victim. He had left his country, after the army had come to his village and abducted and killed most of the boys. A year later he came to know that his elderly father and his younger brother had been murdered by the military. U.B. made a suicide attempt. After hospitalization he was referred for therapy. In the conversations with U.B. what had happened in the third phase of traumatization—the traumatic loss of two of his relatives— was the most important theme. U.B. felt both helpless and guilty about the death of his father and brother.*

During exile, a refugee may experience a lot of stress which is not directly traumatic but adds to stress related with traumatic experiences. For one thing, refugees encounter physical conditions (climate and landscape) and social and cultural conditions (norms and customs) which are different to those they were used to in their own country. This may lead to adjustment problems. The specific content of these adjustment problems depends, among other things, on the cultural background of the refugee.

For example, in tropical countries people spend much of their time outdoors. The chances of being involuntarily alone are therefore limited. In Western Europe and North America things are different, and a refugee who comes from a tropical country has to acquire a new set of social skills in order to find company, and learn to deal with being alone more often than he was used to.

To give some more examples: the way in which European girls associate with boys is quite different from what is considered proper in Iran and Sri Lanka; in Chile guests are received very differently than in England; the way in which Europeans and Americans treat their dogs and pets is considered crazy and unhygienic by most people from the Middle East; in Vietnam one tries to avoid contradicting other people, especially in public, rather than being assertive; and the way in which Europeans and Americans discuss personal matters on television is embarrassing for anyone who used to live east of the fifteenth degree of latitude.

Cultural differences can cause serious confusion for refugees who are not yet used to them. Misunderstandings and embarrassing situations can occur between such refugees and the inhabitants of the host country. How to behave in normal everyday situations can therefore become a problem to the refugee: it is something he has to think about and this requires some energy.

Refugees who, for various reasons, are not very energetic, are tempted to restrict their contacts with the host population to a minimum.

Moreover, refugees are not always treated with respect in Western countries. From time to time they are confronted with racial prejudice, xenophobia and an image that portrays them as thankless profiteers of the social security system who are too lazy to work but, paradoxically, are also the cause of unemployment because they steal the jobs of the indigenous population. They find that many people consider their native country to be backward and them to be less civilized. Such unpleasant experiences sometimes cause new emotions which are difficult to deal with.

The language barrier makes contact with the indigenous population difficult, and this contributes to the social isolation of the refugee. On the other hand, the refugee himself may shy away from new emotional relationships—and this applies to the therapeutic relationship as well—for less obvious, intrapsychic reasons. He may, for example, experience the establishment of a new friendship or relationship of trust as disloyalty to friends and relatives who have remained behind, or to the political cause for which they were persecuted.

The average West European or North American is unaware of the details of the situation in the countries from which refugees come, and will hardly take the trouble to find out more. This does not stimulate refugees to seek contact with inhabitants of the host country. Some of them experience this lack of knowledge and interest as particularly offensive, or become embarrassed when people ask them 'stupid' questions.

Friendship with other refugees from the same country may be strained because of political differences. Refugees who belong to political groups sometimes find that their political friends do not understand their problems and demand more effort from them for political activities than they are capable of. They therefore feel emotionally abandoned by their friends. Others do at first receive emotional support from their comrades but become isolated when they adjust their political views as a result of their experiences and education in the host country. Still others maintain their political views and their militancy but feel terribly frustrated because there are not many possibilities for political action; they are deprived of an important source of inspiration in their lives (cf. Cienfuegos & Monelli, 1983). Meeting political friends then becomes a depressing event and increases feelings of loneliness.

Most refugees come from a cultural background in which talking to outsiders about traumatic experiences or emotional problems is just *not done*, and this attitude is not very helpful in overcoming their problems through seeking social support. The resulting feeling of loneliness and the fear of having a mental disorder may also have a traumatizing effect (Brown, 1986).

Moreover, some refugees are afraid—and sometimes they have good reasons—that agents of their native country's secret police may have infiltrated their social circle and that what they do or say could have consequences for relatives and comrades back home. Finally, a refugee may have an ambivalent attitude towards contacts with other refugees because they remind him of painful experiences with which he has not yet come to grips.

V.B. had periods of dejection and sometimes felt very lonely. He came from an Asian country and had been detained for a long period for political reasons while he was still very young. He did not want to be reminded of the past in any way and therefore avoided listening to music from his native country or watching the news on television. For the same reasons he preferred not to associate with compatriots. He seemed to adjust fairly well in his contacts with peers in the country of exile, but these contacts remained superficial, partly because of the language barrier, but also because he refused to talk about himself, especially about his past.

One may suppose that V.B. tried to put the past out of his mind and therefore denied the roots of his personal identity. For this reason he held back in establishing more intimate contacts with peers, and had to do without the emotional support of an intimate friendship.

In addition to the factors mentioned above, government policy relating to granting asylum to refugees may also cause or aggravate psychological problems.

The refugee is uncertain about his future until a final decision is made about his request for a residence permit. Not being able to make any real plans for the future may lead to serious psychological problems. Moreover, the procedures involved in making a request for asylum may aggravate the psychological problems caused by traumatic experiences before or during the flight into exile. Refugees have to relate traumatic events to officials, and in doing so they re-experience them, but in the absence of those conditions which would make this re-experiencing liberating.

In this connection it should be noted that some refugees remain silent about their traumatic experiences in such situations because they are unable to discuss them with someone with whom they do not have a relationship based on mutual trust. Sometimes they feel intimidated or humiliated by the official who is questioning them or by the interpreter. The interpreter may make mistakes in translating information which is relevant for the request. Unpleasant experiences with officials in the native country can also interfere with communication in these interviews. This influences the way they react to officials in the country in which they have requested asylum, particularly if they wear a uniform, are impatient, or give the impression that they do not believe the refugee's story in the first place. As a result they do not tell the truth, or the whole truth, when providing information which could be important in the decision to grant them asylum.

X.B. only mentioned that he had been tortured after his request for asylum had been turned down. It was in the sixth interview with the therapist that he was

able, with much emotion, to talk about his traumatic experiences during deten-
tion. Shocking battlefield experiences, which were also relevant for his request,
were only discussed during therapy months later.

The feelings related to the stress that results from applying for asylum are comparable to those that result from traumatic experiences like imprisonment, torture and so on. Complications in the asylum procedure also cause feelings of powerlessness and anger, because they are experienced as humiliating and painful and can only be endured. The unpleasant aspects of the application for asylum therefore often remind the refugees of traumatic experiences with which they could not cope, and they intensify the problem of unassimilated traumatic experiences. They increase the chance that feelings of powerlessness and anger will come to dominate the refugee's whole attitude to life.

Y.B. had been tortured for a short period before he went into exile. After psy-
chotherapeutic interviews his complaints reduced significantly. He no longer had
nightmares, he slept well, was more cheerful and could concentrate on his stud-
ies. He also had more contact with his compatriots. Then he was informed that
his request for asylum had been turned down. He appealed against the decision,
but his nightmares and insomnia returned and he became depressed. He neg-
lected his appearance and said he doubted whether further treatment would be
useful.

In this connection Keilson's study of the different phases of traumatization gives interesting starting points. His research was concerned with the significance of the experiences during each of these phases for the development of psychological problems in Jewish children in The Netherlands who were separated from their parents during the Second World War. According to Keilson (1979) what happened in the third phase of traumatization was crucial for the subsequent mental functioning of the children concerned. Those who experienced a relatively favourable second phase and an unfavourable third phase were found to have a less satisfactory adaptation 25 years later than those who experienced an unfavourable second but a favourable third phase.

Generalizing from these results it can be assumed that the experiences in the third phase of the traumatization process really make a difference, and that they influence the subsequent psychological functioning of refugees to a significant degree. And this presents an interesting challenge to professionals and others who are responsible for the admission and well-being of refugees in our society.

Uprooting

Uprooting can also be described as a process with three phases. The first phase starts when the refugee leaves the familiar environment, often hoping that this is only for a brief period. What follows is often a sequence of displacements; sometimes under very difficult conditions. The second phase is the first period after arriving in the country of exile, before the refugee has the certainty that he can stay. During this phase many refugees initially feel relieved because they are saved and have escaped acute danger. However, after some time the restrictions connected to being an asylum seeker are experienced as very annoying. Often the fear of being expelled becomes more paralysing; also feelings of powerlessness, sadness, anger as well as aggressive and self-destructive impulses may increase. These feelings and impulses interfere with efforts to adapt to the new environment, such as learning the language or building up a social network.

The third phase starts when the refugee has a permanent residence permit. For most refugees, receiving this document is a big relief, bringing new energy for all kinds of efforts aimed at adaptation and building up a new life. Sooner or later however, many refugees have to face the fact of new problems, for example in relation to housing or finding a job, that can trigger feelings of helplessness or anger. Also it may become apparent that psychological problems the refugee attributed to fear of mandatory repatriation do not just fade away.

Uprooting is not only a sequence of negative experiences. It also may have the character of a challenge; it may result in achievements which bring a feeling of competence and in personal growth (Eisenbruch, 1984; Akhtar, 1995).

Culture Shock

The difficulties related to uprooting sometimes are characterized as a culture shock. This term is used to refer to the violent emotions occurring in people who find themselves in a strange cultural environment. It describes the emotional upheaval and identity problems that may be the consequence of cultural uprooting (Garza-Guerrero, 1974).

Sometimes the emotions provoked by being in an unfamiliar cultural surrounding may be limited to amused amazement, as in the famous speeches of the Samoan chief Tuiavii about his meetings with Europeans (Tuiavii, 1985). According to Coelho (1982), who did research on culture shock among foreign students in the United States, often these emotions have a much more negative meaning for the individual. They may be characterized by the word *loss*. By this he means:

1. The loss of love and respect as this was experienced in the relationship with friends and family.
2. The loss of social status, which may or may not be accompanied by discrimination.
3. The loss of a familiar social environment with its mutual obligations and dependencies which gave meaning to life.

Refugees suffer the same kind of loss. The loss of love and respect may be experienced, for instance, in connection with companions whom they left behind in distress during detention or combat. The loss of social status occurs almost certainly because most refugees have to start at the bottom of society in the country of exile. Also, the students among refugees sometimes experience a decline in social status through a fall in their academic achievements due to language difficulties and the necessity of adapting to a very different educational system than the one they were used to. And many refugees who request assistance take the risk they will lose the respect of some of their compatriots just because they are seeing a psychologist or psychiatrist.

Among other things, the loss of a familiar social environment is experienced through the ignorance and lack of interest of the people in the country of exile regarding the situation in the refugee's country. Moreover, immediately after arrival refugees are often directed to reception centres organized in a manner which deprives them in many ways of the possibility of making their own decisions (cf. Marx, 1990). For some time they are not free to decide where they want to settle. They may be denied opportunities for mobility, work or study. This is also a form of loss. On the other hand, in many respects the more affluent country of exile usually provides increased opportunities for personal decisions than refugees used to have in their own country. In order to be able to make the correct decisions and impose restrictions upon themselves, different abilities are required than were needed for adequate adaptation in the native country (cf. Bettelheim, 1960). The gain in opportunities is combined with a loss of clarity and security.

The ability to integrate new experiences is reduced as a result of the loss of familiar cultural backing: familiar frames of reference cannot be applied to the flood of new experiences and impressions.

Because it is also a form of loss, culture shock and cultural uprooting can be compared with the way people cope with bereavement (cf. Eisenbruch, 1984). In the process of adaptation to cultural uprooting, one can distinguish phases of denial, anger, depression, and finally acceptance (Lin, Masuda & Tazuma, 1982).

Besides losses, uprooting results in the refugee being cut off from people who are important for him. He feels strongly concerned about relatives and friends who stayed behind, but at the same time is unable to actually support them.

In relation to culture shock, Hertz (1987) distinguishes between intrapsychic and interpersonal aspects of this phenomenon. The intrapsychic aspects relate to inner conflicts about norms and values. Someone who settles in a different culture will come into contact with norms and values deviating from those in his own culture. He will be under pressure to adopt the new norms and values and this leads to inner conflict.

Inner conflicts are often resolved through communication with others. This brings us to the interpersonal aspects of the problem: communication can be impeded by cultural differences. First, there are cultural differences in non-verbal communication. For example, a British or Dutch boy would be less likely than an Iranian or Vietnamese young man to express sympathy towards a friend by holding his hand. Moreover, language differences can easily lead to problems in verbal communication. During therapy in a language foreign to the refugee, various subtle expressions of emotion, affection and appreciation will be difficult or impossible to express or to understand. As a result both the therapist and the refugee may feel uncertainty and even helplessness.

This means the communication necessary to solve inner conflicts is hindered and as a result the conflicts may linger. Eventually these communication problems can become a source of preconceptions on both sides. For example, after a few unsuccessful attempts to communicate with a Tamil refugee, the European therapist may get the impression the Tamils are inscrutable. The refugee may get the idea Europeans do not want to understand his problems, or are incapable of doing so.

The role of women in society demonstrates a great deal of intercultural variation. Many of the experiences brought together under the heading culture shock are related to gender interaction. Culture shock may be a very different experience for men and women. Men from non-Western cultures are often unacquainted with finding women in managerial positions. Often, women are in danger of becoming isolated because they no longer have the network of female neighbours or relatives who supported them in caring for their children. On the other hand, Western society offers them opportunities exceeding the limitations placed on them by traditional roles. Women taking these opportunities may come into conflict with their husbands who feel weakened in their position as head of the family. In many cases such problems result in divorce (Groenenberg, 1991).

Adaptation to the New Cultural Environment

Adaptation to the new cultural environment may proceed along diverging trajectories. In one trajectory, the refugee starts to learn the language of the country of exile. He also builds up a supportive social network and establishes new emotional relationships with inhabitants of the country of exile. He gets adjusted to the cultural situation in the country of exile (acculturation), without denying his own cultural heritage. He develops a capacity for good-humoured ambivalence towards both the native country and the country of exile, and feels increasingly comfortable in simultaneously associating with individuals from both of his cultures (Akhtar, 1995). In that way he forms a *bi-cultural identity*.

A second trajectory can be labelled *partial adaptation*: the refugee adapts to his new environment, but only in selected ways. For example, he learns the language and manages to mobilize citizens of the country of exile who help him to find better housing, but avoids more personal contacts with them, and strongly rejects many cultural values of the country of exile. His only friends are compatriots, and he sticks rigidly to traditional values.

A third trajectory can be referred to by the term *over-adjustment*. Some refugees adapt very quickly to the habits of the country of exile, while they strongly reject any behaviour they associate with their own cultural background. For instance, they avoid compatriots, try to conceal that they are not European, and speak about their native country in a derogatory manner. Some of these refugees seem to attach a great deal of importance to the acquisition of material wealth, and like to possess all the paraphernalia they think to be characteristic of a modern Western individual. Sometimes they want to change their name to make it sound more European. From a psychodynamic viewpoint, it could be argued, this form of adaptation is not adequate because the loss of the familiar environment has not been worked through (cf. Garza-Guerrero, 1974).

Adaptation to the country of exile can be supported by a counsellor who is able to communicate his respect for the refugee, his appreciation of the refugee's former social status and for his capacities. He can help the refugee by explaining about cultural differences and by giving information about values, norms, customs in the country of exile. Some education about the way institutions work may also be useful. A counsellor can encourage the refugee to explore situations he considers as strange, and help him to acquire all kinds of practical and social skills that are adequate in the country of exile. Moreover, he can try to help the refugee to meet people from his own cultural background. In that way the refugee can build up a social network in which he finds emotional support, through informal meetings, but also by participating in rituals: such as rituals around birth, death, religious events and commemorative meetings. But a social network does not always work like this. Some refugees are reluctant to share their feelings about personal losses with people of their own cultural background: they are afraid that they will not be taken seriously or will become a subject of gossip (cf. Rohlof & Jasperse, 1996).

CHAPTER 2

Traumatization and Uprooting: Theoretical Views

In this chapter we will look at the psychological consequences of traumatization and uprooting. It is based on the conceptual frameworks provided by various theoretical approaches, which present points of departure for counselling and psychotherapy. In order to give a concise review, the vast domain of psychology and psychiatry is crudely reduced to six approaches. These are labelled as: the psychiatric classification approach, the developmental approach, the psychodynamic approach, the family therapy approach, the learning theory approach and the cognitive approach.

The Psychiatric Classification Approach

Disorders Frequently Seen among Refugees

In principle, refugees can suffer from any mental disorder found among human beings. It is possible they already had some mental disorder before being traumatized or forced to leave their homeland, and that traumatization and uprooting did not really change the quality of this disorder. A schizophrenic person will still be diagnosed as schizophrenic after traumatization or uprooting. The same goes for someone who is mentally retarded. In addition, it is possible that traumatization or uprooting is an aetiological factor, but only of secondary importance. An individual may function on a level that cannot be considered optimal, but is sufficiently adequate to be labelled as a variation of normal functioning. One may think he behaves a bit oddly or is unadjusted, or that he is rather unhappy. His behaviour may remind us of a particular mental disorder, but it is not deviant enough to speak of any disorder. However, psychosocial stress, like the stress related to traumatization and uprooting, may overburden this individual or remove the protective factors stopping him from becoming worse. In this way he may be pushed over the edge, developing more symptoms justifying the diagnosis of the mental disorder to which this individual seemed to have a predisposition.

Within the psychiatric approach, it is thought that a traumatic experience can result in a specific kind of disorder, called Post-Traumatic Stress Disorder. The symptoms and other characteristics of this disorder are listed in the DSM-IV (APA, 1994) under Code 309.81. The symptoms include re-experiencing of a traumatic event, for example through recollections, dreams, and acting or feeling as if the event were recurring, in combination with persistent avoiding of stimuli associated with the trauma and symptoms of increased arousal such as difficulty in falling asleep, concentration problems, or outbursts of aggression. Sometimes the symptoms of Post-Traumatic Stress Disorder are manifested almost immediately (within six months) after the traumatic experiences. Such cases are referred to as acute Post-Traumatic Stress Disorder. But the complaints may appear only much later, and then they are referred to as delayed Post-Traumatic Stress Disorder. In the case of some war victims, the disorder manifests itself both as an acute reaction (shortly after the war, on average five years) and a second reaction manifesting itself after a period of 15 to 25 years, during which time the victim did not have any complaints (Op den Velde, 1989).

Various investigators have concluded that the diagnosis of Post-Traumatic Stress Disorder is often applicable to refugees who present mental problems (Glassman, 1988; Kinzie et al., 1984). Among refugees, however, the symptoms of Post-Traumatic Stress Disorder may be accompanied by the symptoms of Major Depression (Mollica, Wyshak & Lavell, 1987a; Vladár Rivero, 1989). The most important symptoms of Major Depression are a depressed mood and loss of interest and pleasure in most activities, almost all day, every day; as well as the presence of delusions or hallucinations whose content may or may not be consistent with the typical depressive themes of personal inadequacy, guilt, disease, death, nihilism or deserved punishment.

In addition to this, refugees who have symptoms of Post-Traumatic Stress Disorder sometimes have auditory hallucinations, which are not necessarily accompanied by other psychotic symptoms (cf. Mueser & Butler, 1987). Infrequently, the symptoms of Post-Traumatic Stress Disorder may be accompanied by bizarre behaviour with a delusional and paranoid content, or by visual hallucinations that may be related to the trauma, but cannot be considered as flashbacks (Kinzie & Boehnlein, 1989). Moreover, tactile and bodily hallucinations with a fright-inducing content (e.g. a sensation of being bitten) have been reported (Bailly, Jaffe & Pagella, 1989). Both depressive symptoms and symptoms such as hallucinations and delusions may conceal symptoms related to the persistent re-experiencing of traumatic events, avoidance of trauma-related stimuli, and symptoms of increased arousal.

In the ICD-10 (World Health Organization, 1992), one more diagnostic category is described that might be useful in describing the consequences of traumatization: *Enduring personality change after catastrophic experience.* This category refers to an enduring personality change, present for at least two years, after catastrophic stress. For example, trauma caused by concentration camp experience, disaster, prolonged captivity with an imminent possibility of being killed, prolonged exposure to life-threatening situations such as being a victim of terrorism, and torture. The disorder is characterized by a hostile or distrustful attitude towards the world, a chronic feeling of 'being on edge' as if constantly threatened, and estrangement. This category suggests a certain irreversibility and, therefore, does not inspire much therapeutic optimism. It could easily be abused as an alibi for not treating those victims of trauma who are less attractive or charming than average.

The DSM-IV does not mention disorders which are specifically related to cultural uprooting. However, Acculturation Problem (Code V62.4) is mentioned under the Axis I category 'other conditions that may be a focus of clinical attention'. Also 'Difficulty with acculturation' is mentioned under the descriptions of Axis IV: Psychosocial and Environmental Problems.

Utility and Limitations of the Psychiatric Approach

The psychiatric approach offers a useful first characterization of the problems of many refugees who request assistance. It supplies the therapist with lists of symptoms. These can be transformed into questions in order to help refugees express complaints. Then the therapist will also convey the message to the refugee that his problem is in some way 'familiar' to him, the therapist, and treatment is possible. Usually this has a reassuring effect.

> E.C. presented his problem as follows: 'I cannot sleep, and I am afraid I am going mad.' He illustrated this by mentioning he had lost all interest in his hobbies, felt alienated from his former friends, and had the feeling of being trapped in a cage from which he would never escape. Also, he said he was unable to read a newspaper or watch television because he could not concentrate for more than a few minutes. The therapist asked E.C. if he was having nightmares, which he confirmed. Talking about the content of these nightmares it became clear they were related to the traumatic experiences (months of torture) which had forced him to leave his country.
>
> The therapist concluded Post-Traumatic Stress Disorder was a useful provisional diagnosis. He decided to explain to E.C. that he understood his complaints as a result of his traumatic experiences, and did not consider these complaints to be a sign of madness, but an understandable reaction to traumatic symptoms as a result of months of torture. The therapist also told E.C. he had been right in seeking help, because he thought that E.C.'s problem was indeed serious. Also, the therapist told him he was thinking of various methods of treatment to help alleviate E.C.'s symptoms.
>
> In this way he offered E.C. a first explanation for his symptoms, and hope that he might overcome them in the future.

The psychiatric approach, especially the concept of Post-Traumatic Stress Disorder, can help us to explain to the refugee what is happening to him. It helps us also to exclude the possibility that the refugee suffers from some other type of mental disorder. What he experiences as madness or extreme weakness, or what his environment may have been interpreting as hysteria or malingering becomes understandable as a 'normal', and thus respectable, reaction to extremely sad or painful experiences. Moreover, the psychiatric approach offers a point of departure for considering the prescription of psychotropic medication.

A limitation of the psychiatric approach is that it does not as yet offer satisfactory and generally accepted descriptions of the possible pathological consequences of uprooting. Moreover, the DSM-IV manual states this psychiatric classification system must be used with caution when evaluating the psychological functioning of persons from different ethnic or cultural backgrounds. Symptoms of distress can be very culture-specific, and behaviour seemingly pathological in a Western context may be common and adaptive in the original cultural environment of the refugee. For instance, when one works with refugees it is not unusual to see a patient who feels possessed, or troubled by a spirit. These feelings can often be understood as a normal sign of cultural bereavement (Eisenbruch, 1989) or as a culture-related way of expressing distress.

A second problem is the diagnosis of the Personality Disorders. Refugees from non-Western countries sometimes show behaviour that impresses as fitting in the picture of Avoidant Personality Disorder (e.g. being reticent in social situations because of fear of saying something inappropriate or foolish, or being unable to answer a question) but that is perfectly understandable as a way of coping with an unfamiliar situation. Behaviour that is associated with the Histrionic Personality Disorder (e.g. expressing emotion with inappropriate exaggeration) might not be considered deviant within the culture of the refugee, because that culture uses other standards for what is exaggerated, and what is not. When applying this diagnostic label to a refugee, actually one should have a heteroanamnesis which is evaluated by a person from the same cultural background. Otherwise, more or less adequate coping behaviour of refugees can be misinterpreted as signs of a Personality Disorder, or the other way round. Organized violence may cause decent, gentle and conscientious people to do things one considers at a first glance to be indicative of an Antisocial Personality Disorder; while people who had an Antisocial Personality Disorder in the first place, may later be traumatized by organized violence and manifest the symptoms of a Post-Traumatic Stress Disorder. Also, behaviour such as reading hidden demeaning or threatening meanings into benign remarks or events that in some cases refers to a Paranoid Personality Disorder may be perfectly understandable as adequate coping in a situation of terror. When trying to diagnose or to exclude a personality disorder, it is important to get information about the onset of the behaviour in question that is indicative of a particular disorder: whether it was long before or only after the traumatic experiences or the flight.

Another limitation of the psychiatric approach is that it does not claim to offer much of an explanation about the psychological mechanisms responsible for the development of psychological problems as a consequence of traumatic experiences. However, some research has been directed to the biological and physiological causes of the symptoms of Post-Traumatic Stress Disorder. It has been shown, for example, that the autonomous nervous system of patients with Post-Traumatic Stress Disorder does not function normally (Van der Kolk *et al.*, 1985a,b). This type of research belongs to a long tradition in which post-traumatic symptoms are related to factors such as the physical effects of protracted malnutrition during detention, or brain damage as a result of blows to the head. Van der Kolk's research on the physiological effects of pain and fear is a modern variation on this approach. However useful the results of this research may become or already are for the psychiatrist considering the prescription of psychotropic medication, they do not offer clearly visible points of application for psychotherapeutic techniques. Psychological approaches providing causal explanations of the problems of refugees are needed for the construction of a detailed treatment plan. These approaches help to describe individual differences in the way the psychological consequences of traumatization and uprooting are manifested. They provide concepts and a theoretical framework for understanding and evaluating the 'healthy' aspects of psychological functioning. These 'healthy' aspects, as it were, provide the basis for the application of psychological treatment methods.

The Developmental Psychology Approach

Developmental Interference

From a developmental point of view it can be hypothesized that traumatization and uprooting may easily interfere with the normal developmental process. Both processes may complicate the mastering of developmental tasks the individual is facing at a particular moment. Therefore, it could be interesting to obtain information about the functioning of the person just before he was traumatized or uprooted, and about the developmental tasks he is facing at the time he requests assistance.

Developmental Tasks

By developmental tasks we refer to the idea that, as they get older, children and adolescents have to respond to new challenges, learn new skills, or solve new problems. For the therapist working with refugees it can be an eye-opener to assess which developmental tasks his clients are facing at the time they seek assistance. In the case of children and adolescents, it can also be relevant to consider their problems in relation to the developmental tasks their parents or foster parents are currently facing (cf. Scaturo & Hayman, 1992). Counselling and therapy can then be aimed at supporting the refugee and members of his family in dealing with these developmental tasks. Examples illustrating the usefulness of the concept of developmental tasks while working with children and adolescents will be presented in Chapter 9.

Protective Factors

The concept of protective factors has already been introduced in Chapter 1. It could be used to explain individual differences in adult refugees with regard to the after-effects of traumatization and uprooting. It is a promising concept in connection with refugees because protective factors seem to be similar in diverging cultural situations (cf. Werner, 1989). The concept suggests the therapist should not only support the available protective factors. He could also look further than the threshold of his consulting room, and assume an active role in promoting changes in the life environment of the refugee which *create protective factors*. This way psychotherapy could become more productive, or even become unnecessary.

> *F.C., a boy of 16 from an African country, was referred for psychotherapy by his guardian. He was very depressed because he was uncertain about the where- abouts of his family. He suffered from nightmares. At the time of the referral, F.C. was temporarily staying in an institution. The therapist suggested the guardian should find a home for F.C. in which he could stay for at least two years and where he would receive support with regard to practical matters such as cooking food, washing clothes, handling money, and so on. After this had been realized, F.C. had no more complaints, and his achievements at school improved.*

Utility and Limitations of the Developmental Approach

This approach forms a useful complement to the psychiatric approach because it focuses attention on the possibilities for further development and change. The concepts of protective factors and developmental tasks both have diag- nostic value. They also offer points of departure for psychotherapy. However, the concept of 'protective factors' is a typical *post factum* construct. The ways in which these factors protect, and the psychological mechanisms making them effective, have hardly been investigated. A therapist who attempts to create protective factors still depends largely on his intuition. The concept of developmental tasks should be used cautiously, because the content of these tasks may be partly dependent on the cultural situation.

The Psychodynamic Approach

The Consequences of Traumatization: Damage and Repair

Within the psychodynamic approach the traumatic experience is seen as a confrontation between the individual and his environment, in which he encounters 'unbearable stimuli' and experiences 'overwhelming affects'. The usual coping skills and defence mechanisms are unable to deal with this situation. The individual's affective responses produce an unbearable psychic state threatening to disorganize all psychic functions and damage the personality structure. He experiences helplessness and surrenders, which means he becomes totally passive and inhibited (cf. Baranger, Baranger & Mom, 1988). The processes of defence and coping become disorganized. This can result in the disappearance of affective reactions, apathy, or depersonalization. These effects may continue for some time (Furman, 1986).

From the psychodynamic point of view, a traumatic experience has two consequences: damage and a process of reparation. The after-effects of a traumatic experience can be seen either as a result of damage, or as the side-effects of a necessary and useful process of reparation. The repeated reliving of traumatic experiences in nightmares or wakeful imagination can be seen, for instance, as part of a process in which the emotions occurring during traumatization become assimilated. This process can be described as a *sequence of phases* (Horowitz, 1976, 1986).

In the first, short, phase (a few hours to a few days after the experience), which may sometimes be skipped, the emotions stimulated by the traumatic experience are expressed violently. Horowitz calls this the *outcry* phase.

Then there is a phase when the emotions are repressed: the *denial* phase. The individual pretends nothing special has happened, or the events have not touched him. He appears to function normally, but tries nevertheless to avoid situations reminding him of his traumatic experiences. His reactions are shallow and unemotional.

This second phase alternates with a third phase* when memories of the traumatic event and the painful feelings associated with it come forcefully to the surface. In this *intrusive* phase the person has nightmares and it does not take much to remind him of the shocking events he has experienced. [*Note: Horowitz's observations that some individuals skip the first phase, and they may move back-and-forth between the second and third phases, shows his concept of 'phase' has a meaning differing fundamentally from the concept of 'stage' as part of an invariable sequence, as it is used in developmental psychology.]

The alternation of the second and third phase can, according to Horowitz, be seen as a gradual assimilation of the endured emotions. In the third phase, these emotions are made conscious so they can be assimilated. If they become so intense that the person is in danger of being overwhelmed, then the defence mechanisms will be engaged and he will revert to functioning as in the 'denial' phase. After a while, when he has calmed down and had new experiences enhancing his capacity for coping, he will admit more of these emotions into his consciousness so that they can become assimilated. Eventually the intensity of the feelings that are related to the traumatic experiences will decrease and the alternation between the intrusive and denial phases will cease.

After this there is a fourth phase: the phase of *working through*. In this phase, the traumatic episodes become an important part of the person's experience. They are not denied as in the second phase, but they are not dominant either, as in the 'intrusive' phase. During this phase the person learns to live with his experiences and to fit them into his world-view and his self-image.

A.D., a 16-year-old refugee from Latin America, visited the therapist four months after he had been tortured by the secret police. He began the interview by saying he wanted to tell his story. And so he did, in a session of two and a half hours. His behaviour reminded the therapist of Horowitz's description of the 'outcry' phase, although it occurred much later than a few days after the trauma. It was only at the end of the interview that the therapist found the opportunity to ask A.D. about his complaints and symptoms. A.D. then told the therapist that lately he had been having nightmares frequently, as is to be expected in the 'intrusive' phase. In later interviews, the most frequent topics of discussion were A.D.'s adaptation to the country of exile, the problems of his parents and the political situation in his native country. The latter subject brought back memories of torture, but without much emotional upheaval, as in the 'working through' phase. The nightmares had disappeared after the first interview. They had not returned a year later. Other symptoms (lack of concentration, nervousness) also gradually disappeared within four months.

It is the author's experience that Horowitz's descriptions offer many points of recognition. However, the behaviour of refugees does not conform very often to the sequence of distinct phases Horowitz postulated, at least not in all domains at the same time. For instance, after 'working through' one traumatic experience, intrusive memories of a second traumatic experience may occur, which are worked through at a later time.

In addition to these relativizing thoughts about Horowitz's contribution, the following critical remarks can be added. It should be noted that according to the literature concerning emotional responses to undesirable life events, human beings show considerable variation in their post-traumatic behaviour. This variation manifests itself in the particular demonstrated emotional responses. Also, it is a fact that some individuals do not exhibit any emotional reaction at all (cf. Silver & Wortman, 1980). This means that however enlightening Horowitz's descriptions may be in many cases, they should not be referred to as normative. If an individual reacts to a traumatic experience in a way deviating from Horowitz's typification then this does not mean his reactions are therefore abnormal, inadequate or pathological, or that his personality development is disturbed. Finally, Horowitz's descriptions might suggest that a person generally recovers spontaneously from traumatic experiences. The empirical evidence suggests, however, that such an assumption is inapplicable to at least a sizeable minority of the population (Silver & Wortman, 1980).

The Consequences of Traumatization: Impetus for Inner Conflict

The psychodynamic approach offers various other ideas contributing to understanding of the fact that many people continually relive their traumatic experiences during a certain period of time. In this paragraph the ideas of Freud (1955) and of Grinker and Spiegel (1945, see Brett & Ostroff, 1985) will be discussed. In their approaches the concept of inner conflict plays an important part.

Freud was intrigued by the continual reliving of traumatic experiences during nightmares. He became acquainted with this phenomenon through his contact with front-line soldiers of the First World War. Freud saw their nightmares as a primitive defence mechanism against being overwhelmed by emotions: compulsive repetition. (By primitive Freud means: only adequate for very young children.) Freud assumed that, in a certain sense, the organism actively recalled the traumatic experiences into consciousness. This occurred in order to re-experience, or more correctly experience, the anxiety that was originally absent at the time of the traumatic event. This active recollection of very painful experiences which had been passively and helplessly endured contributed, slowly but surely, to the emotional assimilation of the trauma.

Therefore, Freud thought the individual actually tried to remember his traumatic experiences. But the memories evoked so many negative emotions that, in order to avoid becoming conscious of them, the individual simultaneously brought other defence mechanisms into action. There is thus an *inner conflict* between defences: repetition-compulsion as a defence against an overwhelming feeling of passive powerlessness resulting on one hand in re-experiencing, and defences such as denial or repression on the other hand. This inner conflict tends to frustrate the process of assimilation. Recent research has shown one of these defences may be dominant: re-experiencing seems to be dominant in those who have witnessed violence, while among those who have physically experienced or participated in violence, re-experiencing appears to be warded off by denial (Laufer, Brett & Gallops, 1985); although appreciable overlap between these two groups also was found (Eth, 1986).

Freud claimed that traumatic experiences also have cognitive consequences: the traumatized person comes to know aspects of life, human nature, his own personality, and other persons, unknown to him before the traumatic experiences. This new knowledge becomes very important. The person also may discover that what he has learned in the course of his traumatic events is incompatible with his former world-view and self-image. The conclusions he was forced to draw from his traumatic experiences may be incompatible with what he always believed. This causes fear, which is why some memories of the experience are repressed.

The repression of certain kinds of knowledge is also part of the inner conflict mentioned above. The person knows something he would rather not know; something he would like to forget. But at the same time, he realizes that what he has learned from his traumatic experiences can be useful in avoiding similar occurrences in the future. In more abstract terms: the inner conflict also tends to frustrate cognitive coping processes.

> B.D. described an experience occurring just before he fled into exile. It was an experience that still gave him very unpleasant dreams. He had never talked to anyone about this.
>
> It occurred when he was 8 years old. One morning, on his way to school, he saw dozens of bodies piled up on a piece of wasteland behind a shed. 'I remember now the thought which occurred to me at that moment', B.D. said. 'It was: my mother won't protect me.'

Freud's contributions serve to direct the therapist's attention to the inner conflict related to talking or even thinking about traumatic experiences. Grinker and Spiegel (1945, see Brett & Ostroff, 1985) also relate the occurrence of nightmares to inner conflict, though in a different way. Their hypothesis is that nightmares about traumatic experiences can be understood as a form of self-punishment. These authors focus on the interaction which can develop between present inner conflicts and traumatic experiences from the past.

> C.D. had a nightmare in which she re-experienced the pursuit which preceded her arrest. She dreamed that she appealed to her parents for help but they sent her away. In reality her parents had always helped her—they had helped her to flee the country. In the talk which followed she said recently she had started having a relationship with a married man. She suspected her parents would disapprove and was not sure whether she would write and tell them.

The Consequences of Traumatization and Personality Structure

According to the psychodynamic approach, an individual's reaction to traumatic experiences depends on the quality of his personality structure. One factor thought to be important is the quality of his *coping* repertoire, which in turn depends on the vicissitudes of the personality development preceding the traumatic experiences. In a retrospective study of the coping behaviour of victims of the Nazi concentration camps at Treblinka and Sobibor, Schumacher (1982) distinguishes three groups of victims by the types of coping they applied: regression, adaptive defence, and progressive coping. The victims who survived by regression described their behaviour in the concentration camp as passive and apathetic. They said they tried to avoid perceiving what happened around them. The victims who survived by adaptive defence continued to perceive reality. They attempted to adapt to it by submissive behaviour, keeping the relationship with their guards as good as possible, and by considering themselves lucky to be alive. Those who survived by progressive coping tried to analyse their situation, to recognize possible danger before it became reality, to take adequate action to protect themselves from it, to make use of every possibility to improve their situation, and so on. The behaviour of these victims was determined by the aim of getting one of them out of the camp alive, so that he could tell the world what was happening inside.

About the personality development of these three groups, Schumacher concludes that the survivors who used regression were children of good, strong and protective mothers, and this experience had given them the trust that eventually everything would turn out right. The victims who used adaptive defence had weak and helpless parents from whom they had learned to survive by submissive adaptation. They had developed little self-esteem, but a great determination to survive. The victims who used progressive coping had strong, successful fathers who were supported by quiet but confident mothers. The relationship with their parents had enabled them to acquire self-confidence.

The three groups differed also with respect to the consequences they ascribed to their experiences in the concentration camp. Those who had used regressive coping by adopting a passive attitude to ward off the bitter reality seemed to have forgotten most of their traumatic experiences. In court cases against war criminals they could not give much evidence. Moreover, they did not show signs of psychological damage. So Rutter's (1987) conclusion, that cognitive mechanisms to protect oneself against stressful life experiences are probably only effective when they lead to active coping and not just passive acceptance, seems to be open to discussion. People may be able to survive and keep relatively healthy in a psychological sense by ignoring as much as they can. (In that case they are also unable to describe their traumatic experiences. This may be a handicap for a refugee who requests political asylum.)

Returning to Schumacher's study of concentration camp victims: most psychological damage was found in the group that used adaptive defence. They suffered from fears, nightmares, depression, and so on. Those who had used progressive coping did not seem to have much psychological damage. And also they could remember what had happened to them very well.

There are refugees who have experiences that in some ways resemble those of the victims of Treblinka and Sobibor. For instance, refugees from Cambodia and some refugees from Bosnia and Iran who spent a long time in detention under constant threat of being tortured or executed. The author has had experience with the latter group. Among them he saw nobody who seemed to have survived exclusively through regressive coping. This is in line with Schumacher's conclusion, that those who use this coping style do not show signs of psychological damage. A few of the Iranian refugees who discussed their prison experience in detail seemed to have used adaptive defence as a coping style, at least in some situations; sometimes in combination with regressive coping. In relation to prison experiences, they often mentioned fear and helplessness as overwhelming emotions. In line with Schumacher's conclusions, they had problematic relations with their parents, although it would be too simplistic to describe these parents, in Schumacher's terms, as weak and helpless. These refugees also had a rather vulnerable self-concept.

Another group of Iranian refugees described their prison experiences above all in terms of what they had seen the guards do to other people. The feeling they described most often as overwhelming was that of intense powerlessness at moments when they wanted to protect other prisoners. The coping style of these prisoners seemed to be comparable to progressive coping but, contrary to Schumacher's subjects, they certainly had psychological damage.

A second important factor thought to determine an individual's reaction to traumatic experiences is the *presence of disturbances in personality development—*which may or may not have resulted in manifest symptoms—*before traumatization*. The traumatic experiences may become either articulated to existing, manifest problems, or potentiate and reactivate emotional problems hidden for a long time (cf. Kramer, Schoen & Kinney, 1987).

D.D. requested assistance because she had phobic complaints. Also, she was very depressed and haunted by terrible nightmares. Talking about the nightmares, it became apparent that during her early childhood D.D. had been seriously abused by her parents. As a child she had serious depressions and problems in making social contacts. As an adolescent she had been detained for political reasons and maltreated but, as she said, not severely when compared to what happened to some of her friends. Nevertheless, she found it very difficult to discuss her experiences of being in prison. Talking about this recent traumatic past evoked a lot of intense emotions she could hardly verbalize. These seemed to be related to the abuse in her early childhood. The therapist concluded that the recent traumatic experiences had reactivated a latent emotional problem, which it was better not to uncover. He focused, therefore, on the way she had coped with her recent traumatic experiences, which (in Schumacher's terminology) could be described as a mixture of adaptive defence and progressive coping. This had a supportive effect. D.D. regained some of her self-confidence and became less depressed.

E.D. requested assistance for complaints which were similar to those of D.D. His recent traumatic experiences seemed much more severe. He had reacted to the first of these—the destruction of his house and murder of his parents by the government army—through progressive coping, by joining a resistance organization. After another traumatic event—a buddy was killed before his eyes—he had made a serious attempt to kill himself. He became very sad when the therapist asked him some routine questions about his family background. He remembered the close relationship he used to have with his parents, and mentioned the confidence they had in him. E.D. did not seem to have worked through the loss of his parents. The death of his buddy, five years later, was a trauma in itself. Also, it seemed to have reactivated the emotional problem E.D. had with regard to the loss of his parents. E.D. was able to talk about his parents, and therapy became an opportunity for mourning.

The Consequences of Uprooting

Erikson's contributions on the relationship between psychological development and cultural factors make it possible to present some psychodynamic hypotheses about the effects of cultural uprooting. Erikson (1960, 1968) concluded that the course of identity development is related closely to the standards and values of a particular society, and the kind of ideology and future perspective this society offers. He observed also that when the cultural pillars of identity in a society collapse, young people may suffer severe identity confusion. This psychological state may cause them to withdraw into apathy and tempt them to self-destructive behaviour such as alcohol and drug abuse.

It can be supposed that refugees, because of having to live for some time under the kind of anomic repression and violence that forces people to flee, and subsequently being forced to leave their familiar cultural environment, may be struggling with identity problems. These may manifest themselves as: a sense of confusion about standards and values; irresolution, even in trivial matters; ideological doubts; loss of future perspective. Identity problems may result in apathy and self-destructive behaviour. In some cases the complaints, symptoms and behaviour of refugees become more understandable when these are evaluated against the background of identity problems, and the therapist talks to them about such topics as standards, values, political ideals and the future.

F.D., a 24-year-old refugee from the Middle East who belonged to a left-wing political group, became very confused upon realizing his ideas about politics were not very sophisticated, and that some of the achievements of capitalist society were very tempting. He started to visit bars, which led to conflicts with his political friends. His opinion about them changed: 'If they should come to power, they would become the new torturers', he confided to the therapist. He could not feel relieved even after receiving a positive answer to his request for political asylum and being admitted to a university. He felt alienated. He was uncertain when it came to making decisions. For example, he had registered for a course of study he thought would be useful if he could return to his country. But he was not sure about sticking to his original plan. He thought about choosing another subject that would give him more chance of getting a good job in Europe, or following what he called 'an impulse' and studying art history.

Utility and Limitations of the Psychodynamic Approach

The psychodynamic approach offers many useful hypotheses: with regard to the individual differences in the way that individual refugees deal with traumatic experiences and uprooting; the way they think about their problems; and their attitude towards people who want to help them. As a developmental theory, it draws attention to the fact that psychological problems consequent on traumatic experiences mingle and interact with normal phase-specific problems, and can evoke long-hidden emotional problems. Finally, it presents interesting thoughts about inner processes in relation to traumatization and uprooting of which most refugees are hardly aware themselves, but which nevertheless may have decisive importance for their behaviour.

The term psychodynamic approach refers to a complex field of theoretical contributions, which offers insight into the complex nature and interconnectedness of psychological problems. However, the concepts used in these theoretical contributions are often not very clearly defined, and certainly not easy to operationalize. They cannot offer a simple list of questions to ask, or symptoms to check. Understanding the problems a refugee presents in terms of the psychodynamic approach is not a matter of a few structured interviews. For diagnosis the therapist needs time, and he has to enter into a therapeutic relationship with the refugee.

The Family Therapy Approach

In this section thoughts from theoretical denominations with very different backgrounds are brought together. What they have in common is that they focus their attention upon the relations and interaction processes existing between individuals in their primary life environment, and the quality of these relations and interaction processes is seen as an important determinant of individual behaviour.

The Consequences of Traumatization

The following consequences will be discussed: dysfunctional circular inter-action, disturbances in communication, family secrets, overprotectiveness, parentification, the coming into existence of a hierarchy of suffering, and trans-generational phenomena.

Dysfunctional circular interaction.
A basic assumption of this approach is that an individual's family (or the people who surround him as a primary social environment) forms an important factor in his well-being. The interaction with his family can produce a lot of practical and emotional support for the individual, which makes him less vulnerable to stress from the wider environment. But this interaction is not always supportive, and it can also make the individual more vulnerable to environmental stress or it may in itself be the cause of the individual's mental problems. If an individual has a mental problem, this has to be evaluated against the background of the interaction processes within the family.

Another important assumption is that the interactions between people have a circular character (Haley, 1963). The behaviour of all the individuals who take part in dysfunctional interaction tends to complement the continuation or escalation of the dysfunctional quality of that interaction. This means that, in the case of inadequate patterns of social interaction, it is impossible to say which individual is the cause of dysfunction. For example, a refugee has a nightmare about traumatic experiences. He does not want to burden his wife with it, so he does not tell her. Because of the nightmare he is a bit cranky. The wife thinks he is angry. She does not ask him anything, but becomes cranky herself, and keeps her husband at a distance. As a result he starts to think she does not love him like she used to. He becomes afraid of losing her. As a result he gets more nightmares. He does not want to burden his wife by telling her about the nightmares. And so on.

Disturbances in communication.
Some representatives of the family therapy approach state that inadequate family interaction can be seen as the result of disturbances in the communication between members (Watzlawick, Beavin & Jackson, 1967). Communication is the exchange of information, by means of verbal statements and behaviour. This information has two aspects: a message with a certain content, and an expression of emotions which concern the relationship between the persons involved in the exchange. In this sense the meaning of everything which is said has two levels, and can thus become ambiguous.

Misunderstanding can arise when one of the persons involved in the interaction does not notice or understand both aspects of the message. This may happen when the individual who says or does something to another member of the family is not aware of the emotions he simultaneously expresses; or when an individual tends to interpret ambiguous messages in a rigid, stereotyped way. Not telling something is also a message, only, the message is not clear and will often be misunderstood. In the above example: The unspoken message of the refugee to his wife is: I do not want to burden you. But she receives: my husband is angry with me.

Moreover, one misunderstanding leads to another, thus causing conflicts and estrangement within the family.

Secrets.

Communication in a family can also become disturbed when some members share a secret about a very important issue about which the other members of the family are not informed. These secrets usually concern topics such as birth, sex or death (Van de Lande, 1980). For instance, the circumstances under which a member of the family died, the fact that one of the children was born out of wedlock, or the traumatic experiences of one of the parents can be kept secret.

Secrets in the family are kept on the basis of the fear that disclosure of the secret might result in the break-up of the family. Sometimes secrets are kept in order to protect certain moral values embraced by the family. By keeping something secret, the informed members of the family try to escape feelings of guilt, or the fear and grief related to an imminent loss (Pincus & Dare, 1978). Under circumstances of extreme repression, a traumatic experience of a family member may be kept secret from part of the family in order to prevent the family from becoming a victim of more traumatic events. In this case, keeping the secret may be (or may have been for some time) an adequate form of coping (cf. Sluzki, 1990).

Usually it is the parents who keep a secret from the children. What they keep secret are things they believe the child would not be able to handle, or would make him overly anxious or excited.

A.E. a 21-year-old man who had left his Latin American homeland after some very traumatic experiences, told the therapist he was very nervous because his father had not written to him. Instead he had received a letter from his sister, informing him that his father had twisted his right arm and was not able to write properly. When asked why this made him so nervous, A.E. responded that he was afraid this meant his father had died. A.E.'s mother had died two years before, but the family had not dared to inform him. They had decided to prepare him slowly for the loss. First, they had written to him to say his mother was in the hospital for an illness. Later, they informed him the illness was a heart problem. Then, A.E. received a message that his mother's condition was serious. Finally, an uncle arrived in person to inform him his mother had died. When he received this news, his mother had already been buried six months before. Now, A.E. took the news of his father's twisted arm very seriously.

Secrets in the family can become a burden for vulnerable children, especially if the secret activates fearful fantasies. Then it can result in disturbed behaviour or disturbed symptoms. An open discussion within the family, on a level understandable for the child, usually leads to a diminishing of symptoms and problematic behaviour (Dare, 1980).

Overprotectiveness.
The keeping of secrets can be seen as an example of avoidance of open communication about emotions related to traumatic experiences, based on overprotectiveness. For instance, after a traumatic event the discussion of feelings of fear and sadness may be avoided. This will occur when the traumatized individual thinks some members of the family might not be able to cope with the reality and when he is afraid that he might become a burden to his family (cf. Figley, 1988), or when he feels ashamed of what he calls his 'weakness', and so on. The effects of fear on families are described by Becker and Weinstein (1986). Their study is based on experiences during the military dictatorship in Chile, and concurs with what this author observed in the families of refugees. According to Becker and Weinstein, frightening and threatening events are often not discussed, even when they are not just isolated incidents but a part of everyday life. They are kept secret. The emotions which are related to these events are not shared. An emotional distance develops between the members of the family and each feels alone, not understood.

In addition, the way in which family members associate with each other becomes less flexible (see also Dare, 1980). Their roles become rigid. For example, the father acts tough, the mother plays weak, the son is always aggressive and the daughter cries over nothing. But at the same time they hide other feelings and impulses. The father wants to cry but is afraid it will disturb the children. The son has received another threatening telephone call but does not mention it so his mother will not worry. She is aware that her son feels threatened and is very worried, but she pretends not to notice because she does not want her husband to get concerned. To put it more abstractly: because they are unable to protect each other from external violence a form of overprotection develops which impedes communication and mutual emotional support. It seems as though the family is falling apart. In reality, it is an artificial distancing stemming from a mutual concern.

Another consequence of fear and threats in everyday life is that family members become more aggressive in their behaviour towards one another. They are easily irritated. Conflicts and rows develop, but they hardly speak about the threats from outside.

C.E., a Turkish girl of 16, had received a residence permit for humanitarian reasons shortly after she joined her mother who had arrived in The Netherlands a year earlier. After three years her mother, who was a victim of torture, was still waiting for an answer to her request for political asylum. So was her brother of 17. C.E. told the therapist about the daily quarrels in the family. Also, she said that she was afraid her mother might be sent back to Turkey, especially since a political friend of the family had been ordered to leave Holland after waiting four years for an answer to his request for asylum. This incident, she said, had never been discussed in the family. Her mother had not shown any reaction when she heard the news.

Sometimes victims of trauma are just not able to verbalize the feelings of fear related to their experiences. Nevertheless, their daily interaction with other people in their primary environment is coloured or disturbed by these feelings.

D.E., a 21-year-old refugee, had been severely tortured while being detained for political reasons. He often had sudden spells of fear, especially in places like restaurants, discos and cinemas. D.E. was not able to discuss these fears with his girlfriend. He usually became angry when she asked him why he wanted to leave suddenly. She thought he was angry at her. During therapy it became clear that the fears were related to flashbacks. D.E. started to talk about his flashbacks with his girlfriend and she gave him considerable support in overcoming them.

Parentification.
This is a condition occurring when one of the children has to assume the responsibilities of one of the parents (Minuchin & Fishman, 1981). For example, a child who learns the language of the country of exile quicker than his parents and functions as interpreter can easily become overburdened.

Sometimes the consequence of a traumatic experience is that the traumatized individual is treated as a victim by the members of his family, or more or less willingly accepts the role of the victim. Unable to take normal responsibilities they are no longer taken seriously. When the traumatized person is a parent who behaves like, or is treated as, a victim this disrupts the hierarchical organization of the family and may result in parentification.

After returning from prison, where he had some very traumatic experiences, F.E. had a lot of invalidating somatic complaints. His wife and his eldest son took charge of most of the problems the family faced. F.E. felt offended that a lot of decisions were taken without him being consulted. He also blamed his son for not achieving at school. The boy, who was 12, seemed to be rather intelligent. He had learned to speak Dutch in less than a year and acted as an interpreter for the family. However, he seemed to have concentration problems at school.

Hierarchy of suffering.
When a family undergoes traumatic experiences, this may result in a hierarchy of suffering coming into existence in a family (cf. Begemann, 1991). In some

families where one or more members have suffered from traumatic experiences, the members who have had no traumatic experiences, or less spectacular ones, may feel their traumatized relatives think they have not suffered seriously and therefore should not whine. The members of the family who have low standing in the hierarchy of suffering then have the feeling they are merely putting it on when they feel depressed, or under stress, and avoid communication about their problems with the other members of the family.

Trans-generational phenomena.
Some family therapists (Boszormenyi-Nagy & Spark, 1973; Stierlin *et al.*, 1980) focus their attention on the history of the family and the phenomena observed through the sequence of generations. Nagy states that each individual in a family has an existential feeling of *loyalty* to his parents and other members of the family. This influences his decisions in daily life. Parents give their children *legacies*, in the form of expectations about the way they will lead their lives. The individual is not always aware of these loyalties, and the legacies that are connected with them. But nevertheless, he behaves as if he felt the obligation to make decisions in a way which concurs with the expectations, orders or wishes of the parents. This means the individual sometimes makes decisions that are against his own interests, feels guilty about decisions which are contrary to the wishes of his parents, or seems to be unable to make a choice. For example, a parent may order the child to achieve a high status in society. This leads the child to choose a study that is beyond his intellectual capacities, so that he experiences failure after failure.

> *In order to pay for his journey to the West, H.E.'s parents had to sell their house. H.E. felt very guilty about this. He hoped to become a doctor, because that was his father's wish. When his achievements at university fell short of his expectations he became very depressed.*

The legacy of a parent may also take the form of a certain attitude or feeling towards life, or people in general, as a result of experiences developed during their lifetime, and which is transferred to the child. For example, an individual may feel depressed for a long time without understanding why, until he realizes that his mother always seemed to be melancholic after the death of her husband. A similar phenomenon can occur after traumatic experiences: when a parent is unable to face certain feelings related to a traumatic event, he may nonetheless still express them and transfer them to the children (Reinoso, 1985).

> *E.E.'s father died in prison when E.E. was two years old. He had been detained for political reasons, after he had been separated from E.E.'s mother and before E.E. was born. E.E. had never seen his father. His mother, who consulted the therapist*

*because she could not handle E.E.'s problematic behaviour, seemed to have
ambivalent feelings about her ex-husband, but described him to her son as a saint.
E.E.'s behaviour had become disruptive at home since his mother had found a
boyfriend. But also he sometimes became aggressive at school when his peers
boasted about their fathers.*

The Consequences of Uprooting

When a family moves to another country, existing forms of dysfunctional
interaction within families may continue. Also, when a refugee goes into exile
without his family, that does not mean he is in every way independent of his
family. For example, the parentification of an oldest son may continue.

*G.E. saved some money each month to call his mother who lived in Africa. After
the call he was always very depressed. His mother never asked him much about
himself, but only complained about her husband and his family.*

Moreover, uprooting may have the following consequences: communication
problems resulting from differences in speed of adaptation, losing contact
with supportive subsystems, problems attached to the formation of a new bi-
cultural system, and problems attached to the possibility of return.

Differences in speed of adaptation.

Even in families functioning well before uprooting, new communication
problems may develop, resulting from differences in the speed of adaptation
to the situation of exile. Conflicts may be related to the fact that one of the
family members begins to deviate from the cultural traditions all of them used
to adhere to in the past.

*I.E. was referred to the therapist because he had difficulty in sleeping. He was a
refugee from Africa. He and his wife arrived in The Netherlands together. I.E.
had trouble learning the language because of his concentration problems, while
his wife mastered it in a year and went on to university. She made friends with
other female students, and embraced some of their ideas about the position of
women in society. I.E. felt threatened by these ideas. The couple started to have
serious disagreements.*

*J.E. came to The Netherlands from the Middle East with his wife and four chil-
dren. His oldest son soon made Dutch friends. When he reached adolescence, he
started behaving like a Dutch adolescent. J.E.'s wife tolerated her son wearing
torn jeans. But she did not dare to discuss it with her husband because that did
not coincide with her view about the behaviour of a decent wife. J.E. himself considered his son's behaviour to be outrageous, and tried to assert his traditional
authority with physical punishment. The boy ran away from home.*

Loss of contact with supportive subsystems.
The effectiveness of a family system in solving problems may deteriorate because communication between subsystems has become difficult, or impossible.

> *When K.E.quarrelled with his wife, usually he did not speak to her for some days. He was used to reacting in this way and had done so since their wedding day. He told the therapist his father did the same thing when he had a disagreement with his mother. In their family, marital problems were usually solved through the intervention of older brothers, or grandparents, who played an intermediary role and tried to invent some solution protecting the husband from losing face. Because his brothers and parents were far away, he had to do without their interventions. He was afraid to lose face if he admitted to his wife that there might be some sense in her point of view.*

Problems attached to the formation of a new, bi-cultural system.
Finally, when a refugee starts a relationship, a bi-cultural system may come into existence. If a family has its roots in different cultures, it will sometimes be necessary to discuss differences in value systems, ideas about the education of children and loyalty to the cultures one wants to transfer to the children. This may become a problem when the family of one of the partners intervenes.

> *L.E., a refugee from the Middle East, and his wife, a refugee from Africa, had some problems from the beginning of their marriage. The problems escalated when L.E.'s parents came to visit them at the time L.E.'s wife was expecting her first child. The parents stressed that the grandson (they would not consider the possibility of the child being a girl) should receive an Islamic name.*

The possibility of return to the native country as a potential problem.
Refugees are people who feel forced to leave their country and give up the life they built up there. Very often the idea of returning to their native country lives on in the back of their mind. During exile, thoughts about return by the various members of a family can easily develop in diverging ways, depending on, among other things, the level of adaptation to life in the country of exile and the emotional attachment formed with some of its inhabitants. Therefore, the possibility of return is a potential problem, which can become apparent when favourable political changes occur in the native country. It then often becomes clear that there are disagreements about return between parents and children, or between husband and wife. Also, long before return becomes a realistic option, conflicting views on the possibility of return may hinder communication within the family.

During a psychotherapeutic interview M.E., a refugee from a Middle Eastern country, discussed his hesitations around choosing an academic study. It became clear that he knew what he wanted, but was afraid to discuss his choice with his parents. His study would be totally useless in his native country, and he would have to tell his parents that he never wanted to return. He described his father as someone who kept himself going by acting as if the possibility of returning was just around the corner, even though the political situation in his native country had in no way changed in a positive direction. He was afraid his father would not be able to endure an open discussion about this matter.

Utility and Limitations of the Family Therapy Approach

The family therapy approach stimulates us to evaluate the complaints and symptoms of a refugee against the background of his interactions with his primary social environment, his family in the first place, but also buddies from his political organization, or room-mates and friends who have become close to him in the country of exile. It makes us sensitive to rigid patterns in the refugee's interaction with the people close to him. It draws attention to matters about which there is no, or only inadequate, communication.

Unfortunately, the construction of a theory about the consequences of traumatization and uprooting based on this approach has only just started. A therapist who wants to use the therapeutic tools offered by this approach is often handicapped because an important part of the family lives far away.

The Learning Theory Approach

The Consequences of Traumatization

Some of the consequences of traumatic experiences—the reliving of these experiences, avoidance of certain situations or activities arousing recollections of the trauma, the physiological reactivity upon exposure to events symbolizing or resembling a part of the traumatic events—can be seen as the result of learning processes. For example, the repeated reliving of traumatic experiences can be explained in terms of conditioning (see, e.g., Lyons & Keane, 1989). During traumatic events conditioning processes are activated, resulting in neutral stimuli becoming associated with the negative emotions and physiological effects that were a natural reaction to the traumatic experiences. If one of these stimuli happens to occur in a new situation, the painful emotions will be relived immediately and the physiological effects that occurred during the traumatic experiences will reappear. Sometimes the original traumatic experiences are instantly re-experienced as well.

A.F. was a refugee from Latin America. He had been tortured after having been arrested by uniformed policemen who had forced their way into his house. Years later he became very confused when a uniformed postman rang the bell to deliver a parcel. When he told this incident to the therapist he started sweating profusely.

The confrontation with neutral stimuli conditioned to the traumatic experiences generally causes feelings of fear and fear-related physiological reactions, such as sweating, hyperventilation, accelerated heartbeat, and other symptoms. Some of these physiological reactions can cause new fears (of choking or having a heart attack, for example). Moreover, the sensations accompanying physiological reactions during traumatization can also form stimuli that can become conditioned to the traumatic events.

For B.F. any sport or exercise could bring back memories of being tortured. The smell of his own sweat seemed to be the stimulus that had become conditioned to the experience of pain and fear while he was tortured.

When the refugee is able to realize that, in spite of his fears, there is no real danger, then it becomes easier for him to cope with the fear, for instance through the use of conscious relaxation.

According to learning theory, a traumatized person tends to avoid stimuli which have become associated with the trauma. This can be seen as a natural reaction. This avoidance behaviour may be adaptive, especially if there is any real danger. In such cases it may prevent new traumatic experiences. It also can be adaptive over a period of time if it prevents the person from having more frightening memories than he is able to handle. The avoided situations would have overwhelmed him instead of enabling him to realize that there is no real danger. Avoidance behaviour, however, can also eliminate all possibility of extinguishing conditioned fear reactions. This may occur if avoidance behaviour becomes a routine through new conditioning. The avoidance of fear then works as (negative) reinforcement, and the 'natural' avoidance reactions to specific stimuli develop into a broad repertoire of avoidance behaviour which becomes a problem in itself.

C.F. became very upset when uniformed inspectors checked his ticket in the subway. Their intimidating and derogatory behaviour reminded him of his arrest and subsequent maltreatment. He became very anxious.

After the incident in the subway, he was afraid to use public transport. He could not face another encounter with inspectors because he thought he might lose control of himself. He started avoiding all activities obliging him to travel. This led to a reduction in his social contacts, and he became more lonely and depressed than before the incident. In his native country C.F. had, for obvious reasons, learned to hide as soon as he saw a uniform, and to avoid situations in which he might be checked by the police or military. After his arrival in Europe this behaviour had not continued. It was the behaviour of the inspectors that triggered his fear.

On the basis of the learning approach, it can be assumed that post-traumatic symptoms are the result of a conditioning process. The maladaptive effects of these conditioning processes can be diminished by exposing the traumatized person, in a non-traumatic situation, to the stimuli that have become associated with the traumatic experience. This exposure can be accomplished by various behaviour therapeutic techniques, such as flooding in imagination (Basoglu, 1992) or other kinds of therapeutically controlled visual imagery (Yüksel, 1991).

Learned Helplessness

The principles of conditioning may be used also to explain passivity, apathy and the attitude of helplessness sometimes manifested by the victims of traumatic experiences. In this context, reference can be made to Seligman's experiments with dogs that had been caged and tormented with electric shocks (Seligman, 1975).

These unfortunate animals were subsequently more prone to illness than dogs which had not been made helpless and exposed to pain. They also behaved differently to other dogs. They were less socially enduring than the average member of their species. When these traumatized dogs were returned to the cage for more electric shocks, but were provided with the possibility of escape by climbing over a barrier to the other side of the cage, their behaviour differed dramatically from that of their non-traumatized fellows. The latter became active and quickly learned to avoid the electric shocks by moving to the other side of the cage. The traumatized dogs remained passive, simply lying down and whining. Seligman describes this behaviour as 'learned helplessness'. It can be unlearned. By dragging them to the other side of the cage, the dogs are shown they can avoid torment. This has to be repeated many times, however (Seligman, Maier & Geer, 1968).

In similar experiments with humans, in which less painful forms of torment were used, similar reactions were observed (Gielis, 1982).

According to Seligman's theory, learned helplessness goes together with four effects:

1. Reduced motivation to react actively. Helpless people tend to adopt a passive attitude. Their reactions are slow and their thinking is sluggish. This is related to their expectation that whatever they do, it will not have any effect on the unpleasant situation in which they find themselves.
2. Reduced capacity to learn that their actions can lead to the desired results.

3. Negative feelings such as fear, depression, emptiness, absence of desires.
4. Self-reproach and reduced self-esteem.

In order to unlearn helplessness, the human victims of traumatic experiences should be given the therapeutic equivalent of 'dragging them over the barrier' as occurred with the dogs in Seligman's experiment (Van der Kolk *et al.*, 1985a). Of course, this is easier said than done.

Seligman's observations can be summarized by stating that traumatization often results in the passivity of the traumatized individual during certain situations. This passivity may be understood as the result of extinction processes occurring during the traumatic experiences because none of the individual's actions in the traumatic situation were followed by positive or negative reinforcement. It may manifest itself in situations in some way resembling the traumatic situation (for example, an initial interview in which the helping professional tries to gather diagnostic information may resemble police interrogation in some respects).

> *D.F. was 13 years old when he arrived in Amsterdam. His parents had put him on an aeroplane because they feared that he would be conscripted into a local militia. They supposed that an aunt who lived in Europe would take care of the boy, but she did not show up at the airport. Apparently, she had left for Canada. D.F. was first received in a children's home, and after a few weeks placed in a foster family. He was sent to a secondary school attended by some compatriots. After some months he was transferred to another school. The reason given was that D.F. and his compatriots, although they soon learned to speak Dutch, formed a clique. They spoke their own language among themselves, which was thought to be disturbing the classroom routine.*
>
> *D.F. was referred to the counsellor because of his passive attitude. He did nothing unless he was ordered to. He made no friends at the new school. He was a member of a sports club, but during the weekly training he showed the same passivity.*
>
> *In the contact with the therapist D.F. seemed very timid. However, he slowly came out of his shell when the therapist addressed him in his native language. He pretended to be indifferent about living far away from his parents and having been moved around like a parcel. He was able to admit that he did not like his school and considered himself to be a failure. It became clear that at this school he had to learn two foreign languages while speaking Dutch was still quite an effort.*
>
> *The therapist tried to find out what D.F. had liked or considered as interesting while he was still with his parents, but received only evasive answers. There seemed to be an absence of desires. So he concluded that D.F.'s condition was*

similar to 'learned helplessness', the trauma being the sudden separation from
his parents, and later from his friends at school.

The Consequences of Uprooting

Learning theories stress the importance of the environment in which behaviour
is learned. Within this framework it seems justified to assume that specific cultural situations may result in the learning of specific forms of behaviour.
Behaviour adequate in a particular culture may be inadequate in a different one.
This means that, after uprooting, new behaviour has to be acquired, especially
social problem-solving skills (Pellegrini, 1985). It also means that some problem-solving or coping behaviour which was adequate and protective in the
native culture, but inadequate in the new culture, should be restricted to certain
situations (for instance, meetings with compatriots), or unlearned.

> *E.F., a refugee from a South East Asian country, had left his country because*
> *he was a politically active member of an ethnic minority that lately had*
> *become the object of persecution. He was an extremely polite, soft-spoken per-*
> *son, who never contradicted anybody. This attitude had rather negative conse-*
> *quences. For instance, the government official who interrogated him about his*
> *request for political asylum had said to E.F. that he supposed he had never been*
> *in trouble for political reasons. E.F. politely confirmed this, although he had*
> *been detained twice for political reasons. Therefore, E.F.'s request for political*
> *asylum was denied.*
>   *The social worker who was appointed to help E.F. with some practical prob-*
> *lems became desperate. He could never be sure whether E.F. really wanted*
> *something, or was just being compliant. He referred E.F. to the therapist. Soon*
> *it became clear to the therapist that E.F.'s pliant attitude had been very useful*
> *for a member of an ethnic minority in his native country and had become sec-*
> *ond nature.*

The complaints and symptoms of refugees might become more understandable if they are seen as learned behaviour, or as resulting from a lack of
adequate social skills for their present cultural surrounding. That means, the
therapist should discuss the difficulties they experience in daily social
encounters, and must be aware of the possibility that his own behaviour may
not be in line with the social conventions the refugee has learned in his own
culture.

Utility and Limitations of the Learning Theory Approach

Learning theories provide us with clear concepts and formulations which help
us to understand the problems of refugees as well as providing interesting

points of application for psychotherapeutic techniques. However, an important limitation is that these theories have not produced much to facilitate the understanding of the more complicated aspects of refugees' behaviour and inner life, such as contradictory feelings, doubts about the meaning of life, nightmares, self-destructive imagination, and so on. The concept of learned helplessness, as introduced by Seligman, can be seen as an effort to fill this gap. But by using such terms as expectation, self-reproach and reduced self-esteem, Seligman introduces a cognitive element into his explanation. In the following section, it will be shown that this cognitive element becomes the backbone of a more recent reformulation of his theory. Moreover, a cognitive reformulation of the theory of classical conditioning will be discussed which can be very helpful in understanding the psychological consequences of traumatization by political violence.

The Cognitive Approach

The Consequences of Traumatization

In this section, the hypotheses are discussed that traumatization may result in inadequate cognitive representations and self-instructions, disturbances in information processing, and changes in world-view and self-image. In addition to this, the coping styles and explanatory styles of victims of trauma will be discussed.

Inadequate cognitive representations and self-instructions.
Cognitive concepts can be integrated in different ways into the learning approach, by assuming that behaviour, among other things, is determined by cognitive representations that can be conceptualized as inner speech or self-instructions (cf. Meichenbaum, 1979).

When a person has traumatic experiences, these experiences instigate conditioning processes, in which not only bio-physiological reactions, but also cognitive representations and self-instructions become connected with previously neutral stimuli that occurred during the traumatic events. These cognitive representations and self-instructions may have been adequate at the time the trauma occurred, but are often inadequate in the current situation and result in maladaptive behaviour (cf. Korrelboom *et al.*, 1989). This maladaptive behaviour can be changed by changing the cognitive representations by which it is determined. For instance, behaviour can be altered when new self-instructions are acquired through observational learning (cf. Meichenbaum, 1979).

The conditioned bio-physiological responses can be deconditioned by exposing the traumatized individual to a variety of stimuli that have become conditioned to the traumatic events, *under circumstances in which the cognitive representations of the traumatic events are not proven to be adequate at this time.* That is to say, exposure will only work beneficially in a safe situation in which the individual feels protected, respected, is supported in getting control over his reactions and is also encouraged to change his cognitive representations of the traumatic events as well as the self-intructions connected with these cognitive representations (cf. Korrelboom *et al.*, 1989). This is an important correction to the claim that exposure can be beneficial in any non-traumatic situation and that cognitive changes are not necessary.

Classical conditioning is usually defined as a process in which some reflex that is the involuntary consequence of a particular stimulus becomes linked to another stimulus that is contingent with the first stimulus. The stimulus that has the reflex behaviour as a natural consequence is called the unconditioned stimulus (UCS). The reflex behaviour is called unconditioned response (UCR). And the contingent stimulus that becomes linked to the reflex behaviour is called the conditioned stimulus (CS). According to the theory of classical conditioning, the CS is thought to automatically provoke a response (called the conditioned response, CR).

From a cognitive point of view, classical conditioning can be seen as a process in which the organism tries, in an active way, to gain knowledge about its environment (Davey, 1989). The CS is consciously experienced by the subject as a predictor of a UCS. In the case of a traumatic UCS, it is experienced as a precursor of another painful experience of extreme helplessness. The habitual response following the CS is a preparatory response on the anticipated UCS, through which the traumatized individual tries to cope with pain and feelings of extreme helplessness. It is similar to the response he showed during and directly after the occurrence of the traumatic events.

Emanating from both the classic behaviouristic and the cognitive view on conditioning, the effect of traumatic experience can be summarized as follows: A conglomerate of stimuli contingent with a traumatic experience, which can be described in simple terms (for example, the sound of rattling keys or the smell of blood) or have a more complex nature (a tone of voice which suggests humiliation, being alone in a small room) can become conditioned stimuli. The traumatic experience triggered bio-physiological reflexes, such as sweating, an acceleration of heartbeat, hyperventilation and so on, which later can be triggered by the abovementioned types of conditioned stimuli.

Often traumatic experience is not a momentary presentation of a distinct stimulus, but something that may continue for hours or longer. This means that the abovementioned bio-physiological reactions, triggered when the first traumatic stimulus is perceived, become contingent with trauma-related stimuli appearing later. Therefore, the bodily sensations and feelings (for instance, tightness of the chest and oppression) generated by these bio-physiological reactions, but that might occur also under different circumstances, may become conditioned stimuli.

According to the cognitive view on conditioning, the conditioned stimuli also bring the representation of the UCS to awareness. This means that a memory of the traumatic experience comes to the mind. This memory interferes with other cognitive activities (for instance, when the person is reading a book at the time the CS presents itself, the memory may disturb his concentration). Both the bio-physiological reactions and the memory result in emotions (usually fear, disgust, aggression, depression or a numb feeling).

In the case of a traumatic experience the representation of the UCS is not just a memory, but also has a complex structure of thoughts related to the traumatic experience. It contains causal explanations or attributions, a complex of thoughts one may summarize with such terms as self-image and world-view and (usually pessimistic) ideas about voluntary action that could aid an escape from a repetition of the negative sensations accompanying the traumatic experience.

This cognitive representation of the UCS also involves thoughts about conscious, voluntary actions the individual may undertake to cope with his bio-physiological reactions and the accompanying sensations and emotions. In other words: the cognitive representations include self-instructions eventually resulting in some overt responses. Usually these responses have been the best possible reactions in the traumatic situation. But they may be not very adaptive under different circumstances.

Therapy can be focused on changing the UCS representations by discussion, explanation and relabelling. For instance, what a refugee experiences as fear, can sometimes be relabelled as understandable and legitimate rage. Although not bad in itself it has to be canalized in an adaptive way. UCS representations can also be changed by suggesting alternative self-instructions.

U.G. suffered from flashbacks about his experience in a refugee camp that was invaded by soldiers. When he had a flashback, he had the tendency to hide in his room. The therapist explained to U.G. about the phenomenon of flashbacks and their bio-physiological aspects. He taught him several breathing and relaxation exercises. He suggested to U.G. that, at the first sensation of fear, he should instruct himself to say: I have to counter these physical reactions by doing one of the exercises.

Disturbances in information processing.
During the periods that a person is undergoing traumatic experiences, he is perceiving an enormous amount of very complex information. This information includes: physical sensations of pain; emotional reactions such as fear, disgust, shame and sexual excitement; physical sensations and reactions that are brought about by physiological reactions related to the abovementioned emotions; emotional reactions to these physical sensations and reactions; perceptions of environmental attributes in which the person is subjected to traumatic experiences; perceptions of the characteristics of the perpetrator and possible bystanders; the thoughts of the person about himself during the

traumatic experiences; the memories that were revived during the traumatic experiences, and so on.

This bulk of information can easily become overwhelming. Comparing the human mind to a computer (cf. Seifert & Hoffnung, 1987), the following hypotheses could be formulated. The average person's functional capacity for processing information will fall short in processing the enormous amount of information connected with traumatic events. This means, at least part of the information is not transformed and not stored in the long-term memory, but continues to occupy large parts of the short-term sensory store or short-term memory. This condition implies that it stays close to awareness and may easily become present again in the form of intrusive memories, flashbacks and nightmares. It implies also that the capacity of the short-term memory to store new information becomes less: it is already filled with information related to the traumatic experiences. This results in disturbances in information processing, becoming apparent in symptoms such as forgetfulness and loss of concentration with regard to current activities. The condition that the information related to the traumatic experiences has not been transformed into long-term memory has a second effect: when re-entering awareness it is as vivid and intrusive as during the traumatic experiences themselves.

Departing from these hypotheses, recommendations can be made regarding psychotherapy with trauma victims. From an information theoretical viewpoint, the objective of psychotherapy would be to help the victim to transform the information about his traumatic experiences. Then it can be stored in the long-term memory and will no longer disturb his cognitive functioning. This objective could be approached by discussing in an orderly way all the information associated with the traumatic experiences. The information can be arranged and classified. The 'testimony method', which is described in Chapter 7, is a set of psychotherapeutic techniques used with victims of organized violence. In this therapeutic technique the accent is on a chronological ordering of the information. It is an example of a therapeutic method in line with this cognitive approach. Another example is the following.

A.G. was a refugee from a Middle Eastern country who had been traumatized over a period of seven years both during combat and during captivity. One day he started the conversation with the therapist by complaining. During the last week he had had three or four nightmares every night. He added, he kept thinking of these nightmares all day. Then he stopped talking. The therapist asked him to describe in detail the worst nightmare that came to mind. By this question the therapist tried, among other things, to help the refugee to structure his experiential world (in this case, in a hierarchy of bad experiences).

Changes in world-view and self-image.

Victims of traumatic experiences have undergone an experience which, even if they were aware of danger, they did not imagine could happen to themselves (Janoff-Bulman, 1989). They have experienced mortal danger and this has altered their *world-view*. As a result they experience the world as threatening. They feel less safe than before and tend to interpret various neutral phenomena as harbingers of danger. Their *self-image* also changes, to the extent that they feel powerless in the face of these perceived dangers. In order to be able to function properly again victims have to integrate their traumatic experiences into a new world-view and self-image. Their encounters with malevolence, meaninglessness and personal failure have to be assimilated. In this connection, the repeated reliving of traumatic experiences can be seen as an attempt to process new information provided by the traumatic experiences, in such a way that their original world-view and self-image remain intact as far as possible. In this connection, Tailor, Wood and Lichtman (1983) have noted that victims often minimize or even trivialize what has happened to them. Apparently they want to avoid constantly having the impression the world is unsafe. They do not want to seem pathetic or in need of help, either to themselves or to others.

Minimizing traumatic experiences is not the same as denial in the psychoanalytical sense of defence mechanism. Denial means that something which was conscious, or could have been conscious, becomes or remains unconscious. When experiences are minimized they remain conscious, together with the associated emotions. The negative side of the emotional meaning of the experience is relativized rather than simply denied. Ascribing a 'positive meaning' to traumatic experiences is also a way of minimizing their negative side. The victim thinks his experience was useful, even necessary in order to do well later on.

> *N.G. fled his native country after being imprisoned for a few years on the charge of distributing political pamphlets. He was a member of a sectarian political group. His political ideas were based on his study of the only critical book he could find in his country. Once in exile he read a lot about political ideology. His views became more sophisticated. 'It's a good thing that I was forced into exile', he said. 'If I had continued I would have become a terrorist and caused more trouble in my country than there is already.'*

Coping styles.

Coping refers to cognitive activities elicited by psycho-social stress and aimed at adaptation. Traumatization and uprooting are both forms of psycho-social stress and therefore will activate coping activity.

The concept of coping was introduced in the section on the psychodynamic approach. There it refers to an intrapsychic process and the effects of this process on behaviour and cognitive functioning. It was briefly mentioned also in the context of the discussion of learning theory. There it refers primarily to problem-solving behaviour.

In psychological studies coping can also refer to activities with a cognitive component, such as discussing problems with others, consciously trying to stop thinking about certain experiences, consciously trying to 'get over' certain negative feelings or not thinking in a certain way, or looking at the funny side of problematic situations.

Many researchers assume that there are different *styles* of coping. In the section on the psychodynamic approach Schumacher's (1982) descriptions of regressive coping (which, because it includes the avoidance of perceiving traumatic circumstances, is partly described in cognitive terms), coping by adaptive defence, and adaptive progressive coping were mentioned. Regarding the behaviour of people in extreme circumstances, a distinction can also be made between those who try to influence the situation in which they find themselves, those who direct their energy to controlling their own emotional reactions, and those who—in cognitive terms—come to view their painful experiences differently, thus reducing their influence (Miller *et al.*, 1985). Another categorization (Folkman & Lazarus, 1988) is even more cognitive in its terminology. It integrates some of the previously mentioned descriptions.

According to Folkman and Lazarus the following dimensions of coping style can be identified.

1. Coping by the deployment of attention. This refers to coping activity diverting attention from the source of distress (avoidance strategies), or directing attention to it (vigilant strategies).
2. Coping by changing the subjective meaning or significance of a person–environment transaction. This involves transforming a threat into a challenge, denying its existence, emphasizing the positive aspects of the situation, or distancing (for example by making jokes about it). Distancing may be very adaptive in situations where nothing can be done.
3. Coping by changing the actual terms of the person–environment relationship. This can be done through either 'confrontive coping' (an assertive or even somewhat aggressive interpersonal form in which the individual defends his rights or makes clear what he wants, possibly generating negative emotions in the person who is being confronted), or by 'planned problem-solving' (a strategy of using rational problem-solving while at the same time inviting others to provide emotional support).

It can be useful to assess the ways in which a refugee is coping with his problems and to stimulate him to explore alternative ways of coping.

B.G. suffered from intrusive memories of his experiences during captivity. He said he actively tried to put the images of the past out of his mind, but was not able to do so. The therapist concluded that B.G. used coping by deployment of attention in the form of an avoidance strategy. He suggested that B.G. make brief notes, or a quick drawing, of the content of the intrusive memories before he tried to put them out of his mind. The notes and drawings became the subject for discussion during therapy. The intrusive memories soon became less frequent and less disturbing.

C.G. requested assistance because he had uncontrollable outbursts of anger. He had beaten his girlfriend during one of these outbursts. He felt very ashamed about this. At first, the therapist interpreted these aggressive outbursts as a post-traumatic symptom of increased arousal. C.G. had been traumatized severely during the years he was detained and tortured. Later, when he had heard more about C.G.'s behaviour in prison, he concluded that it might be interpreted also as a form of confrontive coping he used whenever he was suspicious. This became clear when the therapist had the opportunity to tell C.G. he had received a residence permit on humanitarian grounds. C.G. was not able to concentrate on the rather complicated legal facts the therapist had to explain, became very suspicious, anxious and finally aggressive. It was the fear perceived in C.G.'s reaction that made the therapist think aggression might be his way of coping with fear, in this case the fear of being cheated and eventually sent back to his torturers.

In the next session, C.G. apologized. The therapist asked him if he had ever had the same feelings as he felt during the last session. C.G. then described some prison experiences. He explained that aggression had been the only way to prevent himself from giving information to the prison guards, especially if they seemed nice and patient. This form of confrontive coping was useful in prison, but became obsolete during exile.

Explanation or attribution styles.
The thoughts about explanation and attribution styles of traumatized people presented here are based on laboratory research about the reactions of human beings to pain and stressful experiences they could not control (for an overview of this kind of research, see Wortman, 1983). They ought to be preceded by a relativizing observation about the possibilities of applying the generalizations of this research to clinical work with refugees. The stressful experiences one can inflict on a person in a laboratory situation differ considerably in intensity, quality, diversity and duration from the traumatic experiences some refugees have undergone (for example, sexual torture or the 'disappearance' of a relative after he was arrested by the secret police).

The laboratory research on explanation styles started as a trial to show that Seligman's theory of 'learned helplessness' in dogs was useful in explaining the occurrence of chronic depressive symptoms in human beings, and led eventually to a reformulation of Seligman's theory in cognitive terms (Peterson & Seligman, 1984). This revized theory focuses on the way people attribute causal explanations to painful experiences they cannot control. It can be summarized as follows.

When people have experienced painful events that they could not control, they usually wonder why the events happened. Their answer, that is the cause they attribute to the events, determines, or is representative of, the way they react to difficult situations. It is possible to distinguish three explanatory dimensions in people's answers to the question: 'Why did it happen to me?' Firstly, the individual can see himself as the cause of the calamity (internal attribution), or attribute it to the situation in which he found himself (external explanation). Secondly, the causal factor may be described as transient and alterable, or persistent and unalterable. Finally, the cause may be limited to the event (specific explanation), or may effect a whole variety of outcomes (global explanation) (Peterson & Seligman, 1984).

> *D.G., E.G., F.G. and G.G. all had the same complaints: they had started having nightmares again. 'It's because I stopped taking my sleeping tablets, I was not really ready to stop completely', was D.G.'s explanation. This explanation implied his complaints would be alleviated by changing only one clearly defined aspect of his behaviour—taking his sleeping tablets. He explained his complaints in terms of a cause he experienced as internal, specific and transient. E.G. remarked: 'Since I began to consider returning to my native country things have not been going well.' In this explanation he gives the impression that he is the cause of the recurrence of his nightmares, and that they are not his only problem. He has an internal, global and transient explanation. In connection with her nightmares F.G. said: 'It's so cold here. It's never as cold as this in the country where I come from. When it's so cold everything goes wrong.' She refers to an external, transient cause—the weather. Because she said that everything went wrong, her explanation is global. G.G. gave the following explanation: 'This weekend I saw a film in which people were tortured and as a result painful memories surfaced.' He refers to an external, specific, transient cause.*

> *H.G., I.G., J.G. and K.G. felt lonely and depressed. H.G. said: 'It's because I have an egocentric character; everything I do goes wrong.' He experiences the cause as persistent, internal and global. I.G. gave the following explanation: 'It's because the people here are so cold. You are never welcome. I will never feel at home here.' He perceives the cause as persistent, external and global. J.G. remarked: 'It's because I can't learn the language, it's just too difficult for me. That's why I don't have any friends and feel lousy.' Here the cause is experienced as internal, persistent and global. K.G. said: 'My girlfriend broke off our relationship because*

she doesn't want to have children. I miss her terribly, I cannot live without her.'
This is a specific, external, persistent cause.

The modes of explanation which an individual uses to account for unpleasant experiences are not, or only to a very limited extent, related to the events in question (Peterson & Seligman, 1984). They tend, rather, to conform to a personal cognitive style.

People who tend to explain unpleasant experiences in terms of internal, persistent and global causes are more likely to react with depression and helplessness. They see the cause of their problems as persistent, therefore they do not see any possibility of changing their situation for the better. They see the cause of their problems as global; this implies that they think it will continue to cause new problems, which, of course, is a depressing thought. Since they view the cause of their problems as internal, they tend to feel guilty or inferior. Of course, psychotherapists will add that reflecting on one's own role in causing the problems need not necessarily lead to feelings of guilt, and can be seen as positive when it results in a change of behaviour.

According to Seligman, a mode of explanation which accounts for experiences in terms of external, transient and specific causes offers more scope for the adequate assimilation of painful events.

This theory has been supported by laboratory and other research using diverse empirical methods and very different samples. Moreover, it has been argued that a maladaptive explanatory style could be shaped by a catastrophic, traumatic experience as well as by a series of mild stressors, such as during childhood receiving the parental message over and over again that one is personally inept and to blame for the difficulties encountered in life (McCormick, Taber & Kruedelbach, 1989). It has also been shown that psychotherapeutic techniques can bring about changes in the mode of explanation used to account for negative experiences.

Refugees may have explanatory models that are unfamiliar to Western therapists. For example: some refugees attribute ther problems to supernatural causes (Handelman & Yeo, 1996). And quite often refugees direct their attention mainly to factors they cannot influence. Powerlessness (and the accompanying feelings of anger and sorrow) is then the dominant emotion. The therapist can use Seligman's theory to analyse the mode of explanation which a particular refugee applies to his problems. However, attributing a problem to a persistent cause and concluding it is unsolvable, may be realistic (cf. Gielis, 1982). When refugees consider the losses they have suffered by going into exile as persistent and unalterable they are sometimes right. Coping with the emotions related to this observation, plus learning to differentiate between what is really unalterable and what may change over time, then becomes vitally important.

By analysing the way in which a refugee explains his problems the therapist can attempt to direct his attention to aspects of his situation which force him to alter his explanation, thereby offering a point of departure for beneficial behavioural changes, and perhaps even for a change in his general explanatory style. For example, the therapist can try to replace a global mode of explanation with a specific mode. This would help to give the refugee a more balanced view of his situation and stimulate a more realistic and adaptive self-image.

> H.G. explained his problems in terms of his egocentric character. The therapist knew from H.G.'s life history that he had been very active in a human rights organization. He asked H.G. whether he thought these activities had also stemmed from his egocentrism. A discussion ensued, as a result of which H.G. concluded he did have egocentric traits, and he was no different from anyone else in that respect. But H.G. also concluded he was capable of displaying less egocentric characteristics as well.

Similarly, an internal mode of explanation can be replaced by an external mode.

> I.G. initially explained his depression and loneliness in terms of the cold and impassive character of the people in his country of exile. Soon it became clear that he was using this to repress another explanation which was on his mind: 'It's because I'm mad.' He found this plausible because he was consulting a psychotherapist. The therapist suggested his problems might be related to events he had experienced a few years earlier. These events had been so terrible that they would cause anyone with a normal emotional life to have depressions for some time afterward. He asked whether I.G. had nightmares. As a result, in subsequent interviews, I.G.'s terrible combat experiences were discussed. He no longer seemed to be troubled by the idea he was mad. Also, he became less ashamed of the emotions which talking about the past evoked.

Sometimes the prospect for improvement is increased if attention can be shifted from unalterable external causes to an internal cause, and the refugee begins to reflect on his problems.

> J.G. was dissatisfied with her life. She felt that her boyfriend was hindering her political activities. They were both the same nationality but they had met when already in exile. The therapist observed that, in spite of her political involvement, from among her many compatriots she had chosen one who no longer wanted to be politically active. He pointed out her responsibility for her own situation. Perhaps she was ambivalent about her political activities? The interview contin-

ued and she expressed doubts about the political views for which she had been active for so long.

Finally, the refugee may explain his problems on different levels simultaneously.

K.G. explained his depressions by the fact that he had been waiting to be granted refugee status for two years. He had a global, external, alterable explanation for his depressions. Interviews with the therapist stimulated self-reflection. After a while it appeared that he could also trace his sombre moods to internal causes. His first attempt to give an internal explanation comes down to the following: another important cause of my problems is I had to flee and go into exile, and that was because I didn't listen to my parents and went and got involved in politics.

The cognitive reformulation of Seligman's theory about 'learned helplessness' has provoked a lot of critical comments. For instance, it has been argued that explanatory styles are not sufficient to describe a helpless attitude. Such an attitude usually goes together with a much more complex pattern of discouraging cognitions and inadequate problem-solving strategies (cf. Dweck & Wortman, 1982). When facing some problem-solving task, people with a helpless attitude tend to manifest more task-irrelevant behaviour. They also tend to direct their attention to themselves, especially to the personality characteristics which they consider to be negative. This means they do not concentrate fully on the task before them, which increases the probability they will fail. They make less effort and give themselves less positive instructions. Moreover, they seem to consider earlier successful experiences to be less relevant. The attributional styles they use to explain failure are not identical to the attributional styles they use to explain success. For instance, they usually ascribe failure to a stable cause, but consider success to be the result of sheer coincidence (Dweck & Wortman, 1982).

Utility and Limitations of the Cognitive Approach

For learning theory, the cognitive approach stimulated an extension of the concept of behaviour. The term behaviour is no longer reserved for overt, observable action. It can refer also to thoughts, self-instructions, convictions and cognitive strategies for solving problems. This means that the cognitive categories discussed above are seen as susceptible to modification through special training, instruction, or education. This cognitive-behavioural perspective offers new ideas for the psychological treatment of refugees and other traumatized persons.

With regard to refugees, the cognitive approach also suggests that the explanations refugees give for their symptoms can become an important obstacle to their recovery, and their explanatory style can be altered by offering them plausible alternative explanations. For instance, symptoms evaluated by the refugee as a sign of going mad can be explained to him as the usual side-effects of a normal process of repair. When the refugee starts to recover he can be prepared for relapses, in a similar way, by explaining to him that the process of recovery often follows an uneven course that is best described by some variant of 'three steps forward, two steps back' (Simons *et al.*, 1986).

Summary and Conclusions

The problems for which refugees seek help can be clarified by making theoretical extrapolations about the consequences of traumatization and uprooting. These extrapolations result in diagnostic categories which may help the therapist in obtaining relevant diagnostic information, and also suggest points of departure for psychotherapy.

Each of the theoretical approaches mentioned above highlights some special part of reality, and ignores other parts. Also, they structure reality in different ways, on different levels of abstraction. That way they are complementary.

CHAPTER 3

Diagnostic Appraisal

The starting point for any kind of assistance to refugees is to listen carefully to the complaints they present. These complaints can initially be simply transcribed as the refugee relates them, then later amplified by the observations of the therapist or social worker, and finally completed with the professional's interpretation of what he heard and observed in terms of the various practical or theoretical approaches he feels comfortable with.

In the first contact with the refugee the helping professional will usually try to come to an agreement with the refugee as to the nature of his problem. He tries to summarize the complaints of the refugee in terms that are recognizable for both the refugee and the professional and which suggest the direction in which their cooperation can develop.

The articulation of the problem in terms that make sense for both parties will suggest topics about which the therapist needs to know more, in order to reach an understanding of the circumstances and processes that brought the problem into being in the first place. Talking about these subjects will also provide him with information about the necessity of assistance, and possible starting points for therapy.

The term diagnostic appraisal refers here to this process of gathering information in order to gain insight into both the problem itself and points of application for professional help (cf. De Wit & Tak, 1996). It is an effort to look from a certain distance, with as much objectivity as possible, at the problem of the refugee, and to interpret what is seen and heard in such a way that the phenomena can be related to one another in a meaningful way.

In order to be able to choose a therapeutical approach, the therapist also has to make an estimation of the capacities and limitations of the refugee, in relation to his own professional capacities and limitations. This means among other things that the therapist tries to make an estimation of the motivation of the refugee to change certain aspects of his behaviour or to make certain opinions a subject for discussion, and observes how the refugee reacts to tentative proposals for tackling his problems.

Diagnostic Appraisal as a Regulative Cycle

At the end of the first interviews, diagnostic appraisal results in a series of provisional statements about the coming into existence of the problem and starting points for professional help for the individual refugee. These statements form a hypothesis. Often it is possible to look at the problem from more than one angle, and to formulate more than one hypothesis. These hypotheses may amplify one another, or be contradictory. In the latter case more information is needed to decide which of them is most credible and offers the clearest perspective for therapy.

A diagnostic statement worded or written at a certain moment does not of course have unlimited validity. It tells 'with a reasonable amount of certainty' the ins and outs of the problem, but its contents should be continuously tested in the light of all new information that becomes available in later therapeutic sessions. New data may generate new insight, which forces the therapist to adjust his approach or even change it radically. Thus diagnostic appraisal will continue just as long as the assistance process. It is a process of adjusting one's course to every new signal, in order to help as effectively as possible.

In order to avoid turning in circles, the progress of this process needs to be accounted for. It is important to give explicit descriptions of each decision that is taken during the course of the helping process, so that the therapist can justify his interventions. In making reports about these therapeutic interventions, the professional reconstructs his patterns of decision-making in relation to the modifications made in the diagnostic hypotheses due to the reception of new information.

Making these reconstructions after each interview is called the 'regulative cycle'. Its components are: the complaints, the diagnostic hypotheses, the questions aimed at obtaining more information or other therapeutic interventions made on the bases of the diagnostic hypotheses, decisions made on the basis of new information, an evaluation of their effects, and reappraisal of the original diagnostic hypotheses.

A.H., a refugee from a South East Asian country, had lived through a long series of traumatic experiences, starting with the killing of his father for political reasons. After the death of his father, he fled and lost contact with his family. He was 15 at that time. In the following years he had many traumatic combat experiences. He requested political asylum at the age of 20. When he first requested psychological assistance, he was 24.

He suffered from nightmares and spells of panic and looked very depressed. He nevertheless continued his studies at a technical school, played his weekly game of volleyball and continued to have an intimate relationship with a girlfriend.

The following diagnostic hypothesis was formulated: Post-Traumatic Stress Disorder, aggravated by the continuing traumatic uncertainty about his request for political asylum and the very realistic fear of being sent back to his country, in an otherwise adequately functioning young adult.

A.H. at first was treated with anxiolitic medication and supportive therapeutic techniques. After he had received a residence permit, the therapist applied techniques directed toward working through traumatic experiences by discussing his nightmares and the memories related to those nightmares. During this phase of the therapy, A.H. managed to find out where his mother was living and started to correspond with her and other relatives. After eight months A.H.'s complaints had disappeared and therapy was concluded.

Two years later, A.H. requested assistance again. This time he complained of spells of anxiety, depression and thoughts of suicide. These complaints had started after a compatriot had put pressure on him to return to his country as a guerrilla. In the meantime A.H. was still functioning well at his work and the relationship with his girlfriend continued. The therapist failed to look at the story from the family process point of view, and forgot to ask how his girlfriend reacted to the returning of his problems.

The therapist started treatment from the diagnostic hypothesis that A.H. had not worked through parts of his traumatic experiences, which had been brought back to his memory through the meeting with his compatriot. This hypothesis at first seemed to be correct: A.H. spontaneously started to talk about some horrifying incidents which included the killing of close friends. But this time the discussions did not result in any improvement of his condition.

In the sixth interview anti-depressive medication was prescribed. This had an unforeseen effect. A.H. took the medication only once and it made him a bit drowsy. This drew the attention of his girlfriend. She asked him what was wrong with him, and A.H. told her about things he had tried to conceal from her: his depressive feelings and his thoughts of suicide. 'After that night', A.H. said in the seventh interview, 'I decided to pull myself together. I realized I was not alone and helpless, that there are people who stood by me. I realized that I had to take care of my girlfriend, that she needs me. I do not feel suicidal any more. The fear still comes occasionally, but then I think: it will go away, and so it goes.' He also told the therapist that his girlfriend and he had decided to marry as soon as possible.

After this interview, the therapist concluded his original diagnostic hypothesis had not been proven wrong, but that part of the problem had been a disturbance in the communication between A.H. and his girlfriend (a hypothesis from the family process approach). A.H. had concealed his problems, and it might prove worthwhile to know his motives for doing so. It turned out that he had been ashamed, and that the return of his symptoms had confirmed his view that he was essentially a weak person for whom other people would have contempt. So a diagnostic hypothesis could be added in terms of the psychodynamic approach: traumatization had resulted in a negative self-image.

In the tenth interview, A.H. told the therapist that he had decided to go back to the part of his country that was under control of an anti-government group in order to visit his mother whom he had not seen since he was 15. He said that he had the feeling that his mother needed to see him. The therapist noted the coincidence between the fixing of a date for the marriage and the decision to visit his mother. He concluded that another psychodynamic diagnostic hypothesis could be added: reactivation of inner problems related to the forced separation from his mother.

Which Information is Needed?

What kind of information is needed for diagnostic appraisal? The answer to this question is in the first place dependent on the theoretical approach of the helping professional, and probably also not independent of less rational beliefs or stereotypical views he may have. Nevertheless most therapists who work with refugees will agree about a basic 'shopping list' which is useful in making a rough screening during the first interviews. The items on this list are:

1. The therapist's first impression of the refugee.
2. Complaints and statements about problematic behaviour, the concrete situations in which both these complaints and this problematic behaviour manifest themselves, and factors or conditions that make the disturbing effect of the complaints or problematic behaviour more or less severe.
3. Information about aspects of the psychological functioning of the refugee which are not problematic, but adequate or even charming, and about environmental factors that suggest points of application for professional help, like the availability of a social network, such as a family or a compatriot community, which can provide emotional support (Boman & Edwards, 1984; Figley, 1985; Wren, 1986).
4. Information about the way in which both the refugee and people in his social environment experience his problem, and their ideas about what caused or provoked the complaints or problematic behaviour.
5. Information about traumatic experiences that the refugee may have undergone.
6. Information about the course of the refugee's personality development, and the level of his development in various dimensions.
7. Information about the political field of forces to which the refugee is a subject, and other environmental stress factors that are burdening him, such as uncertainty about his legal status, having to live in a neighbourhood with a high incidence of delinquency, worries about relatives who have remained behind, illness of a family member and so on.

8. Signals that indicate the possible presence of psychiatric symptoms, like disturbances in perception and reasoning and so on.
9. Statements about the kind of help the refugee himself asks for or explicitly rejects, in relation to experiences he possibly had with other helping professionals.

This information has of course to be evaluated against the refugee's cultural background. The therapist also has to be aware of the possibility that the setting may restrict the information he gets. For example, a refugee may not talk about sexual trauma when members of his family or an interpreter are present, and some topics might be omitted because of the sex of the therapist.

Diagnostic Tools

The most important source of diagnostic information is the clinical interview with the refugee. Diagnostic interviews sometimes have to be conducted with the assistance of an interpreter. In such cases there is always the possibility of translation errors, disturbances in the refugee's reasoning, the refugee being misunderstood by the translator, or the refugee withholding relevant information because he does not trust the interpreter for political or other reasons.

Additional sources of diagnostic information are people in the direct environment of the refugee, like members of his family who are also in exile, or other people who assist the refugee. These could include, for example, his lawyer or language teacher. Sometimes, notably in the case of children, it can be useful to contact relatives in the native country.

Diagnostic questionnaires can be useful, especially if they are worded in the native language of the refugee. Standardized tasks, such as projective tests or the instruction to make a drawing, can be very helpful in the contact with children.

Observation is an important diagnostic tool, either during interviews in the consulting room or in the refugee's home. It can for example be very useful to note the frequency and quality of eye contact, signs of tension, and the refugee's general appearance.

Finally, tentative interventions are an important diagnostic tool. In a first diagnostic interview one can for example try to find out the refugee's reaction to advice by giving him advice on some minor point of his problem, and then asking him about the effects at the following meeting.

The Diagnostic Interview

In the diagnostic interview two things are important: to maximize the active contribution of the refugee to the conversation, and to stimulate him to give relevant information about his personal problems. With regard to these two goals the following suggestions are useful.

It is essential that the helping professional should have a 'warm' attitude, which he expresses in both words and non-verbal behaviour, and which represents his genuine care and interest. Next to this basic attitude, in the first contacts it is usually more stimulating for the refugee if one frequently reacts with short statements or asks simple questions (cf. Pope & Siegman, 1972), than when one just sits back and listens—although the latter approach seems to be indicated in the odd case.

> *B.H., a 17-year-old boy, hardly gave the therapist the opportunity to introduce himself before he started to talk about what had happened after his arrest in a dictatorship in the Middle East, four months earlier. He did not seem to want any interruption. The therapist's only reaction was to sit close to B.H., but without physical contact. After half an hour of talking about the torture he had undergone, he started to cry, and this was the first opportunity for the therapist to intervene verbally.*

In diagnostic interviews, open-ended questions (e.g. *What is your most important problem at this moment?*) often result, after some hesitation, in longer answers than questions phrased in a more directive way (e.g. *Did that happen in prison, or after your escape?*). The answers to open-ended questions generally also contain more personal data. But when the topic of conversation is highly emotionally charged for the refugee, directive questions produce more information than open-ended questions (cf. Pope & Siegman, 1972). In the latter case, however, the answers will often not be more than a series of facts. To obtain an impression about the feelings of the refugee concerning these facts one needs to ask open-ended questions (cf. Cox & Rutter, 1985). Sometimes suggestive additions to open-ended questions (e.g. *How did you feel when this happened? Didn't you become very angry? Or were you just flabbergasted?*) can be stimulating, at least if they are empathetic and allow alternative answers.

The Content of the First Interviews

The topics for the first diagnostic interviews are of course dependent on what the refugee wants to tell the therapist. Apart from that, they are dependent on the theoretical approach(es) the therapist embraces. In common sense terminology the content of the first interviews can be summarized with the following key-words: problem-analysis, situation-analysis, incident-exploration and position-analysis.

The term *problem-analysis* refers to a discussion of the refugee's current problems. The therapist tries to get an overview of all persons, conditions, and happenings that are related to his current problems. He asks questions about the part which the refugee himself plays in these problems. The therapist also gathers information about the role of other persons and the possible influence of rules and regulations to which the refugee is subjected when his problems develop and continue.

Situation-analysis refers to the discussion of the context of the refugee's problem, with respect to the present situation. It concerns matters which may at first sight seem unrelated to the problem, but nevertheless can make it more understandable, or which help the therapist to get an impression of the levels at which the refugee is functioning adequately, and of factors that might prove helpful in coping with his problems.

Situation-analysis may also refer to a situation in the past. In that case the historical background of the problems is discussed, either in relation to complaints (e.g. *When did you have these nightmares about prison for the first time?*), or less directively, by biographic questions. Montessori (1987) states in this connection that in the case of traumatized clients it is important to acquire a detailed biographical case-history: 'This should not be carried out in a formal manner. One must show interest and explain that it is necessary to know more about a person before he can be helped; it is preferable to let him speak spontaneously. The data can be ordered later, and it is not necessary that the patient be present. If anything is lacking it can be supplemented the next time.' Biographical questions may also lead to a conversation about non-problematic aspects of the refugee's personal history, and provide useful information about special strengths and capacities which the refugee possesses.

In the case of refugees, traumatic experiences often form a part of their life history. In the first interviews the therapist will also carefully ask some questions about possible traumatic experiences in order to obtain relevant information, to make it clear to the refugee that he has knowledge about the kind of things that happen during torture, combat and so on, and that he is prepared to discuss these kinds of topics if the refugee wants to.

The conversation about the context of the refugee's problem may of course include a discussion of relevant aspects of the political situation in both the native country and the country of exile.

Incident-exploration refers to the exploration of an occurrence that had great emotional impact on the refugee, usually something that happened just before the interview. The incident, for example a conflict with another person, often shows in a nutshell where the problem lies, and is in a sense representative of the way in which the refugee experiences his present situation.

Incident-exploration involves systematic questioning by the helping professional about details of the incident, until he can visualize it like a film. During the conversation both the therapist and the refugee get an overview of what happened, and insight into the role played by the refugee and other persons who were involved. The therapist pays attention to the feelings the refugee experienced during the incident, to his behaviour, and to his cognitive interpretation of the behaviour of other people who were also involved.

The term *position-analysis* refers to the conversation about the respective standpoints of the refugee and the helping professional and the political field of force in which both function. Topics for discussion would include the kind of help the refugee expects and wants from the therapist, the way in which the therapist could, and is, willing to help, and what the refugee himself can do to contribute to the solution of his problems. Sometimes it is necessary to discuss the restrictions forced upon both parties by the political reality of the day. For example, a refugee seeking asylum has nightmares about being sent back to his country. The therapist cannot provide a great deal of support because those nightmares are in fact at least partly based on a realistic judgement of the situation. The therapist might be able to give some advice about how to react to the nightmares, or even more effectively use his status as an expert in helping to obtain a residence permit for the refugee, thereby eliminating the source of his fears.

The Use of Various Approaches

The theoretical approaches discussed in Chapter 2 each suggest diagnostic categories which may help the therapist in obtaining relevant diagnostic information, and also suggest points of departure for psychotherapy.

The *psychiatric approach* leads to observations of, and questions about, specific signs and symptoms, in order to exclude disturbances that have a primarily organic cause, and to identify possible mental disorders.

Although refugees can be suffering from any mental disorder, one must be on the lookout especially for symptoms and signs of Post-Traumatic Stress Disorder, while keeping in mind that some refugees tend to minimize the impact of their traumatic experiences. Nightmares may be forgotten, and intrusive memories or flashbacks often remain hidden behind other complaints, such as concentration problems, being distracted, headaches, alcohol abuse and forgetfulness. The use of this approach leads to diagnostic hypotheses in terms of mental disorders. A mental disorder like Post-Traumatic Stress Disorder can sometimes be treated with psychotropic medication. Therefore, this approach also suggests an investigation of the refugee's attitude to medication.

The *developmental approach* invites the clinician to assess the refugee's level of development with regard to various developmental tasks and to make diagnostic hypotheses about the possible interference of both traumatization and uprooting with the mastery of these tasks. It focuses the attention on skills a refugee possesses in order to use and enlarge those skills. It suggests exploration of the daily environment of the refugee, in order to find possiblities for the creation of protective factors and fostering competent behaviour.

The *psychodynamic approach* focuses attention on the feelings of the refugee and the specific personal meaning that events may have for him. Some specific diagnostic questions suggested by this approach are:

- Is there any reason to presume the refugee's personality development was disturbed before he left his country, or before he was traumatized?

- How can the psychological functioning of the refugee be characterized in terms of Horowitz's phases?
- Is there any indication about the coping styles (such as regression, adaptive defence, or progressive coping) the refugee was using during traumatization?
- Is his present psychological functioning understandable in relation to this coping style?

The psychodynamic approach will lead to diagnostic hypotheses in terms of inner conflicts, intrapsychic processes and their relation to social functioning.

The *family therapy approach* leads to questioning the refugee about what he experiences as his primary social environment, and to arranging diagnostic interviews in which both the refugee and his primary social environment are present. If that is not feasible or possible, this approach leads to questioning the refugee about his relations with his family and with the persons who at present constitute his primary social environment. Some questions from this approach are:

- Is there physical separation from the original primary social system?
- Has the refugee found or formed a new primary social system?
- Which stereotyped, circular interaction patterns or inadequate forms of communication can be identified that impede social support for the refugee?
- Is there reason to suspect that the family has some secret?
- Which members of the family have been traumatized? Has the structure of the family been disrupted because of traumatic events?
- Is there a functional hierarchy? Is one of the family members overburdened? Or, are there signs of parentification?
- Which loyalties influence the decisions of the refugee? Does the refugee have legacies that form a burden?
- Are there signs of overprotection by avoiding open communication?
- Is there reason to presume a process of trans-generational traumatization?
- Is there reason to believe that some patterns of interaction have existed for a long time and are being continued after the flight?
- Could some of the communication problems be the consequence of a difference in speed of adaptation to life in exile?
- Is the refugee part of a new, bi-cultural system?

The family therapy approach may generate psychotherapeutic interventions aimed at changing rigid interaction patterns or difficulties in communication.

The *learning theory approach* suggests diagnostic questions centred around complaints and problematic behaviour and the circumstances under which they occur. The therapist can be inspired by questions like:

- Is there behaviour that can be characterized as conditioned and which is troublesome for the refugee himself or for other people? Is he aware of this behaviour? How is this behaviour reinforced?
- Which behaviour can be labelled as avoidance behaviour?
- Is there any behaviour that indicates learned helplessness (such as a passive attitude under circumstances where activity might be useful, slow movements, sluggish thinking, querulous behaviour, self-reproach)?
- With regard to the conventions in the country of exile, can shortcomings in social skills be identified? (These include: lack of assertiveness in the sense of not being able to contradict another person because it is considered improper in the native country; behaviour that in the country of exile is considered exaggerated and theatrical; excessive expressions of gratitude that make people in the country of exile feel embarrassed; avoidance of giving direct answers to particular questions; not asking things straightforwardly, but vaguely hinting at what one requires; avoiding certain topics of conversation; and so on.)

The learning theory approach results in therapeutic interventions aimed at initiating learning processes resulting in the replacement of inadequate behaviour by more adequate behaviour.

The *cognitive approach* encourages curiosity about the way in which the refugee thinks about the causes of his problems, or interprets failures and disappointing experiences. Some questions suggested by this approach are:

- Could part of the refugee's thinking be explained in terms of 'cognitive representations of unconditioned (traumatic) stimuli' and related 'self-instructions'?
- Are there signs the refugee is able to summarize his traumatic experiences in some orderly way?
- Which forms of coping is he using? Coping by deployment of attention (vigilant strategies or avoidance strategies)? Coping by changing subjective meanings (transforming a threat into a challenge, denying a threat, emphasizing the positive aspects of the situation, distancing)? Confronting by changing the relationship with the environment (confrontive coping, planned problem-solving)?
- Which explanatory styles is the refugee using? Is his way of explaining his situation stereotyped? Or, can he explain his problems on different levels? In which sense are his attributions inadequate?
- Which statements of the refugee can be interpreted as reflections of his world-view and his self-image? Which incorrect assumptions and inferences can be identified from his reasoning?

The diagnostic hypotheses that can be formed on the basis of this approach will be realized in terms of adequate and inadequate ways of thinking or cognitive representation, and inspire therapeutic interventions aimed at promoting cognitive development in certain areas.

Final Remarks

Refugees have problems that are partly based on current stress such as being denied a residence permit, inadequate housing, or difficulties in bringing a family member to the country of exile. Removal of these stress factors may have a dramatic effect and radically change the diagnostic picture.

CHAPTER 4

Working with Cultural Differences

The Refugee and the Western Therapist

Therapy with refugees often entails meeting people from cultural backgrounds with which the therapist is not familiar. The therapist has to face the fact that he cannot be sure in which way the specific cultural background of a refugee has influenced his personality development. Also, he cannot be sure how culturally determined differences in family life and child development may possibly be reflected in specific ways of coping with stress, specific psychological problems or specific forms of transference. On the other hand, there is no reason to let oneself be intimidated by cultural differences in personality development as long as there are strong indications that over and above all cultural differences, the needs, the feelings, and the vulnerabilities we experience as people are the same the world over. The way people react to psychological trauma does not seem to be very dependent on cultural background (cf. Alexander *et al.*, 1981; Somasundaran, 1993).

Everyone who seeks assistance for mental problems wants to be treated by an expert whom he considers trustworthy (cf. Pederson, 1981). But the criteria by which someone is considered an expert and trustworthy are not the same in all cultures. The same goes for specific therapeutic techniques: what is considered as useful and credible in one culture may be thought of as stupid or immoral in another culture. The therapist has to be attentive to these differences, and flexible in the use of therapeutic techniques. For instance, when he wants to use the discussion of dreams as a therapeutic technique, he has to inform himself about the ways in which dreams are interpreted in the refugee's cultural background.

Because of this difference in cultural background, helping refugees also means dealing with the condition of refugees having divergent ideas about mental problems and the way they should be treated. The kind of help a Western therapist can offer to a refugee does not always correspond to what a doctor or healer in his own culture has on offer (Kinzie, 1978). For example, the refugee may expect to be cured quickly. The idea that his complaints will disappear if he learns more about himself through a long series of talks is both strange and difficult to comprehend.

In the eyes of the Western therapist the distinction between 'madness' and 'normality' may be much less strict than is generally believed in some African or Asian cultures (Kortmann, 1986). Some refugees come from cultures where visiting a psychiatrist is proof of madness.

Refugees from non-Western cultures may express their complaints in a manner unfamiliar to the Western therapist. Giel (1984) describes the moaning and sighing of patients in an Addis Ababa out-patients' department. Initially, he found this behaviour theatrical but his interpreter was impressed by their suffering. Further investigation revealed these patients were not just pretending but really were sick. Giel concluded: 'The generally reserved Ethiopian apparently loses his armour of impassivity during illness.'

The same apparently theatrical behaviour can also be observed sometimes in refugees, especially those who have not been in exile for very long. In addition, the refugee may be accustomed to other norms relating to what counts as morally responsible or healthy behaviour. In such cases it is useful to explore these norms (cf. Brown, 1986; Agger, 1988).

A.O., a 25-year-old refugee from the Middle East, was very worried about his younger brother, who had gone into exile with him and for whom he felt responsible. He had caught his brother masturbating and was worried about the consequences of this for his health. The therapist asked A.O. what he thought about the physical consequences of masturbation and how he viewed it morally. Also, he explained that research in the West had shown masturbation to be a common form of sexual behaviour, that it was seen as preparation for other forms of sexuality, and the majority of the population did not view masturbation as morally objectionable.

There are cultural differences also in the causes people ascribe to illnesses. For instance, in Cambodian culture illness is thought to be the consequence of coming into contact with dangerous spirits, witchcraft or sorcery (Eisenbruch & Handelman, 1989; Van de Put, 1997). The same belief can be found in India (Srinivasa & Trivedi, 1982), in some Caribbean (Cancelmo, Millán & Vazquez, 1990) and in African cultures. Occasionally this kind of explanation may be mentioned by refugees. However, traumatized refugees do not often have much trouble in considering the idea that there may be a relationship between their symptoms and their traumatic experiences.

Moreover, cultural differences are present in the ideas people have about the cause of traumatic experiences. In this connection Mollica and Son (1988) report that Cambodian refugees who have been tortured relate this to the Buddhist concept of *karma*. Because of their karma, they feel in some way responsible for their suffering. This is opposed by the Western conception that torture is something done to the individual for political reasons. More generally speaking, it is important for the therapist to understand the cultural framework within which certain symptoms are evaluated, and the causal explanations implicit in any cultural framework (Lee & Lu, 1989).

Another cultural difference directly influencing the contact with the therapist is a readiness to talk about personal matters with someone outside the family. Refugees from Indochinese cultures tend to mask their personal suffering by politeness and smiles (Denley, 1987). In general, Asian clients often seem to avoid expressing their emotions. They tend to express psychic distress through physical complaints. In the first contacts the therapist may mistakenly perceive them as passive; this passivity, however, should be seen as a cultural expression of respect for authority (Tsui & Schultz, 1985).

According to the author's observations, people from Middle Eastern countries may begin by talking about trivial matters, even a bit tediously, before they are ready to discuss what is really bothering them. Therefore, an inexperienced or impatient therapist might underestimate the seriousness of their problems.

Finally, in some cultures it seems to be normal for the client to give the therapist small gifts. Some refugees maintain this habit in their contacts with European therapists. If the latter is not in the habit of accepting gifts, he will have to make this clear in a tactful manner.

Corrective feedback from the therapist can help the refugee to understand what kinds of behaviour are acceptable or unacceptable in particular situations (De Anda, 1984). In some situations, however, it is desirable for the therapist to conform to the expectations of his client.

B.O., an Islamic refugee, always drank a cup of coffee during the weekly therapeutic sessions. During ramadan the therapist offered him his usual cup of coffee, but he refused. The therapist asked him about the way in which he celebrated ramadan. He did not offer him any more coffee that month.

Communication Problems

It is important for the therapist to be continuously aware of the communication problems arising as the result of cultural differences. Sometimes, he may decide to accommodate to some extent to the refugee. In order to avoid under- or overdressing, the therapist may ask himself how his clothing will be viewed by refugees from various cultural backgrounds (cf. Vontress, 1981), or examine the magazine covers in his waiting room from the point of view of an orthodox Moslem.

On the level of treatment techniques (cf. Sundberg, 1981) he should be careful when using a non-directive approach. Many refugees are unfamiliar with this approach, misinterpreting it as a sign of inadequacy, or lack of interest. Also, he should be aware of the fact that people from particular cultures can experience eye contact as threatening or disrespectful. More generally, it is important that the therapist takes the time to explain again and again how his treatment works; why he is asking certain questions; what he expects from the refugee, and so on. In this connection, therapist and counsellors could compare their service to that of a bank. Although at first it may seem complicated to explain all the ins and outs of plastic cards and pin codes, most refugees learn how to cash a cheque. And usually it does not make much of a difference whether the employee of the bank is white or black, male or female.

A therapist cannot always recognize when a misunderstanding has arisen. The consequence may be that the refugee interrupts treatment. Any time a refugee misses an appointment the therapist can ask himself whether some communication problem may exist without his being aware of it. In such cases the misunderstanding can be cleared up sometimes if the therapist takes the trouble to invite the refugee to come again by phoning him, for example, or writing a personal letter.

Sometimes the refugee may have more confidence in the helping professional because the latter belongs to a different culture. For instance, he may think the professional is more objective, more trustworthy, or better educated.

Whatever the cultural background of the refugee, however, there is no need for the therapist to bargain his professional attitude. Genuine interest, respect and tolerance for the anxiety in his client are basic conditions for counselling and therapy. Of course, the therapist has to make sure these features are recognized by the refugee.

Finally, the importance of the cultural factor in counselling and therapy with refugees should not be overestimated. Culture should not be seen as a complete package of meaning totally determining the behaviour and thinking of any individual who grew up in this culture (cf. Knudsen, 1991). An alternative is understanding cultural background as one of the factors contributing to the process of the identity development in each individual refugee. Meeting a refugee does not mean one encounters a sort of representative from an exotic world, but rather an individual with a personal identity.

Moreover, there seem to be certain universal features of therapy. A socially recognized healer, who has a superior status to the client and who is trained in a particular technique, can be an effective therapist in any cultural situation, as long as he shares an explanatory model for the problem with the client, offers him a new perspective, mobilizes the client's sense of hope, provides experiences of success during the therapy, and facilitates emotional arousal (Littlewood, 1992).

To overcome communication problems the therapist must become informed about cultural differences and develop cultural empathy (Dahl, 1989). On the other hand, he has to be aware that cultural sensitivity can become cultural stereotyping when the therapist underestimates the individual differences between people from the same culture.

The helping professional can inform himself about the cultural background of refugees by studying anthropological and other relevant sources about the cultures in question, or by contacting local experts. That way he may pick up all kinds of observations—for example, South East Asian parents may become very anxious if one comments on the beauty or good health of their baby, for fear of attracting evil spirits (Olness, 1986). Of course, the refugee himself can be an important informant. Many refugees are aware that communication problems may develop and are ready to explain things as soon as the therapist shows some interest. For his part, the therapist can prevent compounding the communication problems by explaining rules and standards common to Western society.

Language Problems and Misunderstanding

The ideal therapeutic situation seems to be that both therapist and client speak the same language fluently. Fortunately this is not always true: sometimes it is easier to discuss a private matter or a taboo in a second language, rather than in one's native tongue (cf. Sundberg, 1981). But, however that may be, psychotherapy with refugees often means the therapist has to work with people who have grown up speaking very different languages. Refugees with personal problems often have difficulty in concentrating or they cannot remember what they have been taught. This usually has a negative effect on their efforts to learn the language of the country in which they are in exile.

In the case of refugees who do speak the therapist's language it is necessary to realize they are likely to have only a limited vocabulary of common terms. They do not know or understand many of the terms which they need to describe or express their emotions. This means they are limited in their ability to articulate their problems. The therapist must take care that what he says comes across in the intended manner. He must be constantly alert for misunderstandings stemming from the use of an unfamiliar language. In such cases therapeutic sessions will be slower than usual and often cannot be limited to the usual 45 minutes.

> C.O., who had left Iran a year earlier, had a very limited English vocabulary. He only knew the concept of feeling in the sense of physical sensation, not in the psychological sense. But he solved this problem when he said of his torturer: 'With my heart I thought: I will kill him, but with my head I thought: You should not do that.'

Even if he cannot speak the refugee's native language, some knowledge of its syntax will help the therapist to understand the problems the refugee has and may help to reduce misunderstandings. The therapist can check whether the refugee has understood abstract concepts by asking him to give examples (Kortmann, 1986). The refugee can be taught concepts which facilitate communication in the same way.

Translated questionnaires, such as the Hopkins Symptom Checklist (Mollica *et al.*, 1987b), where mental complaints and feelings are articulated subtly, can help to facilitate communication and find translations in European languages for feelings which the refugee considers important.

Even if the therapist speaks the refugee's native language fluently, there can still be misunderstandings if the therapist is unaware of certain customs in the refugee's culture. Swartz (1987) describes the *hlonipa* tradition among the Xhosa-speaking peoples of South Africa. In this tradition it is taboo for a woman to use certain words, including the names of her male relatives and that of her husband. Therapists who were unfamiliar with this tradition thought the Xhosa women who came to them for help had language problems, or even that they were mentally deranged.

As was pointed out before, cultural bias can be an obstacle to diagnosis. A diagnostic mistake can easily be made in misinterpreting behaviour that impresses the Western clinician as theatrical, manipulative, troublesome, or avoidant. Observations of such behaviour may tempt the practitioner to diagnose a refugee as suffering from a Personality Disorder. In some cases that may be correct. It is also possible the refugee's behaviour is completely adequate when set against his specific cultural background. Post-traumatic symptoms, however, seem to be more or less the same in refugees from divergent cultural backgrounds. Most of the refugees the author attended who suffered from post-traumatic symptoms, such as nightmares and flashbacks, quickly understood the connection between these symptoms and their traumatic experiences. A few of them initially ascribed their symptoms to some evil ghost or djinn, but it was never difficult to awaken their interest in the possible relationship between their symptoms and traumatic experiences.

Often, the refugees the author attended to seemed to be fully aware of his cultural bias. They could live with it, they were not narrow-minded at all.

Working with Interpreters

When the language barrier between therapist and client is so great that they cannot communicate adequately, then an interpreter can be used. This leads to an unusual situation: communication proceeds through a third person, usually not trained to give assistance, but who nonetheless makes a personal contribution to the course of the encounter. Adding a third person will make it more difficult for the refugee to express thoughts he considers as childish, shameful or evil. On the other hand, the interpreter can be experienced by the refugee as a great help in expressing himself. Some withdrawn refugees actually cheer up when the interpreter arrives (Bot, 1996).

The interpreter's attitude towards the client determines the atmosphere in which the encounter takes place. This attitude does not always conform to what the therapist considers desirable. A sympathetic, businesslike, or authoritarian, patronizing attitude on the part of the interpreter may facilitate or impede the development of a relationship of mutual trust between the therapist and his client. The extent of the interpreter's knowledge of the client's culture may also facilitate the process.

The interpreter's behaviour can evoke certain feelings in the client. If the interpreter is a compatriot, the client may be comforted by his presence. But also he may be ashamed of problems considered to be a sign of madness, or a cause for contempt, in their common culture. Sometimes refugees distrust compatriot interpreters for political reasons. If the interpreter has the same political ideology as the client the latter will be inhibited in expressing doubts about his political convictions.

The interpreter's gender also can influence the client's frankness, particularly in regard to sexual problems. Various transference phenomena may also be present in the relationship with the interpreter. For example, a client who feels the therapist does not understand his problems may direct his irritation at the interpreter, accusing him of not translating properly. Also, the therapist may vent his irritation at the client by directing it at the interpreter.

Sometimes the client places the interpreter in a difficult situation, by telling him something and then asking him not to tell the therapist.

Finally, the interpreter may make translation mistakes which have a negative effect on the therapeutic process. Some of these mistakes can be attributed to words not having an exact translation (Sue & Sue, 1987). For example, it is difficult to find a completely satisfactory equivalent for 'disappointment' in Persian. Price (1975) has done research on the mistakes made by three Hindustani interpreters working in a psychiatric practice in Australia. He found translation mistakes very rarely led to the wrong diagnosis being made, but increased the time needed to make a diagnosis. According to Price, more mistakes were made when translating the patients' answers (at most 15.5%) than when translating the doctors' questions (at most 7.4% when they were talking to psychotic patients, 4.2% when they were talking to neurotics). In translating the answers of patients who were diagnosed as acute psychotic or chronic psychotic, the interpreters made more mistakes (15.5%) than with neurotic patients (5.2%).

The most common mistakes interpreters made in translating doctors' questions were: they changed open questions into leading questions, altered the content of questions and added their own comments. Their mistakes in translating patients' answers included: leaving out part of the answer, adding something to the answer, and mistakes because of their limited knowledge of English.

Recommendations

It is important to select an interpreter who is not instantly mistrusted by the refugee. Therefore the therapist needs to be aware of ethnic and political sensitivities. On the other hand, he needs an interpreter who can be neutral and objective. For that reason friends and relatives are often less suitable (Putsch, 1985). An interpreter should have an attitude that fits the professional situation: so he should be sympathetic and respectful towards the refugee, not patronizing or impatient.

The therapist will have to build a working relationship with the interpreter. It can be helpful to take time to inform the interpreter about the basic principles of the therapist's approach: for example, that he assumes the client has to make decisions himself, that the topics discussed during sessions are confidential, that silence during sessions may be meaningful, and so on. Also, the counsellor can instruct the interpreter to translate as literally as possible: by using the first person whenever the person speaking does so (Pentz-Moller et al., 1988); by not trying to translate an incoherent sentence as more coherent than it originally was; and by translating short phrases one after the other instead of translating a group of statements by giving a summary. It can be very useful also for the therapist to have a preparatory conversation with the interpreter before a session, in which the objective of the session is discussed. It can be very enlightening to check whether certain questions (e.g. about sexual behaviour) can be expressed at all by this interpreter in the client's language. An evaluation after the session can be aimed at discussing the interpreter's emotions and the difficulties he encountered with regard to the translation.

It may be attractive for a therapist to work together with the same interpreters as much as possible. However, changing the interpreter during an ongoing therapeutic contact may be very useful. A change of interpreter brings different aspects of the refugee to the fore and in that way contributes to the effectiveness of the therapeutic contact (Bot, 1996).

A counsellor working with an interpreter should always be aware that interpreters can make incorrect translations and that they may miss important verbal signals, especially signals that point at thought disorders or covert depression (Sabin, 1975). Moreover, the translator's own problems and experiences with traumatic events or adaptation problems may influence the interaction with the client. For example, the interpreter may avoid unhappy memories for himself by not translating accurately, avoiding certain topics, changing the subject, informing the therapist the interview is too stressful for the refugee, and so on (Westermeyer, 1989).

One way of maintaining the client's anonymity, and thereby increasing the chance he will discuss his problems openly, is to use a loudspeaker telephone and the services of external interpreters. Then the interpreter need not meet the refugee personally; he does not know what he looks like and need not even know his name. The disadvantage of this method is that gestures and other non-verbal aspects of communication are lost. When an unfamiliar interpreter is to be present, the client's embarrassment or suspicion can be reduced if the interpreter introduces himself to the client before the session and they have the chance for an informal chat.

In spite of the language barrier, when speaking the therapist can maintain eye contact with the client. This seems to facilitate the client's understanding of what is being said without the intervention of the interpreter. Keeping questions and remarks concise also helps to improve communication. Long questions mean the therapist has to direct more of his attention to the interpreter than to the client.

It often helps if one can prepare a session beforehand, if necessary in consultation with the interpreter. Sometimes it is useful for the therapist to explain to the interpreter why he is saying, or asking, certain things.

Using an interpreter from the same area as the refugee has an advantage. Not only do they share the same language but also the same cultural background. Also, working regularly with the same interpreters increases the therapist's understanding of other cultures.

The emotional reactions of interpreters during therapeutic sessions are sometimes a useful source of information. If the therapist sees that the interpreter is embarrassed, surprised, or shows some other emotional response he may interrupt the session to consult the interpreter about the reasons for his reaction.

Sometimes it is useful to ask the interpreter for his opinion on the client's emotions during the session. Such interventions break the conventional boundaries of the interpreter's role and he becomes a bi-cultural co-therapist. Proper training is necessary in order to enable him to fulfil this role adequately. In the United States a lot of experience has been gained in the cooperation between American and Vietnamese or Cambodian co-therapists, and in providing special training programmes for the latter (see for example Teter *et al*, 1987).

CHAPTER 5

Treatment Goals and the Therapeutic Relationship

Treatment Goals

Ideally, before mental health care interventions are started, a thorough examination is made of the refugee's background and problems.

Sometimes counselling or psychotherapy are clearly not indicated as a first choice, for example when a refugee is suffering from a disorder such as Schizophrenia, Severe Mental Retardation or Psychoactive Substance Abuse. Other forms of professional help, such as psychiatric treatment and care in order to stabilize the condition of the refugee and to foster the quality of his functioning as much as possible, will then be indicated.

If points of application for psychotherapeutic techniques are apparent, the therapist has to form an opinion about the question of what would be the best setting: out-patient or in-patient, individual, in a group, with the partner or with the family. He also has to make an inventory of the general objectives the use of psychotherapeutic techniques could have in this particular case, and about more specific targets.

As far as the general objectives of the use of psychotherapeutic techniques are concerned, a basic distinction can be made between helping the refugee to change things that can be changed, and helping the refugee to accept things which cannot be changed (cf. Mikulas, 1978). Many therapists (e.g. Bleich, Garb & Kottler, 1986) make a second basic distinction: between stimulating long-term changes in certain aspects of the client's personality, or trying to achieve more adequate functioning as quickly as possible. In the first case therapy is aimed at promoting a reliving of emotional experiences and insight into intrapsychic processes. In the second case therapy is aimed at the behavioural aspects of coping skills and at the cognitive components of adequate and inadequate coping mechanisms; the therapist makes use of techniques which stimulate behaviour modification or the restructuring of habitual ways of thinking.

If it is decided to promote long-term processes of emotional integration of traumatic experiences and personality change then the therapist usually attempts to get the client to re-experience emotional conflicts. In this way the client realizes the effect which they are having on his present situation. The result which the therapist hopes to achieve is that the client frees himself from emotional impediments to his functioning, thus putting his life on a new course.

If the objective is a more adequate functioning in a short term, then the therapist will concentrate on achieving limited changes as rapidly as possible. He will choose this strategy if he considers far-reaching personality changes to be unnecessary, or if it seems likely that such changes will occur as part of the result of the more limited changes. A determining factor which may also play a role is if the client is not considered to be capable of dealing with the emotions which would be generated by re-experiencing conflicts which he has not yet assimilated, if there are not many people in his social environment who could provide emotional support, or if there is insufficient structure in his daily life (e.g. a job or other routine activities) from which he could derive support.

Not all psychotherapists who work with traumatized clients agree with the classification of objectives described above. Ochberg (1988) employs the following division. A first type of psychotherapy is directed at the pre-traumatic personality and the problems which were present before the trauma developed. According to Ochberg this approach suggests that the client's symptoms are partly related to weaknesses and limitations in his personality. A second type of psychotherapy places more emphasis on recent events, on coping skills and the client's stronger characteristics, and on the mistaken but rectifiable ideas which obstruct rapid emotional assimilation. Ochberg prefers to start with the second approach, unless the client is of the opinion that his pre-traumatic problems are at the heart of his present difficulties. He thinks that the first approach places the blame for his problems on the client himself, whereas the second approach facilitates a working relationship between therapist and client.

Ochberg's distinction is very useful in providing assistance to clients who have undergone a single traumatic experience within a limited period of time. Many refugees, however, have experienced a long and continuous process of traumatization which interacts with the normal process of personality development. The result of this could be that personality development has not been optimal, and then therapy aimed at personality changes would be desirable. This does not mean that the client is being blamed for his present problems, which are the result of a long process of traumatization.

An alternative distinction can be made between treatment aimed at well-defined complaints, symptoms and present day problems and crisis situations, and treatment that is not focused in this way and which can be directed to the refugee's total functioning: his emotional stability and well-being. Of course the difference between these two extremes is not absolute: in practice treatment often begins with the use of techniques that are directed at relieving incapacitating symptoms and then expands to include wider objectives; or it is the case that the successful treatment of one symptom has an important effect on the total functioning of an individual. In this study, information about psychotherapeutic techniques is presented in line with this distinction. In Chapter 6 methods aimed at the treatment of crises and symptoms are introduced. The conversation during the therapeutic interviews aimed at crises and symptoms is mostly about the current daily life of the refugee. The treatment includes supportive and symptom-oriented techniques. Chapter 7 is about treatment techniques aimed at restoring emotional stability and well-being. When these techniques are applied, the conversation is often about the personal history of the refugee, his inner conflicts and existential questions that are bothering him. The treatment includes, among others, techniques from explorative psychotherapy. This approach in general is only used on the condition that the refugee has attained a somewhat balanced level of psychological functioning in day-to-day life.

In many cases the indications are to use mixtures of the abovementioned types of psychotherapeutic techniques, or to combine them with other forms of professional help. How techniques of different types can be blended in a responsible way will also be discussed in Chapter 7.

Establishing a Therapeutic Relationship

When refugees ask for help they are usually in need of immediate assistance. Generally the therapeutic contacts will have to commence immediately after the first acquaintance has been made, even though the therapist may not yet know what exactly is required. In such cases he could, to begin with, support the client's motivation to seek assistance and attempt to build up a therapeutic relationship. Such a relationship requires that:

1. the therapist and the client have some affinity for one another;
2. that they trust each other;
3. that the refugee can overcome his ambivalent attitude towards requesting and receiving help;
4. that in their relationship their objective is to overcome the client's mental problems;
5. and—as far as is humanly possible—nothing else.

Some Affinity for One Another

The way in which mutual affinity between people develops has not been studied sufficiently from a scientific perspective. It can be stated, however, that some refugees can experience the presence or absence of a sincere interest on the part of the therapist through certain characteristics of the room in which they are received. If there is a map of their country of origin, reading matter in their vernacular and toys for the children in the waiting-room then this will be viewed positively. If the therapist can speak a few words of the client's language—e.g. the equivalents of 'hello' and 'how are you'—then this will also be seen as a sign of sincere interest. These days refugees are not very popular in most countries. A basic condition for providing assistance to refugees is that the therapist makes them feel welcome.

Mutual Trust

Trust usually develops gradually on the basis of contact between therapist and client, as well as contacts between the client and other people working in the therapist's office. Sometimes the client trusts the therapist right from the start because he has already heard something about him and his methods from a friend or doctor or someone else whom he trusts. Previous positive experiences with other therapists or social workers can also contribute to the ease with which trust develops in a new therapeutic relationship.

> *In her first interview A.I. described, without hesitation or restraint, the details of her experiences as a prisoner. During the second interview she said that she had felt secure on the previous occasion. She had the impression that the therapist knew what it was like in the prisons in her country. Moreover, shortly after her release, but before leaving the country, she had discussed her experiences on a number of occasions with a psychologist, and she had retained pleasant memories of those talks.*

On the other hand, previous negative experiences with a therapist or social worker can have the opposite effect. Such experiences may occur when the therapist—usually unintentionally—arouses expectations which he cannot fulfil.

> *B.I. had serious depressive complaints and isolated himself from the other refugees with whom he shared an apartment. The volunteer who was counselling him was sympathetic and initially ready to help him day and night. But when the burden became too great he tried to refer B.I. to a psychologist. B.I. reacted with anger and suspicion, and the referral took place in a crisis situation, a day before the volunteer went on holiday for two weeks. B.I. let it be known that he considered a talk with a psychologist to be unnecessary. He made use of the occasion to give an exposition on the uselessness of psychology, and—B.I. speaks German—to lecture the psychologist whenever he made a grammatical mistake. In this situation a therapeutic relationship could not develop.*

Trust is often seen as something that just has to grow over time. However, the growth of trust can be stimulated if the therapist tries to connect with the

problems, complaints and symptoms the refugee experiences as most troublesome and offers concrete, practical help whenever this is possible.

The Objective to Overcome Mental Problems

When refugees consult a psychologist or a psychiatrist it is often because they
have been referred by a doctor whom they consulted for somatic complaints.
In other cases it may be members of the family, friends or a partner who were
concerned about his condition and persuaded him to seek help, while he is
convinced he does not have a mental problem. Conflicts with a partner can
also lead to a request for assistance, and in that case the refugee is sometimes
not ready to consider the possibility that his own behaviour might contribute
to the conflict. Generally speaking it is not very common for refugees to say
that they have a mental problem and to express the desire to discuss personal
problems with a psychologist or psychiatrist, even when they are afraid of
becoming insane. Admitting that they have a mental problem, for many of
them seems to be identical with being a lunatic. When they meet a mental
health professional for the first time they often adopt a wait-and-see attitude.
It can take some time before they will be ready to think about their own
behaviour and to reflect on what they are feeling and thinking.

> *C.I., a 20-year-old refugee from an Asian country, had been suffering from
> attacks of shortness of breath for years. His doctor had been unable to discover
> any physical cause, and examinations by a number of specialists had also been
> without result. He was told that his problem was 'mental' and sent to a psy-
> chologist.*
>
> *At his first meeting with the psychologist C.I. asked for medicine for his com-
> plaint. He was prepared to answer questions about himself and the reasons for
> coming to this country. But he did not take up the suggestion that his physical
> illness might be related to the experiences which had caused him to flee from his
> own country, or to the problems of adjustment in exile. He indicated that he was
> reluctant to discuss these topics. However, he did accept the invitation to come
> and see the psychologist regularly, although he cancelled or 'forgot' two-thirds of
> the appointments.*
>
> *In ten interviews spread over eight months he generally told the psycholo-
> gist that he was all right and that he did not need any help. Here mutual trust
> and sympathy were present, but C.I. was not motivated by the desire to over-
> come his mental problems. It was only in the eleventh interview that he told of
> his traumatic experiences after escaping from prison.*

. . . *and nothing else.* One of the fundamental rules of psychotherapy is that
the therapist should be as aware as possible of his own needs and desires in
his relationship with his client. He has the responsibility of preventing his
own feelings from obstructing the main objective of therapy: overcoming the

client's mental problems. And it is just as important that the client also has only this goal in mind during therapy.

> *D.I. had so many complaints that he seemed to manifest the symptoms of three psychiatric syndromes simultaneously. But at the same time he functioned reasonably adequately in his day-to-day life. After the therapist had made clear to D.I. in the course of three interviews that he, the therapist, could not possibly influence the outcome of his request for political asylum, and had complimented him on the way he was managing to cope, in spite of the stress related to his request for asylum, D.I. broke off all contact with the therapist, though they did part on friendly terms. D.I. did apparently have mental problems, but was primarily concerned with avoiding deportation to the country from which he had fled.*

Overcoming an Ambivalent Attitude

In some cases refugees have an ambivalent attitude towards requesting assistance. They seem to experience as humiliating the fact they require help from a mental health expert. When a doctor refers them to a psychologist or psychiatrist for somatic complaints without apparent causes they sometimes feel fobbed off, or insulted, and may have the impression they are not being taken seriously.

So when a refugee finally decides to seek help, sometimes after a lot of hesitation (some refugees postpone or 'forget' appointments for registration interviews a few times), he is confronted with a therapist who demands a lot of him. The therapist has to evaluate the problem—even if this is only to estimate whether the refugee has come to the right person—and, therefore, cannot avoid asking a number of personal questions. This means the therapist has to ask about exactly those things the client is ashamed of, or those experiences he would rather forget. On the other hand, this show of interest and concern is not without effect. If it leads to the client releasing some of his suppressed emotions then it may be difficult to stop him. There is a chance he will regret and be ashamed of this openness afterwards. It is from this somewhat precarious position that a therapeutic relationship must be built up.

> *E.I., a 23-year-old refugee from Africa, complained, in his first interview with a psychologist, of headaches, insomnia, nightmares and an inability to concentrate on his studies. When the therapist (suspecting traumatic experiences, given the information he had received from the referee) asked him why he had left his country, E.I. replied decisively, saying he would prefer not to talk about that. He said he would rather talk about his present problems with housemates and girls. He started to talk about these problems, but after two sentences went on to give an emotional account of the painful events leading to his flight. Afterwards, the*

therapist had the impression he had not been sufficiently in control and that it had been a painful experience for E.I.

In a second interview a week later, E.I. recognized his ambivalence: 'On the one hand I want to keep it all inside, and on the other hand I want to get it all out', he said. That interview and the next one were more tranquil. E.I. started the fourth interview with the statement that he wanted to terminate the therapy. The therapist listened to his reasons and asked him to sleep on it. When E.I. did not keep his appointment the following week the therapist sent him a personal letter. Two days later E.I. called in unexpectedly 'to say good-bye'. On that occasion—the fifth interview—he said that the therapist did not understand his cultural background. The therapist agreed with this and asked E.I. to inform him. He had the impression E.I. was looking for excuses to keep coming without having to admit he needed help. This interview concluded with the agreement that E.I. would come and see the therapist the following week at the usual time and tell him more about his country. It was only in the seventh interview that he mentioned his problems again. He stated that he would be prepared to discuss his traumatic experiences only once a number of practical problems (such as housing) had been solved. The therapist agreed.

In the eighth interview E.I. spontaneously told the therapist of a nightmare referring to his traumatic experiences. At the end of this interview he asked for sleeping tablets. Later it became apparent he had not taken them. E.I.'s complaints about his insomnia led him to talk spontaneously about his traumatic experiences. He seemed to be relieved after the interviews and his mood improved visibly.

In the example above the client's ambivalence appears to have been determined primarily by his embarrassment at having expressed emotions, and his need for assistance. This ambivalence can also be coloured by suspicion.

F.I. had asked his doctor to refer him to a psychiatrist because he was suffering from depression. The first interview took place in a pleasant atmosphere, and F.I. described how his problems were manifested in his day-to-day life. In the second interview, he had a lot of questions about the institute for which the therapist worked. Because it was partly state subsidized he was afraid there might be some contact with the embassy of the country from which he had fled. All this was discussed in a calm manner. The therapist had the impression these fears were justified and not merely delusions, given this refugee's world of experience. The therapist also had the impression that the client was sounding out his political views.

The development of a therapeutic relationship is a necessary condition for any type of therapy. At the same time, it is also part of the therapy. The experience of the attention and effort of the therapist, and the regular appointments which have to be kept, provide emotional support and help to structure the client's life.

> *G.I. was a refugee who complained about depressions and anxiety attacks. In the course of ten therapeutic interviews an attempt was made to promote more adequate short-term psycho-social functioning. But the results remained limited. G.I.'s comment on this was: 'At least there is one day in the week when I get up at a normal time, take a shower, and get the feeling that I am treated like a human being.'*

Even in its later stages the therapeutic relationship may still be fragile. This needs to be recognized and some effort made to maintain it. In the first instance, the establishment and maintenance of a therapeutic relationship is a question of time, real concern on the part of the therapist and respect for the conflicting feelings of the client. It helps if the therapist succeeds in recognizing the nature of the client's ambivalence. Moreover, it is advisable for the therapist to ask himself whether he feels personally threatened, rejected or hurt by the behaviour of the client, and is, therefore, less capable of taking an open attitude to the client's conflicting feelings.

Refugees who have been traumatized have often felt very powerless and dependent on the whims of other persons during traumatization. They know how horrible it can be to be dependent on somebody else. They may fear to enter a therapeutic relationship, or leave this relationship when they start to feel dependent upon it. Therefore, it is sometimes useful to discuss the client's conflicting feelings immediately and convince him that his ambivalent feelings are respectable. This applies also if they are related to previous unpleasant experiences in contact with other helping professionals or volunteers. Talking about conflicting emotions is sometimes a great relief for the client. It gives him the feeling that he is understood, at least as far as conflicting feelings are concerned. Also, it gives the therapist the opportunity to dispel possible misunderstandings.

CHAPTER 6

Treatment of Crises and Symptoms

Crisis Intervention

When refugees request assistance, they rarely do so at the first sign that something is going wrong. Most refugees initially try to solve their problems on their own or with the help of friends or relatives, or just hope that they will go away by themselves. It often happens that a refugee only asks for assistance after minor problems have escalated over time and a major crisis occurs.

In other cases, the treatment of a refugee is already going on for some time when, because of new events, such as bad news from the native country, or problems with institutions in the country of exile, a crisis situation comes into existence.

The problems a refugee faces in a crisis situation are usually a complicated mixture of mental problems, social problems, such as lack of adequate housing, and material problems that have all become very urgent. The refugee therefore needs to be helped as quickly as possible. Usually treatment of the mental problems cannot be postponed, while on the other hand, real improvement only becomes possible after the material and social problems have been resolved, or are at least in the process of resolution.

A psychological crisis is usually described as a condition of confusion, in which a person has to cope with very strong and uncontrollable emotions (cf. Butcher et al., 1988). It is the result of a problem situation which, if attempts to solve the problem fail, may result in extensive personality disorganization or emotional breakdown (Caplan, 1964). In a such a situation, traumatized refugees usually suffer from severe post-traumatic symptoms such as nightmares, flashbacks, sleep disturbances and concentration problems, as well as symptoms like delusions and loss of control over aggressive and self-destructive impulses. A crisis usually means a heightened risk of violent, suicidal or bizarre behaviour.

> A.N. was 30 years old, when he asked for treatment because he was very nervous, had severe concentration problems, and was unable to sleep. He told the psychotherapist that he was haunted by intrusive memories, related to several

*periods of political detention during which he was sexually abused. He also
complained of nightmares with a content related to the abovementioned memories. A.G.'s request for political asylum had been denied, and for two years he
had been waiting for his case to be considered by a higher authority. A.N. was
very worried about this.*

*A.N. obviously needed and liked to talk. The first three interviews the thera-
pist devoted to listening to his complaints and the associations he spontaneously
expressed in relation to his nightmares; this was just in order to support his
motivation for treatment while at the same time gathering some diagnostic
information. The therapist also taught him a few exercises for quiet respiration
and relaxation, which at least during the interviews had a positive effect.
Moreover, he called in a psychiatrist who prescribed Temazepam in order to
counter the insomnia.*

*After the third interview, a friend of A.N. was denied the status of refugee and
expelled from the country. Three days later A.N. arrived for the fourth interview
an hour early. He clearly was in crisis: he did not want to sit down in the waiting room, because he wanted to be ready to run in case the police came to kick
him out of the country. He told the therapist that he had not been sleeping for
three days and nights. Then he started to talk about the news he said he had
heard the day before: that the country of exile was in armed conflict with his
native country, which would be a reason for him to be sent back to his native
country at once. It was however, possible to convince him of the fact that there
was no war going on, and that it was very unlikely for the police to grab a refugee
from the waiting room. After, at least for that moment, contact with reality had
been restored, the therapist consulted a psychiatrist.*

*The psychiatrist on duty was wearing big leather boots that day. So A.N. stood
up when he came in, hid behind his therapist and asked him if the psychiatrist
wasn't a policeman. This fear being removed by some quiet talk, the psychiatrist
prescribed anti-psychotic medication, which quickly had the desired effect. The
therapist also informed the immigration authorities about the condition of A.N.,
which resulted in his receiving a residence permit. After this a therapy aimed at
promoting emotional integration of traumatic experiences was started.*

Crisis: the Present and the Past

The problem that causes the crises often has two components: an actual problem, and a problem that is related to the past. The first component belongs to
present day reality: the refugee is faced with some factual problem which
blocks his plans for the future, or confronts him with a feeling of impotence—
occurrences such as a confrontation with television news about war in the
native country, a racist incident in the country of exile, problems in finding a
job or adequate housing, and incidents related to the request for a residence
permit. The second component has to do with the past: the refugee has not

been able to come to grips with some traumatic events or a lasting traumatic ordeal, or at least not completely. The factual problem of today triggers unpleasant memories of these traumatic events, to a degree that the refugee is not able to handle.

When a therapist is confronted with a refugee in a condition of crisis, his interventions may go in three different directions. The therapist may address himself to

- the individual refugee
- the social environment of the refugee, for example his family, partner or close friends
- institutions that have the authority to take decisions that may contribute to the solution of the factual problem of the refugee.

Interventions Aimed at the Individual Refugee

The first therapeutic reaction to a refugee in a crisis situation is to offer him the opportunity to tell the therapist what is on his mind. The therapist starts by listening. While listening, he may sometimes observe (or suspect, if the refugee phones while being in a condition of crisis) that the refugee is walking around agitatedly. So he will advise the refugee to sit down. The therapist may also observe that the refugee is hyperventilating. In that case he may try to draw the attention of the refugee to this fact, explain to him what is happening, and convince him to join in an exercise that promotes adequate respiration (this can also be accomplished by phone).

While giving the refugee much opportunity to express himself spontaneously, the therapist can ask questions in order to identify the direct precipitator of the crisis (e.g. the refugee drank too much alcohol, received mail from his family, felt offended by the immigration police; cf. Butcher *et al.*, 1988). In the meantime the therapist can observe the psychological state of the refugee and assess whether there are signs or symptoms that might indicate that the refugee is psychotic. These observations help him to decide whether it is necessary to consider admission of the refugee to a psychiatric facility or the prescription of psychotropic medication.

After some listening, the therapist will try to make more active interventions. He will ask some questions, in order to get a clear view of what is bothering the refugee. In doing this, the refugee may also succeed in looking at his problems from a certain distance. In combination with this, the therapist is sometimes able to provide factual information relevant to what the refugee perceives to be his problem and to correct misunderstandings. If necessary, he can give explanations about post-traumatic symptoms.

After the problems have been clarified and brought back to realistic proportions, the refugee can often see some new perspective. That is the time the therapist will try to mobilize the adaptive coping skills of the refugee in relation to his present day problems. If necessary, he can give specific suggestions about coping with post-traumatic symptoms. He will also try to set realistic limits to self-destructive behaviour. At the end of a successful first interview in a crisis situation, the therapist has the feeling that he has more deep rapport with the refugee than when the conversation started.

In later interviews, the therapist may go for various interventions, depending upon the indications he perceives pro or con various types of psychotherapeutic techniques at the time the interview takes place. For example, in the framework of uncovering psychotherapy based on a psychodynamic approach, he may try to clarify what transference processes were going on when the refugee entered in a condition of crisis. Or he may, departing from a cognitive-behavioural approach, focus on interventions aimed at the relief of incapacitating symptoms such as nightmares and intrusive memories.

Interventions Aimed at the Social Environment

Sometimes a refugee in a condition of crisis is accompanied by a member of his family, a friend or a partner. In that case listening to them may serve to get additional information. This information could include observations of possible stereotyped ways in which the concerned persons are relating to the refugee and therefore unknowingly are contributing to the condition of crisis.

Interviews with persons who play an important role in the daily life of the refugee also present the opportunity to enlist their aid and cooperation in helping the refugee to cope with his problems. This may be accomplished by explaining to them the condition of the refugee and the therapeutic approach. For instance, the therapist can discuss in which way the refugee's wife can help her husband to interrupt his brooding, or how she may cautiously assist him to come back to the reality of here and now when the refugee is caught in a flashback.

When relational problems are contributing to the crisis, the therapist will have to resort to interventions derived from the various schools of family therapy.

Interventions Aimed at Institutions

Refugees often have to live in uncertainty about their future for some considerable time. As long as they don't have a secure legal status in the country of exile, they have realistic reasons to fear mandatory repatriation. This fear frequently can be seen as an important cause of the refugee entering into a condition of crisis. That means that the therapist can decide to contact the authorities who are responsible for the continuation of this fear.

In his contact with authorities, the therapist faces the task of stimulating civil servants to assess an individual case, and to do this as soon as possible, even when this implies a deviation from some fixed rule or procedure. This job is complicated by the circumstance that he cannot restrict himself to addressing medical professionals, but has to communicate with people who can't be expected to possess special empathic capacities for understanding the reactions of someone who is suffering from a psychiatric disorder. If contact is made with a medical professional, one may of course not expect him to have much detailed expert knowledge on specific manifestations of psychiatric disorders in refugees from various cultural backgrounds. The contact with institutions usually requires a lot of patience, perseverance, tact, and also genuine interest in and understanding of the dynamics in which the civil servants concerned are functioning.

Some Specific Problems

In crisis situations, the therapist is faced with problems that require extra attention, not because they only present themselves when a client is in a condition of crisis, but because they manifest themselves more intensely and require extra vigilance or an instantaneous reaction from the therapist.

First, the therapist has to evaluate scrupulously whether the reactions of the refugee that at first sight impress as overdone and theatrical, are to be considered as normal against the background of his cultural roots, can be waived as a passing form of overreaction, or should be considered as signs of a Personality Disorder (e.g. a Histrionic Personality Disorder).

Second, when a refugee is in a condition of crisis, the therapist has to appraise the risk of suicidal behaviour. Factors which correlate with the risk of suicide among refugees are (cf. Curtis Alley, 1982; Diekstra, 1983):

1. The presence of a Reactive Depression, related to the loss of a familiar environment, alienation from the native country, changes in socio-economic status and forced settlement in a different culture.
2. The loss of someone who was important, through death, divorce or abandonment. In the case of children and adolescents this includes enforced separation from parents and the fear of never seeing them again.
3. The feeling of not having a goal in life, that everything is meaningless.
4. Feelings of anger or rage.
5. Feelings of guilt about having survived while others were killed.
6. Earlier attempts at suicide in the refugee's life history. These earlier suicide attempts may have been very serious ones, that occurred as the result of extremely traumatic experiences the individual had tried to repress. In such cases questions about previous attempts to commit suicide can evoke strong emotions, related to these traumatic experiences. In addition, some refugees come from cultures in which suicide is taboo and therefore not easily discussable.
7. Thoughts and images of suicide. Suicidal images occur sometimes only in nightmares, for instance nightmares in which they are invited to commit suicide by friends or relatives who have been killed.

While working with the refugee in a condition of crisis, the therapist should be aware of what is happening between him and his client in terms of transference and counter-transference. For example, when a crisis occurs the helping professional may be tempted to act as a saviour, give more help than is strictly necessary and in that way reinforce the helpless attitude of the refugee. Or: an insistent appeal for help from a refugee may provoke an aggressive counter-transference, which tempts the therapist to make a wrong diagnosis which results in inadequate treatment.

> *C.N., a refugee from an Asian country, was suffering from nightmares, insomnia, concentration problems and obsessive brooding. Sometimes he lost control over his aggressive impulses. Therapy at first brought some improvement. But after his request for a residence permit was denied, C.N.'s symptoms became worse. He then said that therapy was useless, and he became quite angry and threatening. After C.N. left therapy, the therapist at first was rather sulky and contemplated the idea of dropping the case completely: he had the feeling that C.N had an antisocial personality. A conversation with a colleague, in which the therapist ventilated his irritation, made him change his mind. He remembered that C.N. usually behaved in a very responsible way, and understood that his aggression indicated that he was in a crisis situation. The therapist made an intervention to the immigration authorities which turned out to be successful. C.N received a residence permit, and the therapeutic contact was restored.*

This example also shows that the aggressive behaviour of a few traumatized refugees also constitutes a problem for the therapist. Sometimes, the aggression that the refugee ventilates is directly aimed at the therapist. But even when this is not the case, the aggressive outbursts are not pleasant to witness. They are however often unavoidable, either as aspects of the transference relationship, or as a rather desperate way of coping with feelings of fear and helplessness that in the condition of crisis have become unbearable.

When a refugee is in a crisis situation, the therapist will have to deal with strong emotions in his client that will inevitably trigger strong emotions in himself. That can make crisis intervention a tough job. The therapist may try to comfort himself with the thought that many crises, although they bring a lot of emotional upheaval for both the refugee and the therapist, eventually will prove to have been a decisive turning point, a fresh start for a positive development for all the involved parties (cf. Erikson, 1968; De Wit, Van der Veer & Slot, 1995).

Supportive Techniques

Not all refugees who seek help are in a crisis situation. Nevertheless, in the first interview it often becomes apparent that stress has increased to the point that the refugee is no longer able to rationally reflect on his problems. Under such circumstances the helping professional may decide to direct his attention to short-term goals: trying to promote more adequate functioning on the level of ordinary, everyday behaviour and the reduction of symptoms. Sometimes this seems to be sufficient. In other cases, these therapeutic methods are used in order to prepare the refugee for other forms of therapy. By promoting more adequate functioning in everyday life the therapist tries to create favourable conditions in which to tackle those problems that cannot be solved with these relatively simple techniques.

There are various therapeutic or therapy-supporting methods which can be directed to short-term objectives and require only an intermediate level of expertise from the helping professional (see Winston, Pinsker & McCullough, 1986).

1. Discussing overpowering negative feelings and making them understandable for the refugee by relating them to everyday occurrences.
2. Prescribing psychotropic medication.
3. Providing the concrete assistance which is part of social casework.
4. Discussing the refugee's ideas about the development of his mental problems in order to relativize feelings of helplessness and powerlessness.
5. Explaining the development of refugees' mental problems in general, in order to reduce the possibility of the client developing a negative self-image, and to relativize the fear of being or going mad.
6. Discussing the positive side of his functioning, to strengthen adequate coping skills.
7. Analysing recent, everyday experiences of associating with other people, so that the refugee gains more insight into the way in which people socialize, and how to avoid unpleasant situations and create pleasant ones.
8. Stimulate orderly thinking about the political and social aspects of human existence (Beets, 1974), so that the refugee realizes his special position, both in relation to his native country from which he has fled and in relation to the country in which he has gone into exile.

A.J., a refugee from an African country, was referred by his doctor after he had reported wanting to commit suicide. In the waiting-room he made a tense and depressed impression. But during the first interview (the day after he had seen his doctor) he opened up. Since going into exile he had been troubled by insomnia. He said that he could not sleep for more than three hours a night. He brooded a lot and spent the whole day at home watching television (he lived together with a number of compatriots). During the first interview the therapist examined the possibility of short-term changes in A.J.'s daily routine. He asked him what his daily routine had been when everything had been all right.

It appeared that he had played a lot of sport in his native country and the therapist pointed to the possibilities for taking part in sport with other people from a similar cultural background. He offered actual help by picking up the

*phone and calling a sports club, then passing the telephone to A.J., who made an
appointment to go and train the next day. The therapist also introduced him to
his medical colleague, who prescribed medicine for his insomnia.*

*A few days later, during a second interview, A.J. looked healthier and more
cheerful. He had slept better, spent less time in front of the television and taken
part in some sport. During this interview he gave more details about his reasons
for fleeing his country and spoke of his anxiety about relatives who had remained
behind.*

*In a third interview he told of sometimes being overcome by fear and thinking
that he was going mad. The therapist explained that this did not mean that he
was going mad but that it was a normal reaction to the frightening events which
he had experienced during his flight. It became clear that this fear was related to
bad news about the political situation in his home country and the fact that he
had not heard anything from his family.*

*During a fourth interview A.J. said that he was still sleeping well and had not
experienced attacks of fear or depression, even though he had stopped taking his
medicine. He then spoke of his uncertain position as a refugee whose request for
asylum had not yet been granted, and his disinclination to learn the language
until he was certain he could stay.*

*The discussion then moved on to government policy relating to granting polit-
ical asylum to refugees and the controversy about this in the society.*

*In the fifth interview A.J. said that he was feeling all right and that he was
now ready to do a language course. He was disappointed that there was a waiting list. He still had difficulty with the idea that his request for asylum might be
turned down. Nonetheless he thought that he did not need any more psychological help at that moment.*

In this case medication served to break a vicious circle of tension and
exhaustion. In the case of some clients relaxing exercises or martial arts can
have the same effect.

The advice to A.J. about his daily activities was meant to provide situations in which he would have positive experiences, thereby using existing
skills—social skills in this case—to overcome problems. By contacting the
sports club himself the therapist briefly intruded into the domain of social
casework. By talking about the overwhelming attacks of fear which he experienced it became easier for A.J. to understand their origin. He explained his
fears as 'going mad', an explanation which is, in the terms of the cognitive
approach, internal, global and persistent and thus connected with feelings of
helplessness. The therapist's questions enabled A.J. to relate his fears to specific occurrences, such as waking up from a nightmare about his detention,
or receiving a letter from his family. Once he saw the relation between his
fears and certain specific causes then these fears no longer automatically

resulted in a negative self-image. In this connection the therapist told him something about the mental problems of refugees in general. This had a calming and supportive effect, while at the same time inviting him to say more about his traumatic experiences. The discussion about the situation of refugees in general helped A.E. to feel related to those in a similar situation, and to understand his own ambivalent feelings towards the people of the country in which he was in exile.

Discussing Overwhelming Negative Feelings

One of the first and most important things which the therapist can do is to give the refugee a chance to tell his story and express related negative feelings. This does not automatically lead to immediate behavioural changes or insights which will improve the refugee's situation, but its therapeutic value must not be underestimated. The fact that the therapist listens to the refugee's story and is interested can give him the feeling that his emotions are justified and understandable, and that his actions are not being morally judged.

To put it differently (in Krystal's, 1987, terminology): the client's tolerance for his own emotions is increased. As a result, experiencing unpleasant emotions no longer automatically leads to more or new negative emotions such as shame, fear of going mad, or of being seen as putting on airs. Instead the client can reflect on his emotions and start to integrate them.

> B.J., a middle-aged Latin American refugee, had an argument with a colleague, who had made racist and discriminatory remarks about him. B.J. was angry and grieved. He remembered all the instances of discrimination which he had experienced during his seven years in exile, and concluded that none of the people of the country in which he had been given asylum were to be trusted.
>
> During the next interview B.J. thanked the therapist, a native of that country, for giving him the opportunity to express these feelings. He said that it was only now that he realized that his recurring depressions were related to the condescension with which he was sometimes treated.

However, do not expect an outpouring of emotions whenever you talk to a refugee. Some of them are numb or focused on somatic or other symptoms in an effort to ward off strong negative feelings (Kinzie & Fleck, 1987).

Prescribing Psychotropic Medication

The prescription of psychotropic medication can be indicated for a brief period in crisis situations or as part of longer psychiatric treatment (Vladár Rivero, 1992). In crisis situations, insomnia is often an important complaint; then the prescription of benzodiazepines is a possibility. When there are signs of a psychosis, anti-psychotic medication can be prescribed. For long-term psychiatric treatment, benzodiazepines are not preferred because of the risk of dependence. After protracted use (longer than four months) withdrawal symptoms (e.g. depersonalization) may occur (Schoepf, 1981). Some authors (Rohlof, 1997) warn against the use of tranquillizers in daytime in cases where there are signs of dissociative disorder because dissociative symptoms may become worse. If a refugee continues to have serious depressive complaints then an anti-depressant should be prescribed. Anti-depressants are also proven to be effective in Post-Traumatic Stress Disorder. More information about criteria of choice can be found in a review by Silver, Sandberg and Hales (1990).

If medication is combined with psychotherapy, it is necessary to consider the way in which they interact and the possibilities for attuning them. Medications are most helpful to refugees when the prescription is fully integrated in the therapy process. According to Southwick and Yehuda (1993) anti-depressants 'can dampen down involuntary re-experiencing symptoms such as flashbacks and nightmares, particularly when used in conjunction with insight-oriented therapy. By modifying involuntary re-experiencing symptoms that follow intense and painful memories in psychotherapy, anti-depressants allow patients to more freely experience, work through, and master the trauma.' Prescription of medication may also be related to the stage of the psychotherapy: it can be advocated that medication is very effective in reducing symptoms at the beginning of psychotherapy, while later on the introduction of psychotherapeutic methods (e.g. relaxation exercises) can reduce the dependency of the refugee on medication.

When psychotropic medication is prescribed for refugees, it is necessary to devote extra time to explanation (Vladár Rivero, 1992). The printed instructions enclosed with the medication are usually in a language which the refugee has not yet fully mastered and are incomprehensible to him. It is important that the person taking the medicine should be fully aware of why it has been prescribed, how it works, and what effect it will have on his condition. Also, he should know the correct dosage, how long it may be used, and what possible side-effects there will be (Vladár Rivero, 1992). However, when refugees are well informed about the consequences of using medication and their possible side-effects, often they are able to deal with the abovementioned reactions. Of course, they should be allowed plenty of time to discuss the side-effects from which they are suffering. If a co-therapist is involved, he should be informed about all the possible effects and side-effects of the medication, the kind of information that has been given about this to the refugee, and which procedure has been agreed in the event that the refugee feels he cannot handle the side-effects.

Some refugees have an aversion to the use of psychotropic medication and to the doctors who prescribe it. This aversion against medication can sometimes be understood as an urge to stay alert—an essential contribution to survival in the life of many refugees. In other cases, the aversion against medication can be interpreted as a healthy distrust. It may be based on experience with doctors who 'treated' them so as to enable the torturers to continue their work, doctors who forcibly administered psychotropic medication and/or other drugs such as pentothal, scopolamine, curare derivatives and LSD (Vladár Rivero, 1986), or the use of drugs before combat.

People from different ethnic or cultural backgrounds may react in different ways to psycho-pharmaca: Asian people may react to lower doses of anti-psychotic or anti-depressant medication than Caucasians (Lin, Masuda & Tazuma, 1982; Vladár Rivero, 1992; Rohlof, 1997).

Concrete Assistance

Within the context of supportive psychotherapy it does no harm for the therapist to occasionally give direct assistance, for example by contacting social organizations for the refugee, helping him to write a letter or fill in a form. But in the case of time-consuming problems, or matters which require detailed knowledge of the social system or the methods of social casework then it is advisable to bring in an expert.

> *C.J., a 24-year-old refugee from the Middle East, had been in exile for two years. Recently his 13-year-old brother had joined him. C.J. had difficulty in caring for his brother but did not want to be separated from him. The therapist brought him into contact with an organization which was concerned with caring for young refugees.*

Discussing the Causes of Psychological Problems

Some refugees have very clear, but inadequate ideas about the causes of their problems. As was pointed out in Chapter 2, the cognitive approach provides a point of departure for offering the refugee more adequate explanations which will make behavioural adjustment possible.

There are also refugees who say they do not know the cause of their complaints. They are aware that they behave differently or do not function as well as they used to, but are often unable even to say when these changes first started. They obviously have negative feelings about these problems, which are sometimes transformed into a negative self-image and have a patina of helplessness. This becomes apparent from expressions like 'I have become weak' or 'I no longer have the perseverance'. A detailed look at the time when the first symptoms were manifested can be useful in stimulating the client to think about the genesis of his problems, and this may in itself lead to a reduction in feelings of helplessness and powerlessness. By doing this the therapist implicitly shows that he thinks the problems can be solved and that the client's own intellectual activity can play an important role in this. In this way feelings of helplessness can be relativized.

Explanation and Information

Many refugees who ask for assistance are afraid of going mad or already being mad. This fear may be related to the fact that the refugee does not understand his own emotional reactions and personality changes (Eitinger, 1960). The same idea, but then more specifically aimed at the problems of refugees who had been tortured, can be found in the work of Genefke (1984). She claims that refugees' fear, nightmares, insomnia, headaches and concentration problems stem primarily from the fact that they do not understand why they feel and act differently since they were tortured. The changes can be spectacular: people who have always been extrovert become introvert; active, independent individuals become passive and dependent; optimists become pessimists; social altruists become egocentric.

Genefke considers it of vital importance to explain to refugees that torture is aimed at breaking the victim's personality. She points out to her patients that torturers often explicitly threaten their victims, for example by predicting that they will never be able to sleep well or have a normal sex life again. Moreover, she stresses that such personality changes are the reaction of healthy individuals to inhuman experiences. Her explanation is meant to help the refugee to accept that, as a result of torture, his personality has been partially and temporarily damaged and altered, and to use this acceptance as a basis from which to restore his identity.

The same kind of explanation can be given with regard to the refugee's integration in the country of exile. Some of the inexplicable emotions and personality changes or the deterioration of academic achievements which the refugee notices in himself can be explained by the fact that he suddenly finds himself in a very different, sometimes confusing, cultural situation. Here one can also speak of normal reactions to radical changes in an individual's situation. The aim is then to work towards restoring his identity, which has become vulnerable as a result of cultural uprooting.

Explaining the cause of symptoms and placing the client's experiences within a conceptual framework is often called *psycho-education*. Using this technique, one should always be aware that the client may interpret the explanation wrongly. For example, some may see a particular explanation as proof that there is no hope of recovery. If the therapist uses professional jargon, such as Post-Traumatic Stress Disorder, in his explanations then there is the possibility that some clients will go and look this up in the literature without having the proper knowledge and professional distance to determine whether what they read is applicable to their own case.

Discussing the positive aspects of the refugee's functioning

Discussing the positive aspects of a refugee's functioning is aimed at the re-examination of the refugee's negative views of himself (Boehnlein, 1987) and at increasing his self-esteem. In addition it gives some impression of the adequate coping skills which he already possesses. The therapist can make suggestions about the application of existing coping skills to new areas, thereby increasing the area of behaviour in which the client functions adequately, as well as the number of activities which contribute to his general well-being.

The refugee can make use of this repertoire of activities to structure his daily life, which improves his ability to cope with the problems he is facing.

A discussion of the positive aspects of the refugee's functioning can only develop if he has the impression that the therapist understands how serious his problems are. This means that the therapist must usually first discuss the overwhelming negative feelings with which he has to cope.

Analysing Recent Experiences

Analysing recent experiences in associating with other people (i.e. discussing what has happened in the last few days) is aimed at improving the refugee's insight into the way in which he functions. It may also serve to help the refugee distinguish between the past and the present life situation. As a result he may gain insight into how to alter his behaviour in certain situations.

> *The D.J. family had a lot of problems. The father had somatic complaints as a result of being tortured by government officials in the dictatorship from which he had been forced to flee. There were conflicts relating to the upbringing of the youngest children. The oldest son made a depressed impression and had difficulty in making contacts with peers. In a family interview it appeared that he did associate with his classmates at school but could not hang around with them after school. He had to go straight home because the family, following the tradition of their native country, had their main meal at 4 o'clock. They agreed to alter this routine and have their meal at the time that was considered normal in their country of exile.*

Discussion of Political and Social Matters

In order to be able to function in a psychologically adequate manner it is necessary to have a realistic picture of everyday reality. This includes the political and social aspects of that reality. A refugee can achieve a better understanding of everyday reality once he realizes how the reality of life in exile differs from life back home, and how it came about that he had to exchange one everyday reality for another. For example, it is useful for the refugee to realize that he is now part of a society of which he, at least initially, did not want to become part; that this society seems strange and frightening to him; and that some members of that society consider him to be strange, frightening and unwanted. This knowledge makes his own behaviour and that of the indigenous population more understandable.

> *E.J., a young woman who had been in exile for 12 years, had still not learned to speak the language properly. The topic was broached when she complained of not being able to find a job. When she spoke she often purposely used a number of Spanish terms to show that she was foreign.*
>
> *In the course of a number of interviews it became clear that she was resisting the necessity to learn the language properly. She experienced this necessity as a direct result of the dictatorship in her native country which had forced her to go into exile, and it was against this that her resistance was aimed.*
>
> *She then realized that she was still letting the dictatorship dominate her life. The need which she felt to resist impeded her social contacts with people. She began to realize that some people interpreted it as a sign of disrespect that she kept using Spanish terms in spite of the fact that the vernacular equivalents had been explained to her.*

Conclusion

The therapeutic methods which have been described in this section have been formulated in common sense terms and occasionally have been explained in terms of various theoretical approaches. These methods are not only useful for promoting more adequate short-term functioning. They form a set of basic tools, that often also have to be used when a therapist is using therapeutic methods that require more expertise.

Lastly, all these therapeutic techniques can be adjusted to a group setting. Contact with those who have had similar experiences can contribute to more adequate functioning. The group provides emotional support, offers the opportunity of recognizing shared experiences, reduces the feeling of deviance and supports cultural group identity (cf. Barudy, 1981; Bruers, 1985; Santini, 1985b). In particular, groups that are composed of people with a similar background, for example with respect to their age or cultural background, are effective. The same can be said about groups of people who share the same kind of problems, like refugees who are waiting for the answer to their request for political asylum, or refugees who are considering returning to their native country after some years of exile (Santini, 1985a,b). These groups seem to mitigate the disintegrating effect of a forced separation from family and friends. They provide an environment that makes gradual psychological reorganization possible, through the sharing of common values and beliefs. They provide the opportunity to discuss traumatic events in an atmosphere of mutual understanding. The group process may result in a diminishing of feelings of guilt and helplessness, when these feelings are discussed in relation to the conditions in which they came into existence. The therapist can contribute to the effectiveness of the group by introducing interventions aimed at the reduction of the intensity and frequency of symptoms (cf. Fischman & Ross, 1990), like the ones that will be discussed in the next section.

Psychotherapeutic Techniques Aimed at such Symptoms as Nightmares and Flashbacks

In this section special attention is devoted to various psychotherapeutic techniques that can be used while discussing nightmares about and intrusive memories (flashbacks) of traumatic experiences. The term nightmare here refers to any terrifying dream which results in the individual awakening while feeling horrified. A flashback can be defined as an intrusive memory, that results in a re-experience of a traumatic situation of the past, so that the individual for a restricted period (varying from a few seconds to a few hours) partly or totally loses contact with the present reality.

Nightmares and flashbacks can be important symptoms, even when they are not reported by the refugee. This happens sometimes when a refugee is ashamed or afraid of talking about this subject.

> A.K. first denied having nightmares, because he sometimes wetted his bed when he had one. He also suffered frequently from flashbacks, but at first denied having them because he was afraid that the therapist would consider him to be a lunatic.

It also happens that a refugee is not aware of having a nightmare, because he forgets the content of it almost instantly after waking up. A similar process can be observed with regard to flashbacks.

> B.K. had left his country after two years of obligatory military service. During these two years he had had many traumatic combat experiences. In the initial interview B.K. had denied having nightmares.
>
> During the second interview he reported that he had felt depressed and agitated since he woke up, but could not remember he had had a nightmare. Later during the interview, while discussing his physical sensations after waking up, he remembered that he had indeed seen a nightmare.

> C.K. had left his country after escaping from the prison where he had been detained for political reasons. During the initial interview he said that, during the last week, it had happened several times that he was sitting in a chair for an

hour, with a book in his hands, but not reading one line. He could not remember what had been on his mind during that hour.

When asked how he felt after he came to himself again, he said he felt very anxious and was profusely sweating. The therapist explained to him that he possibly might have had flashbacks from his experiences during detention.

In the next interview, C.K. reported that he had a similar experience some days after this discussion, but then became aware of having had a flashback.

In some cases, a refugee does not mention flashbacks, because he is more worried about his behavioural reactions to having a flashback.

D.K. had been referred to the therapist because he had outbursts of aggression he could not control. His unpredictable behaviour resulted in problems with the compatriots with whom he shared an apartment. D.K. at first felt that his anger was provoked by his housemates. After some discussion, it became clear that the aggressive outbursts were reactions to flashbacks of his experiences in prison.

Why Discuss Nightmares and Flashbacks?

The discussion of nightmares and flashbacks is an important method for helping refugees and other victims of violence, for various reasons. First, these symptoms bring a lot of suffering. Therefore discussing them in detail links up with the motives of the refugee in requesting assistance. Moreover, the relieving of these symptoms often results in other improvements. For instance the individual becomes less depressed, can concentrate better on his work, acquires more patience and pleasure in the contact with other people and so on.

Discussing the contents of nightmares and flashbacks with a person who is ready to listen and does not become overburdened by the matter, diminishes the loneliness the victim is feeling with regard to his painful experiences. In that sense, it brings comfort. This is why some refugees appreciate it when one listens to their stories, *even when it does not result in an immediate relief of symptoms and the therapist himself feels rather powerless about these symptoms.* Talking about nightmares and flashbacks may also help the victim to understand better why he has these symptoms, and he feels less overwhelmed by them. It often results in a diminishing of the victim's fear that he is going mad.

The above reasons are formulated in common sense terminology. On the basis of the theoretical knowledge presented in Chapter 2 of this study, the following reasons can be added.

From a psychodynamic point of view, the content of a nightmare (e.g. it is about being tortured) is very important. This content has a personal meaning for the victim (e.g. the torturer was a friend from primary school, which made the torture much more than physical pain). Discussing the personal meaning which the content of the nightmare or flashback has for the individual, includes talking about what the various ingredients of the nightmare and the original traumatic experience to which the nightmare refers mean for the refugee. The nightmare in some way illustrates how the traumatic experience has influenced the refugee's self-concept, his world-view, his attitude towards other people and towards life in general. When these topics are discussed, this contributes, in psychodynamic terms, to the process of working through the traumatic experiences. After a nightmare has been discussed in this way, it usually does not repeat itself the following nights. The same things can be said about the discussion of the content of flashbacks. After discussing one flashback in detail, it often becomes easier to control later flashbacks because the emotional upheaval caused by these flashbacks has diminished.

From the theoretical approach of family therapy, it would be interesting to discuss whether family members or close friends are aware of the refugee having flashbacks and/or nightmares and how these symptoms influence the communication in the primary social system of the refugee. This discussion might produce ideas about the ways in which family and friends can help the refugee to bear up against these symptoms.

Discussing the personal meaning of the content of the nightmare or flash-back results, in the terminology of the cognitive approach, in cognitive restructuring. That is to say, the victim may start to think differently about important matters, such as the cause of the traumatic events, his self-image and world-view, and his ideas about voluntary actions that could help him to avoid or to escape from traumatic events in the future. The information about the experiences that are relived during the nightmare or the flashback, can become processed and integrated in the view the person has of himself and human existence.

From the approach of learning theory, the bio-physiological reactions that accompany nightmares and flashbacks can be seen as learnt responses, that have been acquired by conditioning processes. Discussing the way these symptoms came into existence and the way they are interpreted by the refugee, may produce suggestions for more adequate ways of coping with these symptoms.

Sometimes, however, talking about nightmares and flashbacks does not bring much relief. This happens when a refugee has very contradictory feelings about discussing private, emotional matters and soon feels embarrassed. In these cases the refugee is not able to speak his true mind and mentions only a part of what is on his mind during the therapeutic sessions. Afterwards he can be obsessed for hours with memories that came to his mind while he was discussing a nightmare or flashback, but that he did not dare to share with the therapist.

Nightmares and Flashbacks: How Do They Come into Existence?

Nightmares and flashbacks in principle have an adaptive function (Blitz & Greenberg, 1984). From a psychodynamic point of view, it can be supposed that they develop because of the presence of strong defence mechanisms, which may have been necessary for a long time, but now impede the integration of traumatic experiences. The refugee's having a nightmare means that his resistance is decreasing and a process of integration is starting. From a cognitive point of view nightmares and flashbacks can be viewed as a form of information processing during sleep or waking life, through which the individual tries to prepare himself for situations that are just as bad or even worse than the traumatic experiences he has undergone.

A nightmare or flashback may be related to incidental, everyday events or sensations which actualize traumatic experiences. For example: receiving a letter from a family member who stayed behind, reports about the deportation of refugees or the rise of right-wing political parties in Western countries, tidings of war or violence. This phenomenon has also been described by Glover (1988), who observed that Vietnam veterans' nightmares about fighting or fleeing are often related to everyday incidents in which they feel out of their depth and desperate. This phenomenon can, as far as flashbacks are concerned, be explained within a cognitive-behavioural framework (see Chapter 2). The incidental, everyday events or sensations can then be seen as conditioned stimuli (CSs) that trigger conditioned bio-physiological reactions and cognitive representations, including emotions, memories and self-instructions that result in some behavioural response. With regard to nightmares, a psychodynamic explanation can be given: the events that happened during the day triggered anxiety-provoking memories that were repressed immediately. During sleep the defences are weaker and the anxiety-provoking memories come to the fore.

Nightmares are partly the result of an absence of interactions which facilitate cognitive and/or emotional assimilation of the traumatic experiences during the day. To put it more concretely: the traumatized person feels that there is no one to whom he can talk about his traumatic experiences. For refugees this impression is often based on an accurate assessment of their social environment. But it can also be an inaccurate one based on communication disturbances within the family, which might become a target for therapy.

The occurrence of nightmares and flashbacks may be related to social interactions which impede the process of overcoming traumatic experiences, because they trigger feelings of being overwhelmed and helpless. For example, experiences with ethnocentric prejudice and negative experiences as a result of cultural misunderstandings, which are not immediately recognized as such. When the refugee feels overwhelmed and helpless during these experiences, he may later have nightmares and flashbacks in which these feelings are re-experienced. A second example: the therapist stimulates the refugee to talk about his traumatic experiences, but is unable to structure the conversation sufficiently or to contain what the refugee is saying. The result is that the refugee becomes overwhelmed by his emotions and feels helpless and/or misunderstood. He later has nightmares or flashbacks in which the latter feelings are re-experienced.

A social position which makes it more difficult to cope with the traumatic experience also contributes to the occurrence of nightmares. For example, the position of those seeking asylum leads to feelings of powerlessness, uncertainty, fear and, in certain respects, restricted freedom. Within a psychodynamic framework, one can say that these feelings are very similar to the emotions that are associated with the traumatic experiences. Therefore it becomes very difficult for the refugee to apprehend that his traumatic experiences are something of the past. This interferes with the process of emotional assimilation of traumatic experiences, and may obstruct the helping process almost completely. It is the author's experience that feelings of uncertainty, fear and powerlessness related to the request for political asylum cause specific nightmares, in which the refugee dreams that he has been sent back to his native country and is once again being persecuted.

Giving Information

It can be helpful to discuss with the refugee what a nightmare or a flashback is. In the course of various interviews the therapist can ask the opinion of the refugee about this matter. Relating to the opinions of the refugee, the therapist can give explanations with regard to the following points of view:

- That these symptoms are a normal result of abnormal experiences.
- That they are related to other symptoms such as concentration problems and forgetfulness.
- That although they are disrupting daily life they have an adaptive function.
- That they mean that the person is trying to overcome his bitter experiences.
- That they are no reason for panic, but have to be observed as quietly as possible, although this sometimes may be very hard for the person concerned.
- That flashbacks are usually triggered by some perception which brings back bad memories, for instance smelling something (like the smell of blood or burning flesh when you are grilling a steak, or the smell of one's own sweat as it was smelled during torture), hearing a noise (like the sound of an alarm signal, the sound of a key in a lock), seeing something (like a uniform, a police car, a film about war, or the news on television), reading something (like the name of a friend who was executed), having a physical sensation (like when a part of the body which was touched during torture, is touched by another person or becomes sensitive for some

other reason), or having a more complex feeling (like having the feeling that one is humiliated, or having the feeling that one has to choose between two unacceptable alternatives).

• That nightmares in a way are much like flashbacks, in the way that they are often triggered by some perception; either while the person is sleeping (for instance the alarm signal of a passing police car), or during the previous day. For instance, a nightmare can be composed of elements from a film one has seen on television, and memories of a prison experience. In that case the nightmare can be seen as a kind of delayed flashback.

General Discussion about Gaining Control

To support the motivation of the refugee, the therapist can raise the matter as to how therapeutic interviews can contribute to the refugee gaining control over nightmares and flashbacks. The therapist can start by asking the refugee about his expectations and/or doubts regarding this point. Reacting to these thoughts, he can advocate the following opinions:

• Control of the symptoms will come when the person, in one way or the other, can face the facts to which the symptoms refer.
• That gaining control is a step-by-step process which takes time.
• That control can be gained as a result of thorough observation.
• That gaining control is a very individual thing, for which the therapist can only offer suggestions for starting to learn by trial and error, and that watertight advice cannot be given.
• That gaining control over physical symptoms by means of exercises often precedes gaining control over disturbing thoughts.
• That improvement tends to come in a spasmodic way, something like three steps forward, one step back, three steps forward, four steps back, which may seem like no progress at all, but has as a net result the proof that movement is possible, and one step ahead that is permanent.

Discussion about Behavioural Reactions to Nightmares

The conversation about nightmares may also include the refugee's reactions to his nightmares or flashbacks and the possibilities of behavioural changes.

> When E.K. awoke from a nightmare he usually lay in bed for a while, petrified. The first change of behaviour which was discussed was that E.K. would try to move his right little finger and then, bit by bit, the rest of his body. At the same time he would start to control his breathing (this part was rehearsed during the interview). After that E.K. would get up as soon as possible, and look out of the window to verify that he was not in prison, but in his new home in the country of exile.

The next step was that E.K. would write down what he had dreamed. He would do this in whichever was the easiest way for him: writing it down either in his native language or in English. The writing should be finished within five minutes. If the writing should make him anxious, E.K. should interrupt it by some quiet deep breathing. The therapist gave the advice that he should not again read what he had written before the next interview. Moreover, it was agreed that after writing down the content of the nightmare E.K. should drink a glass of water and, if he felt like it, have a hot shower. The result of these behavioural changes was that E.K. found it much easier to go back to sleep, without the nightmare's recurring the same night.

The suggestions for behaviour change are aimed at two targets: breaking an attitude of passive helplessness, and restoring the contact with present reality. Writing down the content of a nightmare can be seen as a form of information processing. It also produces interesting material that can be discussed during therapeutic interviews. It often has a beneficial effect (cf. Delany, 1979). But a few refugees will not be able to stop ruminating on their nightmares once they start to write about them. It may be helpful for them to express the feelings that seem to be related to the nightmare, for instance by writing down what is on their mind after waking up from the nightmare, or by expressing their feelings in a different creative production, such as a drawing.

Discussion of the Content of Nightmares

When discussing a refugee's nightmares the therapist can ask him to describe them in as much detail as possible. After that, he can ask the refugee to describe the feelings and associations which the nightmares evoke as a whole. If he considers it necessary the therapist may ask for the associations evoked by all the details of the nightmares as well. These often relate to memories of traumatic experiences.

F.K. said that she had felt tense from the moment she got up. The therapist asked her whether she had dreamt. She said she had had a nightmare in which she met the man who had maltreated her during her detention. In her nightmare she burned him with a flame-thrower. During the discussion the memory of the moment the man had burned her face with a cigarette lighter surfaced.

Nightmares often also reflect the refugee's present emotional problems or inner conflicts (Lansky & Bley, 1995).

G.K., an unmarried refugee, had nightmares in which he was married and his wife betrayed his political activities to the police. He related his dream to a trau-

matic experience which he had had. He had been arrested at a place only his best friends knew about, and he therefore thought one of his friends had betrayed him. During detention he had been tortured. He did not know which friend had betrayed him, and as a result was very distrustful of other people. There was also a second association. He had received a letter from his father, who was pressuring him to get married. G.K. did not yet feel ready for marriage and did not know what to write back.

It should be noted here that dreams may also reflect the denial of feelings of sadness, particularly those related to bereavement (Van Ree, 1987). Such dreams are, obviously, not nightmares.

After H.K. had received a residence permit he dreamed that he was back in his native country. He was visiting a friend who was, in fact, dead. They told each other jokes and H.K. woke up laughing.

Sometimes the content of a nightmare can be interpreted as a metaphor for the fear of the refugee of his own aggressive impulses.

After a long series of nightmares that were related to his traumatic experiences in prison, I.K. had two nightmares of a different kind. In the first nightmare, he was robbed of some money by a man much bigger and stronger than himself. In the second nightmare, I.K. dreamed that he had a vase of flowers on his table, which he touched by accident. As a result, the flowers became pulverized. This made I.K. very afraid, and he woke up wet with sweat and with his heart beating fiercely.

In other cases, the content of a nightmare may be considered as a metaphor for the self-concept of the refugee.

J.K., a refugee from the Middle East, reported the following nightmare: 'I had a birthmark on my body. It was very big, it extended over most of my body. It was ugly, dark brown, and swollen. It seemed to be filled with pus. It was hurting. I noticed that my left leg was the most painful part. Then I woke up. I was covered with sweat, my heart was beating like a drum. But I did not feel pain in my leg.'

The therapist asked J.K. if he had ever seen something like this birthmark. J.K. answered that it reminded him of the way the soles of his feet looked after they had been beaten with an electric cable. While discussing his thoughts about this nightmare, J.K. casually remarked that he was suffering from eczema. Although this problem was under control since he used a special cream, he had the feeling that the eczema made him very unattractive. When the therapist commented that the eczema was hardly visible, J.K. replied that his appearance wasn't attractive anyway.

If the therapist decides to discuss the possible psychodynamic interpretations of a nightmare, he has to be familiar with the specific problems that are connected with the use of techniques from uncovering psychotherapy. Moreover, in order to understand the personal meaning of a nightmare, he must be aware of the fact that a particular attribute may have a symbolic meaning within the cultural background of the refugee.

The therapist asked J.K.: 'What do people in your country say about birthmarks?' J.K. then explained that a birthmark on the head was considered to be a good omen, and a birthmark on the sole of the foot a bad omen. 'I don't believe those things', he added. 'And where is your birthmark located?', the therapist asked. 'On the sole of my left foot', said J.K.

Making up a Happy Ending to the Nightmare

In play therapy with children, progress is sometimes made when the child can think of a happier ending to a traumatic situation he plays over and over again. A similar approach can be used during the discussion of nightmares (Strunz, 1987) and in at least some cases it results in the disappearance of a recurrent nightmare.

K.K., a refugee from the Middle East, suffered a lot of torture during the time he was in custody. He had also survived very traumatic combat experiences. Several times he had the same nightmare: he was entering the house of a friend, who in reality had been executed in prison before his eyes. In the house there were six other friends, all buddies of K.K. who had in reality been killed during combat. All these friends wore white clothes. K.K. associated these clothes with the shrouds of the dead. He also was wearing white, and therefore concluded that he too was dead. This made him very afraid.

The therapist invited K.K. to express his sadness about the death of his friends, and from that point the conversation turned to K.K.'s fear of making new friends. 'My friends always die', he said with tears in his eyes.

Finally, the therapist asked K.K. whether there were other circumstances in which the people in his country usually wear white clothes. K.K. said that these white clothes are often used when one is sitting and having a cup of tea with friends in the evening. After this K.K. could think of a happy ending to his nightmare: he just sat with his friends as in the old days, making jokes and having

*tea. In different words: the scene he originally had interpreted as a sign of immi-
nent danger, was reinterpreted as a happy memory.*
After this discussion the nightmare did not return.

Discussion of Events that Trigger Flashbacks

When a person knows in which kind of situations he often gets flashbacks, he
will become less overwhelmed when he gets into such a situation. He will be
better prepared and consequently will not panic. He may also decide to avoid
the situations or events in question at times when he feels vulnerable.
Therefore, it is useful to describe the variety of events that can possibly trigger a flashback and ask him to think what might be the triggers in his case.

> *L.K. had been successfully treated for his flashbacks. But 13 months after the ther-
> apy was concluded, the war in the Persian Gulf broke out. L.K. started to have
> flashbacks again. These were triggered by pictures of combat he saw on television
> and the accompanying sounds. He told the therapist that he was watching televi-
> sion for hours, including during the night. While discussing this, he decided to
> restrict himself to one broadcast of television news each day, at a time he felt relaxed,
> and to practise respiration exercises while he was watching. In a second interview,
> L.K. reported that this way of acting had produced favourable effects, and there was
> no need for further therapy.*

Discussion of Reactions to Flashbacks

It is interesting to discuss the physical reactions a refugee experiences while
he is having a flashback. Common reactions are sweating, crying, accelerated
respiration or hyperventilation, headaches and an increase of tension in various groups of muscles. When the physical reactions are clear, it becomes possible to discuss behaviour (for instance exercises to cut hyperventilation and
to regain control over respiration and to promote respiration by using the
diaphragm, relaxation techniques or exercises from the martial arts) that has
a relaxing effect or may diminish feelings of helplessness.

> *M.K., a refugee from the Middle East, was 21 when he requested assistance. At
> that time he lived in a student home, where he shared the kitchen with fellow
> students.*
> *M.K.'s most important complaints were difficulty in concentrating on his aca-
> demic work and intrusive unpleasant memories of the four years he had spent in
> prison, where he had been severely tortured and had witnessed the killing of a
> friend. These memories caused accelerated heartbeat, sweating, blushing or flush-
> ing, a feeling of oppression and hyperventilation. He summarized his complaints
> with the words fear and panic.*
> *Anxiolytic medication had been prescribed, but had not brought much relief.*

The therapist analysed M.K.'s problems on the basis of the cognitive-behavioural approach, and departed from the hypothesis that the accelerated heartbeat and other somatic reactions were conditioned bio-physiological reactions. In this case neutral stimuli, that were contingent on the traumatic events and could be considered as CS, were: the smell of blood, the smell of M.K.'s own sweat, the sensation of being humiliated, the sound of an explosion, the sound of a person crying.

M.K.'s cognitive representations of the traumatic events contained memories of the prison environment and what had happened during detention, thoughts of being weak and therefore inferior, thoughts of being helpless and on the verge of going mad. These cognitive representations seemed to result in behaviour as in the following quotation: 'The fear came when I smelled the steak my friend was preparing. The smell of burning flesh reminded me of the interrogation session, when they burned my toes with a lighter. I left the kitchen, passed through the lounge—I did not stay there because I did not want the others to see that I was upset, I was ashamed—and went to my room. I closed the curtains and lay down on my bed. I tried not to think and to feel nothing. It often takes more than two hours before I can get up again.'

Therapy was started by explaining the principles of conditioning. After this explanation, the therapist suggested that M.K. should no longer summarize his problems as fear and panic, but as 'having to learn how to cope with unpleasant physiological reactions'. The therapist also discussed M.K.'s cognitive representations, carefully advocating the opinion that his problem could be considered as a normal reaction to very painful experiences and not as a sign of madness or inferiority. He suggested that M.K.'s behaviour when flashbacks occurred was more or less identical to his behaviour during and directly after the original traumatic events. This was confirmed by M.K. The therapist commented that he thought that this behaviour had been most adequate at the time, but that today, under totally different circumstances, another type of reaction could possibly be more adequate. After ample discussion, he proposed that M.K. should experiment with the following reaction: 'If something like this happens this week, go to your room, but leave the curtains open. Lie down on your bed, but do a relaxation exercise with the help of the cassette I gave you. Then get up, look out of the window, open the door of your room. If you don't feel too bad, proceed to the lounge to see if there is company. If there is nobody, at least go to the kitchen and make yourself a cup of tea.'

After five weeks, M.K. reported that his flashbacks had become less frequent and that he could usually control them within two or three minutes. His concentration had become much better, which resulted in better achievements at school.

The stimulus that was still giving him much trouble was the sound of explosions. When children played with fireworks it took five minutes before he could start to control his breathing. It reminded him of the execution of an intimate friend. The therapist instructed him to say 'I am startled' (in his native language, of course) as soon as possible after the disturbing sound, and then to try to control his breathing. This instruction resulted in a diminishing of his complaints.

Another topic for discussion is the reaction of family members, housemates or other people to the refugee having flashbacks. In relation to this, the therapist can discuss the possibilities for, and the pros and cons of, discussing parts of nightmares, flashbacks and traumatic experiences with one or more of those persons in the direct social environment. Sometimes a family member becomes aware of the refugee having a flashback before the refugee does so himself. In that case it can be discussed whether it would be useful if this family member were to bring the refugee back to reality, and in which way that could be accomplished.

N.K. suffered from flashbacks, which brought about aggressive impulses he could hardly control. His wife could tell from his face when he had a flashback like this.

After some discussion, he decided to ask his wife to 'wake him up' whenever she thought he had a flashback. He instructed her to call his name in a friendly way, but not to touch him. He felt that any intrusive sound or physical contact at such a moment could trigger an aggressive outburst.

Sometimes it is helpful for a refugee to write down the memories of traumatic experiences that form the content of the flashbacks (cf. Pennebaker & Klihr Beall, 1986), because it brings emotional relief. It can of course also be viewed as a form of information processing.

Discussion of the Content of Flashbacks

Flashbacks are troublesome because they make the individual relive very unpleasant feelings such as fear, helplessness or shame that were connected with a traumatic situation the refugee eventually survived or escaped from. However, this last part of the experience is not remembered. It may be useful to discuss this 'happy ending'.

T.K. had flashbacks of an aerial attack he had witnessed five years ago. During the attack, a bunker in which his brother had sought shelter received a direct hit. T.K had seen this. His brother had died. The therapist asked what happened directly after the bunker was hit. T.K. had difficulty in remembering that he had seen the planes turn away and heard the sound of their engines fading away, and that he had felt relieved. After this discussion, the flashbacks became less frequent and intense.

Another topic for discussion is the personal meaning the original traumatic experiences have for the individual. After listening to what the refugee spontaneously tells about this, he can be asked, in one way or the other, what was the worst flashback he had had lately, or what was the worst part of the flashback that is being discussed at the moment. A more intrusive question could be phrased as follows:

'I understand that this is a very bitter memory, it would be bitter for me and for anybody who has human feelings. But maybe there are reasons why this experience has an extra bitter meaning for you as an individual, which I cannot understand instantly. Could you explain to me why this experience was so bitter for you personally?'

The answer to this kind of question may help the refugee to discuss the most important thoughts or feelings related to his traumatic experiences, for example a very distressing feeling.

O.K. had been imprisoned for political reasons while he was 16 years old. He had escaped prison after five years. During his stay in prison he had been severely tortured. When he requested assistance, he was suffering from flashbacks (intrusive memories of traumatic events in the prison) with extreme bio-physiological reactions. These flashbacks were accompanied by a feeling of having fallen backward and hopelessness. Apart from this, O.K. suffered from nightmares, sleeping disturbances, and hair loss.

After some months, the nightmares and sleeping disturbances had almost disappeared. The loss of hair continued, according to O.K.'s dermatologist as a result of psychological stress. The flashbacks had become less frequent, and the bio-physiological reactions had disappeared. But one part of them had remained: occasionally the feelings that formerly were connected with flashbacks came to his mind. O.K. considered his feelings of hopelessness and the feeling of having insurmountable arrears to be realistic.

He mentioned three reasons for this conclusion: he had arrears in paying debts his family had incurred to pay a smuggler that helped him to escape from his native country, he was just starting his studies while he sometimes met former classmates who were already finishing their education, and the loss of hair was still going on.

The therapist asked O.K. whether he remembered having felt like this earlier in his life. O.K. answered that it made him think of the hopelessness he had felt when he was in prison and had heard that he was sentenced to a term of imprisonment of ten years. O.K. also mentioned a childhood experience: he wanted to play soccer with some neighbourhood children, but they did not want him to join because he was not very good at soccer.

In the discussion about thoughts and feelings that in some way are related to the manner in which the refugee relives his traumatic experiences, the therapist can move in two directions. First, he can choose to explore the personal meaning of the traumatic experiences in relation to the personal history of the refugee. He can, to give just one example, explore the hypothesis that the refugee is punishing himself by reliving his traumatic memories again and again, or by focusing all the time on the dark sides of his present life. The therapist then is moving to the domain of uncovering psychotherapy, so he should ask himself if such a move is indicated. As an alternative, the therapist may use a cognitive-behavioural approach. Within this approach, the therapist will first discuss the benefits of the thoughts that are bothering the refugee. Generally this discussion will lead to the conclusion that most of the thoughts in question are useless, and have unpleasant consequences. In that case the therapist can advise the refugee about methods for putting his unwholesome thoughts aside.

The author has favourable experiences with the techniques described by De Silva (1985), who presents a hierarchy of five pieces of advice. Whenever an unwanted, unwholesome cognition occurs, the client has to try the first piece of advice, if that fails, the second, and so on. The advice can be summarized as follows

1. Try to think of something that is opposite to or incompatible with the thought in question.
2. Think of all the harmful consequences of the thought in question.
3. Try some distracting activity.
4. Think of what brought the thought to your awareness and try to think of ways of removing the immediate cause of the thought.
5. Try forcefully to restrain and dominate your mind, concentrate on the thought in a down-to-earth, unsentimental way, and then push it from your mind, if necessary 'with clenched teeth and tongue pressed hard against the palate'.

After some discussion about how the feeling of being backward in comparison to his peers was connected with childhood experiences, the abovementioned O.K. was able to acknowledge that the thought that he had insurmountable arrears was not very productive. He realized that this thought would neither pay his debts nor make him study any quicker, nor make his hair grow more luxuriant. So he agreed to label this thought as an irrelevant, time-consuming one, which he could try to get out of his mind. The therapist then gave him some advice about managing his budget, and introduced him to the programme for thought stopping.

In relation to step 1, O.K. said that it might help if he tried to think of what he considered as his achievements: learning to speak the language of the country of exile almost fluently, having overcome most of his post-traumatic symptoms and having a relationship with a girlfriend.

Talking about step 2, he said that it might be useful to think that ruminating on unproductive thoughts would interfere with his studies. The therapist suggested that he should also remember that the target thought implied that he was humiliating himself, in the same way as his torturers had tried to humiliate him, and that he probably did not really want to continue along that line.

With regard to step 3, O.K. thought that it might help him to do some jogging in a wood near his house.

During the next interview, after two weeks, O.K. told the therapist that he had managed to improve his financial situation a little. He had also been quite successful in getting rid of his pessimistic thoughts. Usually the first two steps of the programme had been sufficient. Once he had had to proceed to step 4. At that moment O.K. had realized that his negative thoughts often started when he saw a compatriot whom he considered to be successful. He then had said to himself that he did not know whether this compatriot was really happy and that he probably would not want to change his own life for that of his compatriot if he knew everything about it.

Evaluation of Results

Discussing the progress which is being made with regard to the treatment of nightmares and flashbacks also has therapeutic value. When a refugee can observe progress, this may diminish feelings of helplessness and hopelessness. And if the progress is not convincing enough for the refugee, observations of progress at least help the therapist to contain the hopeless feelings of the refugee without being overwhelmed and becoming hopeless himself.

Progress with regard to the therapy of nightmares and flashbacks can be deduced from the frequency, intensity and content of the dreams (Hartmann, 1984). In the case of post-traumatic nightmares one may speak of improvement if:

1. The nightmares have become less frequent: for example, once a month instead of every night.
2. The nightmares have become less intense: the refugee still has unpleasant dreams, but they are not as bad as they used to be. He is still afraid when he wakes up, but no longer wet with sweat, and he does not have much difficulty in falling asleep again.
3. The content of the dreams gradually changes from a direct representation of the traumatic experiences to a more symbolic representation, to which other dream elements are added. The dreamer feels less helpless, less alone and more active. At the start of treatment the refugee's dreams are often about persecution and imprisonment, and he wakes up at the point when he can no longer escape and will be killed. Later he may dream that he has been able to escape together with others.

P.K. often dreamed that he was being pursued by soldiers and guerrillas and that he was surrounded. Sometimes he was on the edge of a ravine, so that the only escape was to jump. He was alone.

After three weeks, he dreamed that he was together with a friend and they were both being pursued. He escaped while his friend was killed. A few days later he dreamed that he had managed to escape together with others and that he had become their leader.

Q.K. had spent four years in prison after being detained for political reasons. He had escaped when the prison was bombed by the air forces of a neighbouring country.

After 20 sessions of therapy aimed at nightmares and flashbacks, Q.K. reported a dream in which he was back in his native country, arrested and brought to a prison. Until that moment the dream was fearful. But then he realized that the prison was painted in bright colours, and that there were no bars before the windows. So he opened a window, stepped outside and escaped. Then he woke up, feeling rather happy.

With regard to flashbacks, one can speak of progress:

1. When the frequency of the flashbacks, as monitored by the client, has become less.
2. When the duration of flashbacks has become shorter, or in other words, the person is quicker to realize he is having one, is quicker to become once more aware of the present reality, and more quickly gets control over his behaviour.
3. When the flashbacks have become less terrifying or depressing, and get mixed with pleasant memories.

After six sessions of therapy focused on nightmares and flashbacks, R.K. still had intrusive memories of his experiences in prison. However, this only made him tense for one or two minutes. Sometimes the flashback ended in pleasant memories of one of his fellow inmates.

The Order of Interventions

In this section several groups of topics for discussion are described that a therapist can have at the back of his mind when he talks with a refugee about nightmares and flashbacks. That does not mean that it is useful to discuss every single one of them with every refugee who is suffering from these symptoms. In bringing them up, the therapist can try to tune in to what the refugee has on his mind. This implies that no advice can be given about the order in which these subjects can best be discussed.

However, in order to give a more clear impression of the therapeutic process in which nightmares and flashbacks are the main focus, a more elaborate case example will be presented. It is about a therapy that quickly brought improvement. The success in this case was probably affected by the following favourable conditions: the patient was feeling secure because he had a residence permit; he was happily married and had just become the father of a son; he had had prior experience with therapy which had brought improvement; and the psychotherapeutic process was supported by the prescription of psychotropic medication.

S.K. was a 36-year-old man who was born in the Middle East, and arrived in the country of exile after being in prison for two years. During these years he was severely tortured.

When he met the therapist for the first time, S.K. told him that he suffered from nightmares (he had them almost every night) and compulsive brooding. He did not mention anything that pointed in the direction of flashbacks. At the end of the first interview, the therapist advised S.K. to make notes of his nightmares.

In the following interviews, the therapist asked S.K. to tell about the previous week's nightmares. After this he asked S.K. if the nightmares were related to something that happened in prison, which was always the case. In fact, the nightmares were almost identical to incidents that had happened in prison. In these nightmares S.K. was usually being tortured or at least humiliated.

When S.K. was talking about his nightmares and the related memories, he became very tense and started breathing very quickly, moving his shoulders but not using his diaphragm. Having observed this, the therapist taught S.K. some exercises to improve his respiration. In later interviews, the therapist sometimes interrupted the discussion of his nightmares in order to help S.K. to regain control over his respiration.

In the case of S.K., the treatment did not at first bring about much change with regard to the frequency or the content of the nightmares. Nevertheless S.K. said that the interviews were useful, because this was the first time he had been able to express his experiences without fear of burdening the listener too much.

In the fourth interview S.K. told the therapist that he was feeling worse than ever. At night, when he wanted to go to bed, he was overwhelmed by bad memories that were coming in a random order. He could not sleep more than three hours a night. He continued to have nightmares, but was not able to remember their content. He saw the deterioration in his condition as the result of watching the television news about the revolution in Romania and the habit in the country of exile of letting off fireworks during the last days of December.

During this fourth interview the therapist even considered the possibility of changing to a different therapeutic approach: the testimony method. An advantage of this method is that it helps to invoke the bad memories in chronological order, and also facilitates the rememberance of happier memories.

But the next week S.K. communicated the first signs of improvement. He had only had nightmares during two nights. Their content had been slightly differ-

ent: they were about situations in which S.K. was not the victim, but a bystander. The therapist asked him about the memories that were related to these nightmares, and specifically asked him whether the prisoners found ways to support each other after torture. This reminded him of some positive experiences.

After seven interviews, S.K. did not complain of nightmares any more. But he started to talk about another symptom that was bothering him. It happened about 20 times a day that S.K., unintentionally, suddenly cried out loud. He usually became aware of this by the startled reactions of those around him. It happened at home most of the time, but occasionally also in the library and in the subway.

The therapist gave S.K. the assignment of making notes about the time and place of the occurrence of this symptom, and instructed him to reflect on his thoughts just before he caught himself shouting. During the next interview it became clear that the shouting was a reaction to intrusive memories, related to being tortured or watching others being tortured. That is to say, it was the side-effect of having a flashback. The symptom was already becoming less frequent, and occurred only at home. Over three interviews the therapist and S.K. discussed the notes S.K. had made about the flashbacks preceding the involuntary shouting. The therapist invited him to talk in detail about the worst memory that had come to his mind during these flashbacks. He also taught S.K. an exercise from the martial arts, in which he learned to coordinate his body in an aggressive movement, while shouting at the same time.

After 16 interviews, all symptoms had disappeared. Occasionally S.K. still became aware of the impulse to cry out, but he was usually able to control this impulse. From time to time, S.K. had some unpleasant memories of his years in prison, but he was able to cope with these memories. His achievements in his language course had become much better than before, and he looked quieter and happier. He said he did not need more therapy.

During a follow-up interview 6 months later, S.K. reported that he very seldom had a nightmare or a flashback, but that this did not shake him out of his equilibrium. He said he felt quite happy.

Therapeutic techniques aimed at such symptoms as nightmares and flashbacks often deserve priority because of the incapacitating quality of these symptoms. These techniques may also be used in therapy with other categories of traumatized patients who suffer from such symptoms. Frequently refugees are suffering from ongoing traumatization. This fact implies that refugees, probably more than other categories of trauma victims, have to be prepared for future backsliding.

CHAPTER 7

Restoring Emotional Stability

Discussing Traumatic Experiences

When a refugee's psychological functioning is at an acceptable level and he is not, or not any more, handicapped by symptoms, he may still be suffering from the consequences of traumatization and uprooting. Also, his future development may still be at risk. If that is the case, forms of therapy can be indicated that are aimed at restoring emotional stability and well-being, and in which discussion of past experiences, including traumatic experiences, is a main ingredient. In this chapter we will discuss two therapeutic approaches: the testimony method, which is focused on the discussion of traumatic experiences, and techniques of uncovering psychotherapy, that encourage discussion of a wide range of topics, such as early child experiences, more recent traumatic experiences, inner conflicts, the relationships with the parents, the partner and so on. Both therapeutic methods are based on the idea that unassimilated traumatic experiences interfere with personality development. Therefore therapy should be aimed at working through traumatic experiences, by discussing these experiences and their impact on the life of the client. As Mollica (1987) has stated with regard to Indochinese refugees in the United States:

> Once the patient is ready to tell the trauma story, the narrative begins to give shape to many new possibilities. The patient's previous interpretation of his story as a hopeless loss of control is diminished. . . . The new story that emerges is no longer being a victim of one's own society—it becomes a story about human prejudices and the weaknesses of the so-called human civilisations in which we live. . . . Our clinicians attempt to help our patients bridge this gap between the trauma story of helplessness and despair and the new story of survival and recovery.

Discussing traumatic events may be seen as a *corrective emotional experience*. De Wind (1970) uses this term to point out that it is a dramatic experience for the traumatized individual to realize that the therapist understands his fantasies and fears without rejecting him. Bleich, Garb and Kottler (1986) also speak of a corrective experience. They state that talking about traumatic experiences is so dramatic because it confronts the traumatized individual with frightening emotions. He is afraid of being overwhelmed by these emotions, but during the talk he realizes that he can undergo them and still hold out, and this is a corrective experience. In this connection, talking about traumatic experiences has been compared to the experience of bereavement (Spiegel, 1981), during which previously inaccessible emotions are experienced and expressed. This enables the individual to take leave, as it were, of the traumatic past, thus opening up the possibility of new experiences: a different, positive self-image, a new intimate relationship, involvement in a new ideology.

There is also a cognitive side to talking about traumatic experiences. For example, Piaget (1973) claims that the therapeutic effects of making memories conscious can be explained by the hypothesis, supported by experimental research, that remembering involves cognitive restructuring. Similar views can be found in Allodi (1982) and Spiegel (1981), who both emphasize that talking about traumatic experiences has a therapeutic effect, because it helps the client to realize what those experiences mean to him.

The Testimony Method

The testimony method (Cienfuegos & Monelli, 1983; Lira, 1986) was developed as a result of experience with the victims of the military dictatorship in Chile. It is so tied to the Chilean situation that it cannot simply be applied to the problems of refugees in other countries. But the line of thought behind the method is interesting and it will be discussed in detail below. The testimony method is a directive approach, but it can be used within the context of a therapeutic approach that is essentially non-directive, in the sense that the therapist tries to connect with what is bothering the refugee most.

The point of departure of this method is to encourage the traumatized person to describe his traumatic experiences in as much detail as possible, as though he was giving evidence as a witness for the prosecution. He is encouraged not only to relate the facts, but also to express the emotions related to his experiences. The context of the traumatic experiences—'the life-history of the traumatized person and his reasons for being politically active—is also discussed. Moreover, his capacities, his coping skills and the way in which he copes with difficult situations become a topic of conversation. The declaration is tape-recorded and transcribed by the therapist, who then discusses the transcript fully with the client.

According to Cienfuegos and Monelli, the effect of this approach stems from the possibility of constructively channelling aggression in the form of a charge or indictment. In addition, the client gets a better idea of what has happened to him: fragmentary experiences become integrated in a life-history. Because the experience of suffering has been symbolized in a different form (as a written statement) and its importance recognized by the therapist, the need to express it through somatization also disappears.

The effectiveness of the testimony method can be seen as the result of two forms of reconstruction. There is a cognitive reconstruction of the traumatic experiences in which things are ordered and the individual starts to understand his own strong and weak points. There is also an affective reconstruction of the traumatic experiences in which frightening, and therefore repressed, feelings are re-experienced and assimilated in an atmosphere of mutual understanding and emotional support. According to Agger and Jensen (1990), the result is that 'private pain is transformed in political dignity, . . . shame and guilt connected with the trauma can be confessed by the victim and reframed'. These authors also see the testimony as a cathartic, healing ritual.

Testimony as a Therapeutic Technique for Refugees

The success of this method depends on the client's motivation. It is most successful in the case of those who know exactly what they want to talk about and who realize that it is important to talk about it. Success also depends on the coping skills the client has at his disposal. The testimony method is most successful when used for the victims of torture. The results are insufficient in the case of the relatives of missing persons: here special attention must be given to the process of bereavement (Cienfuegos & Monelli, 1983). In Chile the method worked well in the case of peasants and miners; in other words, in the case of those who had little formal education and who were not used to talking about themselves or their emotions. The method is thought to be less successful with the well-educated, who can write down their own story (Lira, 1986).

Although the testimony method was developed for people with modest verbal abilities, it can also be used with refugees who are used to talking about themselves and their emotions, but who have been in a situation in which they could not confide in anyone for a long time. The method seems to be particularly effective in the case of refugees who still experience repression as a reality in their everyday lives: for example, those who are still awaiting the outcome of a request for political asylum and who have to live with the fear of being deported. Moreover, having a written statement about their traumatic experiences may be helpful for these refugees in several ways. It can help them to give information about their traumatic past in cases where this is necessary, without having to re-experience the traumas if they do not want to. For some refugees, after a while the written statement comes to function as a proof that they have not just had an unbelievable nightmare, but that their experience was true, because it is detailed and well documented.

The method also helps to make traumatic experiences which were severe, though not sensational or spectacular and therefore more difficult to describe, discussable. Finally, the method contributes to making accessible memories of pleasant moments experienced in the same period as the traumatization.

During the first two interviews following the testimony method A.L., a young African, talked about his life in the period before he became politically involved. In the third, fourth and fifth interviews he talked about various experiences with violence and death, but also about the vegetation in his native country, and his interest in poetry.

The sixth interview formed a climax, and he told of the experience he found most terrible: he had not been able to associate with peers for two years.

With refugees, the testimony method can be applied in two different ways. First, the method can be used with refugees who are motivated to give evidence about the political repression and the violation of human rights in their country, either because they want to accuse the responsible authorities, or because they want to defend their request for political asylum. This way of applying the testimony method is characterized as a brief psychotherapy, with a duration of 12 to 20 sessions; although a case with a duration of 35 sessions has also been described (cf. Agger & Jensen, 1990).

Sometimes the therapeutic techniques of the testimony method cannot be applied exactly according to the procedure described above. This happens for instance when a refugee not only has to cope with traumatic experiences from the past, but is also facing problems in the present and/or has to cope with normal developmental tasks. The result is that the refugee will not be motivated all the time to give evidence about his traumatic experiences. In those cases the testimony method can still make a useful contribution to the psychotherapeutic process, but it has to be used in a different way: more flexible and supplemented with other approaches.

In the case of A.L. the interviews which followed the testimony method were interrupted by, and alternated with, talks about various topics. These were apparently introduced by A.L. because he was troubled or excited by them: political developments in his native country, news of friends and relatives, bad experiences with immigration officials, incidents which seemed to stem from misunderstanding of Western customs, somatic complaints and falling in love. In the therapeutic conversations about these topics, the therapist used supportive, symptom-oriented and occasionally uncovering psychotherapeutic techniques.

The testimony method seems effective with refugees who come from a favourable family background and who were functioning quite well before they were traumatized. It appears to be less effective in the case of refugees who have had many traumatic experiences spread over an extended period of time (a number of years), and/or suffer from very incapacitating symptoms, and/or are convinced that they had psychological problems long before they were traumatized by organized violence.

Making Traumatic Experiences Discussable

The main technical problem in applying the testimony method with refugees who don't have a very solid motivation to give evidence, is making traumatic experiences discussable. When a refugee shows signs—however ambivalent—that he wants to talk about his traumatic experiences then the therapist is confronted with the task of helping him. He can of course stimulate those who do not find it easy to talk about what is troubling them, by starting with one of the complaints for which the refugee requested help in the first place. For example, by asking about nightmares and discussing the thoughts, emotions and feelings which these evoke.

It is also possible to talk to the refugee about his normal everyday life and discuss events which have touched him emotionally: the emotional agitation caused by a current event may point to unassimilated emotional experiences from the past. In this connection it is useful for the therapist to be abreast of recent developments in the refugee's native country, and to be aware of other incidents which could stimulate the re-experiencing of traumatic experiences, such as the showing of films about the refugee's native country (cf. Genefke, 1984).

> *The therapist was trying to support B.L. in extending his social contacts and asked him how he had been getting on. B.L. replied that he had not done anything the last few days, just slept. The therapist knew that there had recently been a number of documentaries on television about the situation in B.L.'s native country, from which he had been forced to flee five years earlier. The therapist therefore asked B.L. if he had watched television during the last few days. This provoked a discussion of the many and complex emotions which the films had evoked in B.L. In that way, B.L. started to describe his traumatic experiences.*

It sometimes happens that refugees who are known to have had very traumatic experiences would like to talk about them but that the conversation always breaks down. This is definitely not resistance to the therapeutic process, but the inability to express certain experiences. Explaining that some experiences are so terrible that words cannot describe them, and that the related feelings are inexpressible may have a supportive effect (cf. Puget, 1986).

The Techniques of Uncovering Psychotherapy

Most writers on psychotherapy with refugees seem to proceed from the assumption that the most important thing is listening to what the refugee has to say, and relating this with what appears to be on his mind, but of which he is not completely aware. Some of them hesitate when it comes to asking intrusive questions, as happens in the testimony method or the methods described in the previous chapter. Like those who advocate the testimony method or symptom-oriented methods they stress the opinion that reliving traumatic experiences is painful and that it is useful only in the context of a relationship of mutual trust. However, they expect mutual trust to develop most quickly when the therapist assumes a non-directive attitude and tries to explore the feelings of the refugee, including the feelings he may foster regarding the therapist.

These therapists often use a psychodynamic framework. In their publications they are usually not very detailed in explaining their techniques, but in order to describe their work they distinguish between different phases in the therapeutic process (see e.g. the case studies in Arcos & Araya, 1982; Cienfuegos, 1982; Monelli, 1982; Santini, 1986b; and the more general considerations by Groenenberg, 1984; Somnier & Genefke, 1986). Santini's division is the most elaborate. She distinguishes five phases:

- *Phase 1: Distrust of the therapist.* Many refugees have had experiences that made them lose some of their confidence in other human beings. In some ways they tend to mistrust everybody, including the therapist. They test the therapist's reactions to find out whether he is really interested in their story, and whether he will patronize them. This means that their distrust leads them to hold back or to talk only at a superficial level about their traumatic experiences.

- *Phase 2: Catharsis and reduction of symptoms.* In this phase the refugee talks about the terrible things he has experienced, expressing some of his emotions. This often brings some relief: the refugee becomes slightly less tense and his most disturbing symptoms (such as headaches, nightmares and flashbacks) also become less incapacitating.

- *Phase 3: Working through.* In this phase the psychological meaning of the various traumatic experiences for the individual is analysed. To that end the traumatic experiences are discussed in relation to one another, and against the background of his total life-history and the attitude to life the refugee has developed through the years. Also the consequences of the traumatic experiences as reflected through present attitudes and behaviour (including attitudes and behaviour that are manifested within the relation to the therapist) are considered.

The techniques the therapist uses in this phase of uncovering psychotherapy are described by such authors as Malan (1979) and Greenson (1967). To give a very brief summary: the interventions are directed at bringing to the surface feelings (often impulses) of which the refugee is not aware. These impulses are kept from awareness by feelings of anxiety and by defences. Generally speaking, the therapist tries to recognize the defence, the anxiety and the hidden impulse in that order. These impulses, anxiety and defences can be recognized in relation to three categories: the parents, usually as they were experienced in the past; others, usually as they are currently experienced or as they were experienced in the recent past; and the therapist and/or the institution in which the therapist is working, as it is experienced in the here and now. The experience with traumatized refugees suggests that it can be useful to distinguish a fourth category: the people who were responsible for recent traumatic events (perpetrators and hangers-on).

Which category the work of uncovering is done in first depends on what the client has on his mind (Malan, 1979). Once the hidden impulse has been interpreted with regard to one category, the therapist can try to switch to a different category in order to uncover the defence, the anxiety and finally the hidden impulse. Up to now it is the author's experience that talking about the refugee's feelings about early childhood experiences and about his parents is a more adequate start than talking about his recent traumatic experiences (cf. Santini, 1989).

- *Phase 4: Behavioural changes*. In this phase important topics of conversation are the social relationships of the refugee, for instance with his family, partner, friends (including political friends) from his native country and country of exile. His attitude and behaviour with regard to these persons are discussed, possibilities for behavioural change are considered, and eventually carried out step by step.

- *Phase 5. Restoration*. In this phase the refugee again looks back at his past. Here his feelings of guilt and bereavement are the main topic of conversation. They become assimilated and restoration can then occur: that is the individual gives up the behaviour that was related to the feelings of guilt and bereavement, which inhibited his welfare and adopts new behaviour which enhances his welfare. The latter may include behaviour which is rooted in the assimilated traumatic experiences, such as helping companions who are in a similar situation.

This division into five phases is useful because it provides a description of the many matters which are raised during the therapeutic process. The order of the phases is, however, not fixed: the first phase, that of distrust, may reoccur later in therapy, though in a different form, after there has been some catharsis and emotional assimilation.

While using psychotherapeutic techniques aimed at the emotional assimilation of traumatic experiences and personality change the therapist will be confronted by the following technical problems:

1. Recognizing and managing reluctance to discuss certain topics.
2. Adjusting the extent of re-experiencing.
3. Understanding inner conflicts and defence mechanisms which are not generally known.

Recognizing and Managing Resistance

Resistance refers to the phenomenon that a refugee refuses to talk about certain events or aspects of events, which are relevant to the therapeutic process, even though he does remember them.

> *A.M. said that he saw mental images which reminded him of his experiences with the military regime in his native country. When the therapist asked him about them he changed the subject.*

The Chilean psychologist Lira (1986) gives the following examples of resistance by torture victims. Some refugees minimize what they have undergone. They say that they were threatened and beaten but that 'nothing else' happened to them, and that others have had much worse experiences. Others can give detailed descriptions of the terrible things that have happened to them, but are unable to express the emotions which these experiences evoked.

The therapist can deal with resistance in various ways, depending on the capacities of the refugee. He can try to make him aware of the phenomenon and name it. He can explain that he understands and respects it but hopes that the refugee will be able to overcome it in the future. When the refugee is motivated to overcome resistance the therapist can help him by getting him to narrate his experiences chronologically and in detail.

Adjusting the Extent of Re-experiencing

The re-experiencing of traumatic experiences during therapy can only have a liberating effect if it is adjusted so that the emotions which are evoked are not too strong for the client to cope with. It is impossible to estimate beforehand the intensity of the emotions which discussion of a certain topic will evoke.

> *B.M. wanted to talk about her experiences before she was forced to go into exile. She brought along photos of friends and relatives. During the therapy session she spoke in a rational but emotional manner about her memories. She seemed quite capable of distinguishing her past experiences and the emotions which these evoked in her from the reality of her present situation. At the end of the session she seemed calm and relieved.*
>
> *But that evening, partly as a result of a news report from her native country, she had attacks of acute terror. It had apparently all been too much for her.*

In this connection one must also be aware that when traumatic experiences are discussed it is not only familiar emotions which emerge but also various new emotions which the refugee did not register during his traumatic experiences (Galli, 1984).

Understanding Inner Conflicts and Defence Mechanisms which are not Generally Known

In psychotherapeutic contacts with refugees one may also encounter inner conflicts the content of which is less familiar to the average psychotherapist. For example the following case.

> *C.M. said that she kept trying not to think about prison. But she admitted, somewhat embarrassed, she sometimes longed to be back in prison, though she did not know the reason why. That became clear later in the interview. She explained that she had been seriously maltreated a number of times during interrogation. Afterwards some of the other prisoners had taken care of her: they washed her, dressed her wounds, massaged her and comforted her.*

In some cases, the inner conflicts of the refugee may be centred around feelings of guilt. As Kordon *et al.* (1986), pointed out, those who are tortured compare their reactions during torture to their ego ideal and as a result may retain feelings of guilt or shame.

> *During his detention D.M. had been raped by three prison guards. During the rape he had an erection and because of that he felt very disgusted with himself.*

A relatively well-known phenomenon is the inner conflict victims of organized violence may have about being alive. Having survived, while others died, may provoke such thoughts as: 'Thank god it did not happen to me, but to my buddy.' Thoughts of this kind cause feelings of guilt and suicidal ideation, and will be repressed from awareness (cf. Brainin, Ligeti & Teicher, 1990).

The inner conflicts of victims of organized violence about aggression may be very complicated, and what has been written about it may seem rather confusing. For instance, Schwartz (1984b) claims that aggressive feelings in traumatized patients are sometimes a transformation of guilt feelings, which he describes as aggression of the superego against the ego. Somnier and Genefke (1986) give the example of a man who experienced as frightening the fact that he had not felt any aggression towards his torturers while he was being tortured. Brainin, Ligeti and Teicher (1990) suggest that some victims of organized violence may repress any aggressive impulse, because they experience these impulses as a deformation, brought about by the perpetrators.

For the author of this study, the last mentioned example is more recognizable than the other two, albeit in a slightly different form.

> *E.M. had, during detention, been raped by a policeman. When he became aware of having sexual-aggressive fantasies, he was very disgusted with himself. He saw his fantasies as an inborn deformation, which made him as bad and disgusting as the policeman who had raped him.*

Because the therapist will, during interviews about traumatic experiences, be confronted with inner conflicts and defence mechanisms with which he is less familiar, he may also notice unusual reactions in himself (Krystal, 1984). These unusual reactions will be discussed in Chapter 10.

The Therapeutic Relationship as an Instrument

The relationship between therapist and refugee can function as an important therapeutic instrument for recognizing the refugee's inner conflicts. Once contact has been established the therapist can attempt to determine what kind of feelings the refugee has towards him. The answer to this can contribute to an understanding of the refugee's problems. Sometimes the nature of these feelings seems fairly clear.

> *F.M., a 25 year-old ex-guerrilla, was referred by his doctor because of depressions and insomnia. During the first interviews he evoked in the psychologist the association with a small boy who had fallen and grazed his knee. Moreover, he did not initiate conversation and only gave short answers to questions. He kept looking sadly at the ground.*
>
> *The psychologist had the impression that F.M. initially distrusted him, to the extent that he was afraid of receiving humiliating responses if he spoke too frankly about his depressive feelings and their background.*

The client usually has observable feelings towards the therapist from the first moment. Because he hardly knows the therapist these feelings are usually based more on a basic attitude or emotional barrier than on real experiences in his encounters with the therapist. Within the psychodynamic approach, the expression of a basic attitude during the therapeutic process is called transference. Feelings which are expressed as transference in the relationship with the therapist provide important information about the emotional aspects of the refugee's problems.

These emotional aspects may also become manifest in another way during the therapeutic interviews: in the feelings which the client evokes in the therapist. These feelings are partly determined by the way in which the client behaves: it could be said—in Runia's (1986) terms—that the feelings which the client evokes in the therapist cause emotional resonances which in turn partially influence the content of the latter's therapeutic reactions. These reactions on the part of the therapist, based on emotional resonance, can become manifest in three forms (Abend, 1986):

1. In the form of reactions for which the client unconsciously longs: sympathy, erotic attraction, condescension.
2. In the form of feelings. The client's behaviour towards the therapist may resemble the way in which people whom the client considers important behave towards him, so that the therapist then feels what the client has felt for years.
3. In the form of empathy: 'normal' emotional reactions, given the refugee's descriptions of his experiences.

The therapist's reactions are of course also partly conditioned by his own emotional needs or inner conflicts. His emotional reactions, whether or not they are expressed in his behaviour or attitude, are referred to as counter-transference. By reflecting on these reactions the therapist may gain a better understanding of the refugee.

> The fact that F.M. reminded the therapist of a small boy who has fallen down, and the resulting inclination to take him on his knee and comfort him, says something about the therapist's own inner life. The therapist apparently found it pleasant to adopt a protective father or mother role. This is an inclination which he must keep under control in his contact with the client.
>
> This association also says something about the non-verbal signals which the client transmits: looking sadly at the ground evoked, in this situation, the impression that the he needed warmth, emotional support and reassurance that, in spite of the pain of the moment, everything would be all right.

Some refugees do not show any emotion, either in discussions with the therapist or in their behaviour. Their behaviour is correct and friendly and nothing else. But they do evoke feelings in the therapist, which he may experience during or after the encounter. An analysis of these counter-transference feelings may give some insight into the refugee's own, initially hidden feelings.

> G.M. was a friendly young man of 24, who had a rather vague problem, which he described as follows: 'I'm not enthusiastic about anything'. It appeared that long before he had been tortured, he had very traumatic experiences in the relationship with his father. In his contact with the therapist he was cooperative in the sense that he thought about the questions and gave thorough and balanced answers: in other words he did his best. His tone was serious, flat and slightly sad. During the first three sessions he did not laugh once.

The therapist had the uneasy feeling that he had to do something quickly, otherwise G.M. might sever contact and commit suicide. This led him to suspect that G.M. felt the need for someone who could give him advice and encourage him. To the therapist he seemed to be saying: 'Look, I'm doing my best, don't disappoint me, give me proof that you have something to offer that will give meaning to my life.'

Transference and Counter-Transference in Relation to Refugees

As there is not much literature on transference and counter-transference in relation to refugees, the content of this section is also based on the literature on other victims of political traumatization: victims of the Second World War.

De Wind (1969, 1970) gives a number of examples of the intense transference of negative feelings, in which the client sees the therapist as the person who used violence against him. Refugees also sometimes transfer these negative feelings to the therapist: they may come to see the therapist who stimulates them to talk about their traumatic experiences as one of those who actually caused those experiences.

H.M. said that he wanted to talk about his experiences in prison, but had trouble in doing this. There were two reasons: the memories were painful and he did not expect the therapist to believe him. The latter reason led to a resentful attitude towards the therapist. This attitude could be interpreted as transference once the therapist found out that when H.M. was being questioned in connection with his request for political asylum the government official who interviewed him did not believe his story, and that his lawyer did not take what he said about his experiences seriously either.

Counter-transference phenomena in relation to war victims have been described by Danieli (1980). She describes feelings of guilt (I'm causing the client pain by reminding him of the past), repugnance (what other horrible things will I hear?), shame (how can people do things like that?). She also shows how, in work with war victims, the therapist may come to feel superior or inferior in relation to the client. In therapy with refugees similar forms of counter-transference may occur. In this context, powerlessness is not an uncommon emotion. Powerlessness can in turn cause antipathy towards the client (Lavelle, 1987; Truong, 1987).

I.M. described some of the details of the torture which he had undergone during his detention in a Latin American country. It was a horrible story, but the most frightening aspect was the way in which he tried to suppress his emotions. The therapist was unable to make I.M.'s fear of being overwhelmed by his own emotions discussable at that moment. His own feelings took him by surprise, particularly the feeling that he had nothing to offer in the face of so much suffering, that he had not experienced anything himself and therefore had no right to speak about such matters. He also felt angry with I.M. for putting him into this uneasy situation.

Refugees who ask assistance while their request for political asylum is still pending, and whose problems are being aggravated by the uncertainty about their future and the fear of being sent back to their native country, often feel very powerless. During the registration interview, this feeling of powerlessness can be transferred to the helping professional, who may wrongly, and without making further inquiries, conclude that he cannot help the refugee at all or only by prescribing psychotropic medication.

Another form of counter-transference comes into existence when the therapist himself has been traumatized and experiences some similarity between his own experiences and those of the refugee. He may overrate these similarities and overlook essential differences. And even when he sees the factual similarities in experiences in their proper perspective, he may wrongly assume that the emotional meaning of these experiences for the refugee are more or less identical to his own emotional reactions. A related phenomenon can be described as follows: the therapist has strong emotional reactions to what the refugee tells him about his traumatic experiences, but he is not able to cope with these emotions and to contain them. He then transforms his own emotional reactions to fantasies about the emotional reactions of the refugee, and uses them as interpretations during the therapeutic interview (cf. Bustos, 1990a).

The above example illustrates how counter-transference can impede the therapeutic process. Tiedemann (1987) describes how he attempted to avoid this in therapy with war victims by constantly reflecting on his own feelings. He kept asking himself *whether he felt affection for the client* and *whether he felt at ease* in his presence. If that is not the case then the therapeutic process is threatened; and Tiedemann suggests that this be discussed with the client.

Tiedemann uses the expressions 'to feel affection' and 'to feel at ease'. Other therapists will become alert if they get the impression that they may not laugh, or that they are being hurried, or are becoming bored. Each therapist learns from experience which signals are important for him. But in spite of this it is not always possible to prevent counter-transference from impeding the therapeutic process. By analysing his experiences with the assistance of experienced colleagues the therapist will be in a better position to realize what his own feelings are and to keep them under control. He will then be able to direct his attention back to his client's feelings and help him to express and assimilate them.

Improvisation

In the discussion of therapeutic techniques in this study, we have mentioned how they might be connected with the various theoretical approaches discussed in Chapter 2. It is obvious that the relations between psychological theories and psychotherapeutic techniques are not simple; often the effectiveness of a particular psychotherapeutic technique can be explained within more than one theoretical framework. Therefore, diagnosing the problems of a refugee in terms of one or more theoretical approaches does not automatically lead to the choice of a group of psychotherapeutic techniques. Moreover, diagnostic appraisal is an ongoing process. Therefore choosing therapeutic techniques is often not an isolated event at the start of the treatment, but a process in which the therapist experiments with various techniques, in order to find out what works and what doesn't.

In addition to this, the special problems of refugees often make it impossible for the therapist to stick virtuously to a fixed therapeutic procedure. The reason for this is the complexity in terms of the targets for psychotherapeutic techniques, as well as the influence day-to-day events have on the psychological functioning of refugees. For instance, news about the political situation in the native country or about the condition of relatives who are still living there, may bring back intrusive memories of traumatic experiences that were 'forgotten'. This can lead to a sudden increase in incapacitating symptoms or a revival of inner conflicts. Unexpected experiences with racism in the country of exile may bring adaptation problems to the forefront. Normal life events, such as the birth of a child or the death of a parent, may trigger unexpected emotions, just because they take place while in exile. Therefore working with refugees forces the therapist to integrate techniques from different schools into a pluralistic, multidimensional approach. This multidimensional approach can be described as a process of methodical, justified improvisation. During this process the therapist is constantly making decisions: about making certain interventions and refraining from other possible approaches; about digging deeper in some matter the refugee brings up, or ignoring it for the time being; about staying with or changing the subject, or purposely drifting away on what may be seen as a side-track.

To become aware of his decisions during the therapeutic interviews, the therapist can monitor his own behaviour by using a tape or video recorder. When this is not possible, he can make notes of the conversation. In working with refugees this also may not be possible, especially when the therapist needs all his concentration for conducting the interview (e.g. if the refugee becomes very upset during the conversation, or when the therapist has to use a foreign language). In those cases the therapist can try to reconstruct what happened while he writes his report. The author usually uses the following checklist:

Name: *Interview no:*   *Date:*

1. Intended beginning:
2. Other intended interventions:
3. Content of the interview, beginning: (Who started, and how. Was this conforming or deviant from what the therapist had in mind? This is usually easy to remember.)

4. Content of the interview, middle:
5. Content of the interview, end: (Often it is easier to fill in item 5 before item 4. After writing down how the interview started and how it ended, one can try to reconstruct what happened in between.)
6. Associations: (Entries to be noted here are, for example: 'Why do I keep forgetting the anamnestic data about this refugee?'; 'This man impresses me as being much younger than his chronological age'; and so on.)
7. Feelings of the therapist about being with the refugee, and his speculations about the feelings of the client about being with the therapist: (For example, the therapist may have been bored for some time, he may have had the feeling that he had to say something really clever, he may have felt unfree to ask certain questions, he may have been moved to tears, or he may have felt impatience or aggressiveness. The therapist may speculate that the refugee likes him a lot but is afraid to become dependent on him, or that he at some moment experienced the therapist as an interrogator, or that he takes the therapist for the good guy while he is seeing the therapist's colleague, who prescribes him medication, as a powerful but inadequate woman.)
8. New information with possible diagnostic value: (For example: a refugee tells the therapist casually that he used to be a member of a particular political group. From experience the therapist knows that this group has a very rigid ideology and seems to attract individuals who are in need of a group that can give them a kind of synthetic identity.)
9. Signs of progression or drawing back: (For example, a refugee told his therapist that he missed his last interview because it was a warm day and he went to the beach with some friends. About this refugee the therapist concluded that (a) the refugee's superego had become less rigid, (b) that he was becoming less dependent on the therapy, and (c) that he was making progress in overcoming his inhibitions with regard to social contacts.)
10. Did the therapist consider or effectuate a change in therapeutic strategy, or in any way deviate from the approach he had in mind? Did he think about any intervention that he decided to postpone?
11. Plan with regard to therapeutic strategy and intended interventions for coming interviews:

Sometimes, and with some clients very often, the therapist has to adapt to the actual developments in the life of the refugee. That means he has to change his strategy or at least to deviate for a minute or two. By making detailed reports, the therapist prevents these changes and deviations from being ignored. They will become conscious decisions which can be evaluated later.

Guidelines for Choosing Therapeutic Techniques

Before a list of guidelines which can help the therapist to make his choice is offered, the tentative character of this list must be stressed. The list is restricted to the therapeutic techniques that are discussed in this book, and other kinds of psychotherapeutic techniques that might be useful in working with refugees (such as hypnosis) are omitted. Moreover, which therapeutic techniques are preferred, is also a matter of the personal preference and ability of the therapist.

Whenever a helping professional is considering the possibility of using psychotherapeutic techniques, he has to make an estimate of the motivation of the patient. Motivation for treatment is, in the case of traumatized refugees, almost always ambivalent. Consequently estimating the motivation of the refugee includes thinking of ways in which a very fragile motivation can be supported and stimulated.

Supportive psychotherapeutic techniques will have to be used in almost all cases. Supportive techniques can be used as a sort of safe start, while the therapist is observing the problems and capacities of the refugee, and trying to get a view of the life-world of the refugee (cf. Vladár Rivero, 1989). They will also be the first choice if there are not many people in the social environment of the refugee who can provide emotional support or if there is insufficient structure in his daily life (e.g. having a job, going to school or other routine activities). Supportive techniques may help to reduce symptoms, to improve overall functioning, and to restart developmental processes. They also can be used within the context of therapy aimed at the reduction of incapacitating symptoms, or in combination with techniques of uncovering psychotherapy.

Therapeutic techniques for dealing with nightmares and flashbacks will be used when these symptoms are very incapacitating, and the refugee is able to accept assignments. They are useful in working with refugees who have a massive history of traumatization.

The testimony method is useful when the refugee is, at least sometimes, strongly motivated to discuss his traumatic experiences. This method is only indicated where the traumatic experiences were not too much of a protracted ordeal, and where the symptoms are not too incapacitating. The testimony method seems less effective in the case of refugees who have had many traumatic experiences spread over an extended period of time (a number of years), and/or suffer from very incapacitating symptoms, and/or are convinced that they had psychological problems long before they were traumatized by organized violence.

Use of the techniques of uncovering psychotherapy aimed at promoting long-term processes of emotional integration and personality change is indicated where the traumatic experiences have deeply changed the refugee's attitude towards himself, other people and life in general, in an inadequate way. The use of uncovering techniques requires some psychological-mindedness on the part of the refugee, a capacity to form and sustain relationships, and an ability to form an alliance with the therapist, which implies that the refugee is able to tolerate ambivalent feelings with regard to the therapist. Some refugees have these qualities, but do not appear to do so when they initially request assistance. In those cases the therapist will start with a supportive approach, until it becomes apparent that the refugee needs and has the capacities to benefit from the techniques of uncovering psychotherapy (cf. Schwartz, 1990).

CHAPTER 8

Victims of Sexual Violence

Many victims of organized violence have experienced sexual violence. According to reports from human rights organizations (e.g. Comision de derechos humanos de El Salvador, 1986), sexual violence is part of the regular repertoire of crimes against humanity that are committed by the prison guards, soldiers and policemen in countries where refugees come from. According to a Danish study (Agger, 1989) 80% of the female and 52% of the male refugees seeking treatment at a specialized centre for torture victims had experienced sexual violence.

The special quality of sexual violence lies in the fact that this form of violence lays hold upon a person in matters which in most cultures are not easily open for discussion and are surrounded by shame and irrational beliefs. For female victims, sexual violence often means rape. The reaction to rape by the social environment is partly dependent on the cultural context. If the victim is a virgin, the deflowering may in some cultures result in the woman no longer being considered acceptable as a marriage candidate. A married woman may after rape be stigmatized as a 'whore' and ostracized by her husband and family (Groenenberg, 1992). For male victims, undergoing sexual violence may contribute to serious doubts regarding one's sexual identity, as well as relational problems and disturbances in sexual functioning. The special impact of this form of violation is thought to be a result of the intense feelings (including guilt, shame and self-blame, cf. Roth & Newman, 1990) and the moral conflicts in the victim that are provoked by sexual violence.

With regard to the quality of sexual violence, a distinction can be made between two forms: forcing the victim to take part in sexual activity, and genital torture (cf. Lira & Weinstein, 1986). One form of involuntary sexual activity is *rape*. For female victims, the physical consequences of rape include injury, infections or venereal diseases, deflowering, and pregnancy. Pregnancy is sometimes followed by abortion. Irrespective of the culture from which the woman comes, these consequences are associated with great humiliation and the fear of permanent damage (Groenenberg, 1992). During rape the interaction between victim and perpetrator is very ambiguous: on both sides aggression and lust can both play a role (Agger, 1989). The connection which is made between sex and aggression during sexual abuse makes rape a complex experience which evokes strong feelings of guilt and shame and destroys the image which the woman has of herself as a person who can love and experience sexual intimacy (cf. Lira & Weinstein 1986).

For male victims, anal rape may cause injury, infections and venereal diseases. It inflicts physical pain on the victim, as well as a wide variety of confusing and conflicting sensations and emotions, such as rage, disgust, and powerlessness. Although there is a popular belief that a man with a homosexual preference will enjoy being raped, these victims also suffer when they are submitted to forced anal intercourse or any other form of involuntary sexual activity. In some countries (e.g. Eastern European countries during communist rule) it is more or less a rule that when a prisoner is known to have a homosexual preference, he will be raped by the guards. During rape, the male victim, whatever his affective preference may be, may have an erection or even an ejaculation (Sarrel & Masters, 1982). This can be a very confusing experience, because many men believe that having an erection or ejaculation means that they have enjoyed the experience, which belief leads to feelings of shame or guilt. It may be possible that some victims also have some feeling of pleasure while they are being raped, but having an erection, an orgasm or an ejaculation during anal rape in general can be seen as a pure physiological reaction that comes without the consent of the victim.

Other forms of involuntary sexual activity, such as forced masturbation or fellatio, are not necessarily painful in a physical sense. But they also provoke a broad spectre of conflicting emotions.

Genital torture can be defined as the infliction of physical pain to the genitals which brings the victim to associate pain or panic with sexuality. This form of violence is more often reported by male victims than by female victims. Examples are: blows or kicks at the genitals, wringing of the testicles, and electric torture of the testicles. Genital torture is often accompanied by suggestions from the perpetrator that the torture will have a detrimental effect on the masculinity of the victim, on his reproductive capacities and on his sexual functioning.

The Consequences of Sexual Violence

If one looks at sexual violence *from the psychiatric approach*, it may lead to various symptoms, including a reduction of sexual interest or pleasure, delay or absence of an orgasm, and disturbing thoughts or feelings during sexual activity (e.g. feelings of guilt and shame, flashbacks of the traumatic incident). These symptoms can occur in victims of both sexes. In addition, male victims may experience failure to attain or maintain an erection during sexual activity or premature ejaculation.

From a psychodynamic point of view the following can be formulated. Sexual violence is an interaction in which the parties involved experience conflicting feelings, including lust and aggression. Moreover, in male victims 'the incidents can provoke active sexuality, thereby activating castration anxiety, and/or provoke passive, receptive sexuality, thereby activating homosexual anxiety and identity feeling' (Agger, 1989, p.309).

It must be added here that, from a psychodynamic point of view, the individual meaning of the traumatic sexual experience will be related to the individual's personal history, especially his experiences in relation to sexuality and the quality of his sexual identity before he was traumatized. For example: in male victims there is considerable inter-individual variation with regard to such matters as castration anxiety or homosexual anxiety.

After being raped at the age of 16, A.U., who considered himself to be heterosexual before he was imprisoned, was afraid that he would not be able to have sexual contact with a woman and that trying it would probably result in a fearful, humiliating experience. But he never had any fear of being or having become a homosexual. He said that he heard about boys at his school having a love affair, including a sexual relationship, a few months after he had been raped. He explained to the therapist how amazed he had been that time, because he could not understand that a sexual relation between men could be anything else than disgusting violence.

B.U. was raped at the same age, but he was afraid that the experience might have made him a homosexual, although he frequently had heterosexual contacts after he escaped from prison. He said he had become aware of this fear for the first time after seeing a documentary on television, in which an expert said that some male victims of sexual violence had themselves become sexual offenders.

C.U. was raped at the age of 22. He had considered himself to be homosexual since he was 18. The most disturbing effect of the rape for him was that memories of what happened sometimes provoked aggressive sexual fantasies.

From the point of view of family therapy, the hypothesis can be made that many victims will be reluctant to discuss their experience of sexual violence with their partner. They are burdened with a secret, which will hinder their communication and contribute to relational problems. If the victim has problems in sexual functioning, and the partner is not aware of the background of these problems, she or he may easily misinterpret them (for instance, the partner may become suspicious and think that the victim is having an affair with another sexual partner).

For female victims, rape sometimes leads to the birth of a child. It can be expected that the mother and those in her primary social environment will have ambivalent feelings towards the child. Many female victims of rape were not themselves politically active; they became victims because their husband, father or other male relative was involved in political activities. For these women rape means that they lose the illusion that they will be protected by the men in their social environment. Often very mixed feelings come up. The rage that is evoked by the violence can, often indirectly, be expressed towards the husband. Sometimes feelings of anger related to the rape are transformed to an aversion to all male family members, or men in general (Groenenberg, 1992).

From a cognitive-behavioural point of view, the following hypotheses can be proposed. Sexual violence triggers intense aversive emotions such as panic and disgust, and disturbing thoughts. For many people, these thoughts and emotions are incompatible with sexual pleasure. These emotions and thoughts can become conditioned to certain stimuli that occurred during the traumatic situation. The occurrence of similar stimuli later in life, for example during sexual contact but also in completely different situations, may provoke flashbacks of the traumatic sexual experience which disturb normal functioning.

> *D.U. was raped in a police office at the age of sixteen after being detained for political reasons. Fourteen years later, he was having a romp with the 10-year-old daughter of a friend. The girl accidentally hit his bottom. D.U. shouted: 'don't do that', and was startled by the rage he heard in his own voice. While telling this to the therapist, he recognized he had felt as if he was about to be raped.*

Treatment: Male Victims

Various forms of traumatization may eventually result in sexual dysfunction; therefore the symptom of sexual dysfunction does not always mean that the refugee has suffered from sexual violence.

> *When E.U. requested assistance, he said that his most important problem was that he sometimes failed to attain an erection when he was making love to his girlfriend. Although he had spent some years in prison during adolescence, he denied that he had suffered from sexual violence. In the course of therapy, E.U. talked spontaneously about many traumatic experiences and present day problems. Impotence did not seem to be a very urgent matter, the most important disturbing symptoms seemed to be nightmares and flashbacks. After ten interviews, the therapist reminded him of his problems in sexual functioning. E.U. then said that the problem had disappeared. He thought it had been the result of drinking alcohol before going to sleep, which he had been doing because he had difficulties falling asleep. As soon as his nightmares had become less, he had stopped drinking.*

On the other hand, the therapist should be aware of the fact that sexual violence in prisons and police offices is not exceptional, and that when the refugee does not mention it after a first question, this doesn't mean it has not happened to him.

F.U. had been in prison for three years during adolescence. He said that he had been tortured, but gave a negative response to a routine question from the therapist about sexual violence. During the therapeutic sessions, F.U. told many stories about his amorous adventures with women. Only after a year was he able to tell the therapist that he sometimes failed to maintain an erection during sexual intercourse. He associated this with experiences he had had when he was about 5 years old. After exploring his memories about the experiences, the therapist asked for a second time about sexual violence in prison. This time, F.U. described a severe form of genital torture that had resulted in internal bleeding.

Sexual violence is a traumatic experience, and treatment of the victims of sexual violence may proceed along the same variety of trajectories as the treatment of other traumatized refugees. Therefore the techniques of supportive therapy may be useful, along with techniques aimed at such symptoms as nightmares and flashbacks, the testimony method (cf. Agger, 1989) or the techniques of uncovering psychotherapy.

The traumatic sexual experience is often just one incident during a long process of traumatization. Moreover, the treatment takes place at a time when the refugee has to deal with current acculturation problems and present day difficulties. Therefore, the therapist should take care not to be too selective in his attention to this particular matter.

G.U., a refugee from a Latin American country, had been raped many times during detention. He sometimes had flashbacks, triggered by films on television that showed love scenes. After a first discussion about his prison experiences, ten of the weekly interviews were spent discussing a variety of present day problems. After this, G.U. started to discuss his flashbacks, mentioning only the physical sensations. The therapist taught him some ways for gaining control over these bio-physiological reactions. After another ten sessions, G.U. started to talk about his fears in relation to sexuality and his experience of sexual violence became the focus of attention in therapy.

Treatment: Female Victims

How the process of overcoming the consequences of sexual violence proceeds is strongly dependent on the way in which the woman has been socialized as a woman and the way in which she experiences her own sexuality

(Groenenberg, 1992). All this is influenced by the values and norms of the family or clan in which she grew up. In this connection, the following distinction (Murdock, 1965, cf. Mernissi, 1985) can be used:

1. Societies in which there is a strong internalization of sexual prohibitions during socialization, such as in Western societies.
2. Societies in which the sexual urge is contained by the imposition of external precautionary measures, such as in those societies in which women are supposed to use a veil.

Mernissi (1985) adds that this distinction reflects a different perception of female sexuality in such a way that, in the first case, women are considered as sexually passive beings, and, in the second case, as sexually active beings. If this hypothesis is correct, we may expect that in societies of the first kind, a woman who suffered sexual violence would be considered as a victim. In societies of the second kind, the woman can be blamed for the sexual violence she suffered. This could lead to a conflict with her social environment. For example, in Latin American culture sexual violence towards a woman means loss of dignity for her, and loss of honour for her husband (Groenenberg, 1992). According to Islam women are considered to be strong, threatening, sexually active individuals who should be kept under control in order to prevent them from tempting the men to forsake their social and religious duties (Mernissi, 1985). From this perspective rape is blamed on the woman herself and may result in social rejection (cf. Amnesty International, 1991). To avoid ostracism many women keep silent about rape. The same also applies to women who come from traditional African cultures with an Islamic patina, such as Somalian culture. In addition, women from Somalia and neighbouring countries have often also undergone a genital operation such as circumcision. Various forms of this operation can be distinguished (Thompson, 1989):

- *Incision*: making an incision in the clitoral prepuce
- *Sunna* or *circumcision*: removing the clitoral prepuce
- *Excision* or *clitoridectomy*: excision of the prepuce, removal of the clitoris and all or part of the labia minora
- *Infibulation* or *Pharonic circumcision*: excision of the clitoris, labia minora and labia majora. The two sides of the vulva are then stitched together with thread, or pinned with thorns, leaving a matchstick-sized hole for the passage of urine and menstrual blood

In the last case, rape means that the effects of the operation are violently undone. Some refugees may therefore ask to be referred to a doctor to have infibulation redone—a question that may raise rather ambiguous feelings in the therapist (Groenenberg, 1992).

Special Supportive Techniques

In the treatment of victims of sexual violence, a complicating factor is the reserve against discussing sex-related matters in many cultures. Female refugees in general will not easily discuss sexual violence with a male therapist. For some male refugees, there is an extra threshold to cross in discussing sexuality with a woman therapist, while others feel more awkward when the therapist is a man. Enabling a conversation about sex to take place can be rather difficult, and requires considerable tact.

Talking about sexuality can sometimes start during the first interview. This happens when the refugee himself stresses the importance of the subject.

H.U. obviously wanted to come to the point immediately, and get it over with. He had been referred to the therapist by a student counsellor. He had met this counsellor six times. In the last interview he had told him that he suffered from nightmares about his experiences with sexual violence in a police station. The counsellor had then advised him to seek assistance from a psychotherapist.

H.U. told the complete story in 30 minutes to a therapist who was a complete stranger. Later he said: 'I had no choice, I needed help urgently.'

In other cases, especially when the refugee has other troubles on his mind, the therapist may prefer to wait until a therapeutic relationship has developed before he starts to discuss sexual violence.

In the case of I.U., the therapist suspected that sexual traumatization had taken place because, by coincidence, he was well informed about the situation in the prison where I.U. had been detained. However, he decided not to bring up the subject, because I.U. seemed to be very vulnerable. After a year, in which I.U.'s functioning improved, he cautiously started to explore his experiences in prison. I.U. then confirmed that he had been raped.

In order to make a conversation about sexual violence possible, the therapist often has to take a directive stance 'in which he combines distance with empathy, friendliness with straight professionalism' (Tsui, 1985). This attitude can, to give just one example, be actualized by explaining to the refugee that in order to help him adequately, diagnostic information about very private matters is needed. The therapist may add that he is aware of the sexual violence that takes place in the police stations and prisons of the refugee's native country, and mention some examples. He can also express his understanding of the fact that many people are not very eager to talk about these matters. Then he can ask the refugee if he himself was a victim of any kind of sexual violence, or witnessed other prisoners becoming victims of sexual violence.

It is important for the therapist to have some information about the nature of the sexual violence the refugee has experienced. For this reason, some discussion of the exact nature of the violence is often indicated. If the refugee is not able to talk about (parts of) the traumatic experience, it can be helpful to instruct him to tell the story in the third person, as if he were talking about someone else (cf. Perren-Klinger, 1991).

As soon as it is clear which kinds of sexual violence the refugee has experienced, the therapist can examine whether the refugee is misinformed about certain things, or has questions he never dared to ask.

J.U. had been raped several times by a prison guard. After this, he had to be hospitalized because he suffered from prostatitis. One of the doctors in the hospital had advised him to avoid sexual contact for some time. Since then, J.U. believed that any form of sexuality, including masturbation and spontaneous ejaculations during the night, could be dangerous.

In this context the therapist can also examine the possible realistic components of the fears the refugee entertains about the consequence of sexual violence. An examination by a gynaecologist, urologist or other specialist may be indicated.

K.U., aged 21, had been sexually abused during his detention. He was aware of the fact that this experience had had a negative effect on his sexual relationship with his girlfriend. He had even been able to overcome his shame and talked to her about it. Nevertheless, his behaviour towards her continued to be influenced by unpredictable spells of fear and disgust.

During therapy K.U. said that he had not discussed everything with his girlfriend. He had not told her that he was sometimes afraid of being impure and unclean and of passing this on to her through sexual contact. He considered this fear to be irrational, and a sign that he was going mad. Later it became apparent that it was related to the fear of being infected by the Aids virus. After he had undergone an Aids test (with favourable results) his fear disappeared and the relation with his girlfriend improved.

Another important topic concerns the refugee's norms and moral values with regard to sexuality. It is necessary to explore this topic, because moral condemnation of certain forms of sexuality may complicate the exploration of the consequences of sexual traumatization, and because advice the therapist might consider giving in order to improve sexual functioning should not be irreconcilable with the refugee's moral values.

In the case of L.U., who had been raped during detention, the therapist was hesitant to ask questions about his present day sexual functioning, because

L.U. seemed to avoid the subject. He said to L.U. that he wanted to ask him questions about this, but that, in order to come up with the right questions, he first needed to know something about L.U.'s opinions with regard to various types of sexual behaviour. Then he brought up the topic of masturbation, and gave a brief summary of the differences of opinion in the country of exile about this form of sexual behaviour. Then he asked L.U. regarding his thoughts about these different opinions. L.U. responded to the question, saying that he had always seen masturbation as a sign of moral weakness, but that he now thought that it was a normal thing. At the end, L.U. was ready to discuss his masturbation fantasies in relation to his prior sexual experiences, including the rape.

Discussion of the moral values about sexuality may lead to a discussion about sexual fantasies. A refugee may have fantasies that are coloured by his traumatic experiences. These fantasies are often not compatible with his moral standards, and may provoke an intense fear of being abnormal.

L.U. admitted that he had sexual fantasies about his girlfriend in which he actively approached her. This made him afraid because he associated these fantasies with becoming a rapist himself. The therapist than said that, as a psychologist, he considered sexual fantasies to be a normal and adaptive mental activity. He also said that fantasies can be coloured by memories, for instance the memory of being angry at the man who raped him. He added that fantasies are different from actions and that not every fantasy can or should be put into practice. He then said to L.U. that he had no reason to fear that he would be unable to control his sexual behaviour, and asked if L.U. himself was afraid of losing control. L.U. said he wasn't, since he now understood what was happening.

For refugees who were traumatized during childhood, the sudden upheaval of sexual and aggressive impulses during early adolescence (cf. Blos, 1962; De Wit, Van der Veer & Slot, 1995) may even provoke panic.

M.U., a refugee from an African country, was 16 when his foster parents consulted the therapist. They said that for 6 weeks M.U. had been unable to sleep more than one or two hours. He also suffered from nightmares and flashbacks. Psychotropic medication had been prescribed, but without much effect.

M.U. had been raised in a detention camp for political prisoners, in which he had seen many atrocities, including the rape of his sister and the killing of his father.

In two individual sessions, the therapist taught M.U. various exercises for quiet respiration and relaxation. In a session with M.U. and both foster parents, the therapist explained that all boys of 16 are bound to be very hot-tempered at times, and that they might be startled by their own aggressive impulses. Then the therapist said that he wanted to say something about sex. He explained that all teenagers have sexual fantasies. He added that he had not yet had the opportunity to talk about these matters with M.U. but that he knew from other boys that these fantasies can become very confusing, especially if they become mixed with memories such as the memory of seeing someone being raped. The therapist added that he was ready to talk about matters like this with M.U. if necessary. The session was concluded with some pedagogical advice for the parents.

Three days later M.U. reported to the therapist that he had slept rather well the last three nights. Then he told him that he had fallen in love with a girl he had met a few days ago. After three months, he was still free of symptoms and functioning as a normal adolescent.

CHAPTER 9

Children and Adolescents

Many refugees bring their children with them into exile. In situations of armed conflict, some parents stay in their country, but decide to send a child into exile. Under these circumstances there are also adolescents who themselves decide to leave their country. Like all refugees, these children and adolescents have to cope with the consequences of traumatization and uprooting. Both processes can interfere with their psychological development.

Traumatization and Uprooting: the Experiences of Children and Adolescents

Sometimes refugee children have themselves been victims of violent experiences which could be called traumatic.

> A.R., the 11-year-old son of a refugee from Africa, had been hit by two dumdum bullets during a shoot-out. His brother, who is two years older, was seriously burned when their house caught fire after it had been bombed. A.R. had nightmares.

Other children have witnessed violence in which their parents were involved. For example, they may have been present when soldiers raided their house, took away their father and maltreated their mother (see Santini & Escardo, 1981; Viñar, 1985, for a detailed description of similar cases).

> B.R., an 8-year-old boy, was referred because of bed-wetting. He cried a lot, had temper tantrums and did not play with other children. The problems began after he had seen his father mishandled and arrested. Since this experience he had been very dependent.

Some children are primarily the victim of problems which stem from their parents' experiences with violence and persecution. When their father or mother is imprisoned, children may suffer emotional distress as a result of the sudden, involuntary separation. Parents' traumatic experiences then have an indirect effect on their children.

C.R., a girl of 10, had been in exile with her parents for two years. Her mother claimed that she had changed a great deal recently: she spent a lot of time in her room, was rude to her mother and did poorly at school. Enquiries revealed that she had good contact with her classmates at school and the teachers had no complaints about her behaviour. But serious problems had arisen between her parents: her mother had difficulty in adapting to life in exile and she reproached her husband, who had been seriously maltreated during his detention, for getting involved in politics.

For almost all refugee children, moving to another country means that they have to leave behind relatives, friends, pets and other belongings to which they are emotionally attached. Moreover, they usually do not have the opportunity to say goodbye.

D.R., who was 10 years old, had lived with his grandparents for five years. When his parents began to have political problems they picked him up from school and fled to a neighbouring country, without telling the grandparents. D.R. had not had the opportunity to say goodbye, and the only belongings he had taken along were the clothes he was wearing.

In exile, refugee children have to learn a new language. They also have to get used to a different school system. Sometimes they experience racism. In their relations with peers they become acquainted with different norms and values relating to children's behaviour than those of their parents. If they conform to the new norms this is not always well received by their parents.

Because children learn foreign languages faster than their parents, they often have to play the role of interpreter between their parents and various institutions, which burdens them with various problems. All this taxes the problem solving capacities of these children.

Adolescent refugees have the same kind of experiences as younger children. Those who fled without being accompanied by their parents carry the additional burden of having to fend for themselves without any concrete support or guidance from their parents. Many unaccompanied adolescent refugees lost their parents under traumatic circumstances. Some of them became involved in antisocial activities, or suffered great hardships before they reached the country of exile.

J.W, an African youth, was 15 when soldiers entered his village. He was not there when they came, he had gone fishing at a lake 2 kilometres away. On returning, he discovered the smoking ruins of his house. Behind the remains of the house lay the mutilated body of his father. An old woman walking around said that his mother and sisters had been taken away by soldiers. The next day another group of soldiers arrived in the village. They said that the group that had rampaged the day before were rebels. They told J.W. that he had to go with them to defend his country against rebels. This group was involved in several bloody battles in which many innocent citizens were killed. After a few months J.W. deserted and hid in a cargo ship that after a few weeks arrived in Rotterdam.

Interference with Development

Both traumatization and uprooting can interfere with psychological development. As a result, various processes that are important for development may be impeded or proceed in a less usual way.

Often possibilities for *observational learning* are restricted because the parents are not available as role models either because they are dead or because they are not functioning adequately as a result of psychological problems. The adult caretakers of unaccompanied refugee adolescents often do not have enough time available for direct contact. Language problems and misunderstandings caused by cultural differences can also make it difficult for an adolescent refugee to see a caretaker or a teacher as a role model.

For some adolescent refugees *cognitive development* seems to be delayed, especially with regard to social cognition. They are less capable than most adolescents of looking at themselves and at social interactions from the point of view of a neutral outsider. Also, they seem to be less able to recognize contradictory motives within themselves and others.

R.G., who was arrested when he was 16, still has the physical scars of the torture he endured. He was 21 when he entered therapy. In discussing his relationship with peers, he seemed to see only one type of motive behind their behaviour: to have fun. He thought he was the only one who sometimes wanted to sit quietly beside a friend without talking, or who wanted to talk about his worries, or who sometimes felt ashamed, or nervous.

In this sense, the development of his social cognition seemed delayed. But when the therapist proposed that R.G. should talk in more detail about a particular girl he seemed to like, he became interested in speculating about her motives for seeking his company.

In addition to this, *identity development* may be complicated. Both traumatization and uprooting give rise to the feeling that everything, including their own personality, has radically changed. In Western societies refugees, being members of ethnic minority groups, are in a marginal position. This makes it more difficult for an adolescent refugee to maintain a positive view of himself, especially when he is not part of a social network of compatriots. If the adolescent has such a social network, the life-style and traditions within this network sometimes don't connect with the Western, secular, technological society of the country of exile: this may result in feelings of alienation and disorientation. Losses the adolescent has experienced, such as the loss of social status and losses of career possibilities he had had in his native country but which are not within reach in the country of exile, also threaten the sense of identity. Being forced to change certain habits, for example eating habits, has the same effect (Kouratovski, personal communication). Moreover, adolescents often experience rejection of their request for political asylum as a personal rejection.

Helping Refugee Children and Adolescents: Basic Principles

Helping refugee children and adolescents can be aimed at the following objectives: providing the conditions for optimal development, stimulating development through support, and removing obstacles to development.

Providing Conditions for Optimal Development

The basic conditions for optimal development concern a number of *material* factors such as accommodation in a physically safe, not unhealthy environment; income; heating; food; clothing; personal ownership; opportunities for education and recreation. Equally important are innumerable *intangible* factors (cf. Bartels & Heiner, 1994). Three categories can be distinguished: safety, stimulating social contacts, and opportunities. With regard to *safety*, it is important that the child is in a stable situation that does not change overnight, where he finds continuity in care and guidance, and can get attached to his fosterers or mentors. Moreover, the child or adolescent can only feel safe if he does not live in fear of being expelled from the country. Uncertainty about this matter discourages making plans for the future; it is also experienced as humiliating and painful. *Stimulating social contacts* can be provided by an informal social network with people of the same cultural background, where the child or adolescent can relax and where familiar rituals are carried out concerning, for example, birth, death, annual feastdays and commemorations. Persons working for care-providing institutions and schools can also make an important contribution especially when they are not too nosey, but are genuinely interested in the life-world of the child; when they are ready to take his needs, wishes, and feelings seriously, and do not shy away from the odd shocking story. A structured social environment in which realistic demands are made, that encourages achievements, but that leaves enough space for their own wishes and enough freedom for their own initiatives and experiments, is also quite stimulating. Both informal and structured social environments can provide contacts with adults and peers who can function as the role models that are indispensable for psychological development.

The *opportunities* that are important for optimal development include the opportunity to develop talents, for example in the areas of sport and music.

Shortage of money is often an important obstacle here. The opportunity of meeting agemates in varied situations is necessary for acquiring social skills and the development of social cognition. The opportunity to get knowledge of, and contact with, one's own past is a condition for identity development. For young refugees this means contact with their own cultural background and in some cases contact with people in the country of origin. It sometimes also means that a child or adolescent needs the opportunity to psychologically work through a traumatic past. Last but not least, for optimal development one needs a little luck sometimes. *Treats, small marks of attention, presents, and other strokes of good fortune* are necessary to mark a turning point in a previously very unfortunate life-history.

> *R.W., a youth of 22, described his life as a chain of misfortune, disappointments and abuse. When he enrolled with a housing association he obtained a house within four months. The average waiting time was two years, so this was either pure luck or an administrative error. This was a turning point in R.W.'s life; it led to a change in his self-image.*

Stimulating Development through Supportive Techniques

Children and adolescents are faced with developmental tasks. These tasks concern matters linked to the growing of responsibility and independence which in all cultures is connected to growing older, such as taking care of personal hygiene, moving around without parental supervision, managing aggressive impulses and dealing with aggressive elements around them, and so on. For refugee children and adolescents, these developmental tasks may be more complicated than usual.

The exact content of some of these tasks is related to the society in which one is growing up. In a Western country the mastery of these tasks requires skills that are acquired as a matter of course by children born in that country. But a refugee child may still need to learn some of these skills.

> *O.W., a 12-year-old boy from Ghana, had lived for half a year with his foster parents before they discovered that he disliked taking a shower. He found the water much too cold. After some talking about the problem the foster mother discovered that O.W. did not know how to regulate the water with the type of tap they had. So he had always had cold showers. In the summer this was not such a big problem.*

Therefore it is important to be aware that some skills, for example skills related to using maps, coping with the traffic, telling the time, using a Western toilet, or using a telephone may be lacking and need to be taught.

For adolescents, some developmental tasks are complicated by the consequences of traumatization and uprooting. Three of these, integration of sexual and aggressive impulses, becoming less dependent on parents, and building an independent future, will be discussed in the paragraph on helping adolescents.

Removing Obstacles to Development

The development of refugee children and adolescents can be obstructed by current stress factors, as well as by the consequences of traumatic experiences. Practical help can sometimes be offered to remove current stress; for example supporting the child or adolescent in their contact with relevant institutions or organizations. Specialized therapeutic approaches may be needed for reducing the adverse consequences of traumatic experiences.

Helping Children and their Families

In helping refugee children, supporting their family is the most important ingredient. In working with these families, the therapist must be aware of culture-related opinions in the family. In particular, opinions about gender roles, the authority of the various generations, the connections of the family with networks of friends and relatives, and the autonomy of the individual, may be quite different from the therapist's own opinions (Perelberg, 1992).

Interventions can be aimed at strengthening existing protective factors and creating new ones, changing coping strategies, and restoring contact with the past (Bala, 1996). Strengthening protective factors can be done in various ways. Just mentioning and underlining the strength of the family may contribute to the development of self-confidence and self-respect in the family members. Making the family members more sensitive to each other's needs, pointing out the ways in which they try to help each other, and discussing the support the members expect from each other, can improve their working together and well-being. Bringing the family into contact with resources outside the family (such as community organizations in their neighbourhood) may reduce stress.

Coping strategies the family uses for dealing with trauma-related symptoms can be discussed and changes can be suggested.

> *W.V., a girl of 10, was suffering from nightmares. When she woke up from a nightmare her mother tried to reassure her by saying that these nightmares would disappear. During a family meeting, W.V. was asked to write down the content of her nightmares in a diary, so that she could 'lock them up in the diary'. Mother was asked just to sit for a while with W.V. to comfort her. W.V.'s older brother then started to talk about his own nightmares. (Bala, 1996)*

Many families avoid discussing past traumatic experiences. In doing this, they also blot out cherished memories that could give them hope. Moreover, differences between individual family members with regard to what they have been through are not discussed. If a family can be persuaded to restore contact with the past by talking about traumatic events, mutual understanding will grow. They will understand better how their experiences influence their present behaviour. This opens new opportunities for communication and supporting one another. That does not mean that the traumatic past has been undone, but that a new start can be made in living together as a family.

Helping Adolescents

In providing assistance to young refugees the therapist is confronted with problems similar to those encountered in therapy with other adolescents. The most important problem is their fluctuating motivation: asking for and receiving assistance conflicts with the adolescent need to feel independent (De Wit, Van der Veer & Slot, 1995). Fluctuating motivation requires a flexible and accommodating attitude from the therapist.

> *I.S., a 20-year-old refugee, telephoned for an appointment: he wanted to come and have a talk the same day. The therapist agreed to see him but he arrived half an hour late. The therapist adjusted his schedule, so that they would still have an hour in which to talk. At the end they made another appointment, but when the time arrived I.S. did not show up. The therapist sent a letter inviting I.S. to come and see him, but I.S. did not show up. He telephoned an hour later, apologized and asked for a new appointment, for which he was on time.*
>
> *I.S. who had undergone extremely traumatic experiences and was occasionally very depressed, did not keep two-thirds of the appointments the therapist made with him. Sometimes he took the initiative to make a new appointment and sometimes he left this up to the therapist.*
>
> *In this way a faltering therapeutic relationship developed in which I.S.'s feelings towards his parents were discussed and, occasionally, aspects of his traumatic experiences.*

In the treatment of adolescent refugees the same approaches can be used as were described for adult refugees. However, the problems of adolescent refugees are different because they are coloured by their developmental stage. They can be grouped around three developmental themes: integration of aggressive and sexual impulses, becoming less dependent on their parents and building an independent future.

Integration of Aggressive and Sexual Impulses

According to Blos (1962) adolescence begins with an increase in the strength of both aggressive and sexual impulses. An important developmental task of adolescence is the integration of these stronger impulses, that is to say, finding ways of dealing with them in an adequate, socially acceptable way. This developmental task becomes more complicated when the adolescent has undergone traumatic experiences, either directly or more indirectly.

> *E.S was 14 when he was sent by his school counsellor. He had fallen asleep at school several times in the past two weeks. He said that this was the consequence of his sleeping problems. He never slept more than three hours each night. He was afraid to go sleep, because he often had horrible nightmares. The nightmares were about soldiers burning down the village where he used to live, killing the men, raping the women. The nightmares always ended with a soldier threatening to kill him with a knife.*
>
> *E.S. had undergone some traumatic experiences, but nothing like what happened in his nightmares. However, these kinds of things had happened in his country, and as a child he had probably heard many stories about the rape and killing of innocent civilians.*
>
> *The therapist began therapy, starting from the hypothesis that E.S. was entering adolescence and was experiencing an increasing amount of aggressive and sexual impulses which would produce aggressive and sexual fantasies, which could easily become mixed with memories of the stories he had heard about rape and violence during his childhood. He assumed that he would probably have difficulty in accepting these fantasies, because for him they were associated with violent crimes against humanity.*
>
> *After E.S.'s father had agreed that therapy was indicated because of the deterioration of his achievements at school (E.S. did not want him to know that he was suffering from nightmares), therapy started. The therapist used techniques aimed at dealing with nightmares and controlling aggressive impulses, in combination with giving E.S. information about psychosexual development. The nightmares lost their sexual component immediately, and soon became less frequent.*

Becoming Less Dependent on Parents

Adolescents are confronted with the task of, in a psychological sense, becoming less dependent on their parents. This also applies to adolescents in exile, but for many of them the task is made more difficult because they have not seen their parents for years. Contact with them was severed at a moment when the psychological process of separation and individuation, which occurs during adolescence, had not yet been completed. Sometimes, the parents are dead. If the parents are still alive, the adolescent may be very worried about them and feel that he has failed in his responsibility towards them. Sometimes the adolescents have made promises before leaving—that they will finish their studies, for example—which now they cannot keep. Contact with their parents is very important for them, but difficult to maintain by post. In their native country letters may be opened by the authorities or the postal services are unreliable. Many of the letters never arrive. When they invite their parents to come and visit them in exile all sorts of problems relating to the application for a tourist visa arise. Sometimes these difficulties lead to an alienation between parents and children, which is incompatible with emotional independence.

> *F.S. was 21. His parents had to make great financial sacrifices to pay for his trip to Europe. He later tried everything to get them to come and visit him for two months. Their application for a visa had been made a year and a half previously and they still did not know whether it would be granted. F.S. worried a lot about this delay and could no longer concentrate on his studies. His parents wrote to him regularly and asked him how he was getting on with his studies. He increasingly isolated himself in his room and avoided his friends. He stopped opening his parents' letters.*

If these young people do maintain contact with their parents they are afraid to be too open about their daily life because their parents might, as a result of their traditional attitudes, disapprove.

> *L.W. found it very difficult to write to her parents. She did not want to write about her daily life. She thought that her parents, if they heard that she was living by herself, would be shocked. In her country, the only young women who live by themselves are prostitutes.*

The feelings which young refugees have towards their parents are usually very complex. They miss their parents' emotional support but feel hindered by the expectations and norms which they assume their parents have. They feel guilty about not living up to these expectations or violating these norms. Some of them had to go into exile because of political activities of which their parents did not approve. They reproach themselves and think: I should have listened to my parents. For some political activities were the result of a first attempt to make an independent choice, but if the first step has such disastrous consequences the person is not likely to take a second flippantly. And if they have experienced that those for whom their parents have political sympathies do not shrink from the use of torture, then this will also influence their attitude to their parents.

Other refugees carried out their political activities with the approval of, or more or less under orders from, their parents, and now reproach them for not having provided protection (though they are initially not aware of such negative feelings).

A visit by the parents can sometimes contribute to the assimilation of these conflicting feelings.

Building an Independent Future

Adolescents generally develop plans for their future. This is not easy for young refugees: they are usually very uncertain about their future. The future perspective which they had before going into exile has been destroyed and their world-view and self-image have been shaken by their traumatic experiences. As long as their request for asylum has not been granted they are not sure whether they will be able to build a new future in exile. Some of them fantasize about returning to their native country, but do not know when this will be possible.

The building of a new future perspective is more than just a development task for these refugees, it is also an aspect of dealing with the aftermath of traumatic events. The adolescent has to learn to live with the fact that some of the possibilities he dreamed about are, temporarily or permanently, closed to him because the situation in exile is not suitable for their realization and that the alternatives are not clear.

Studying or learning a trade can be important in helping these youngsters to build a future perspective. The parents of young refugees have usually had to make great financial sacrifices to make their flight into exile possible. They have often given their children instructions to 'achieve something' (see also Bruers, 1985). These youths feel obliged to become very successful for their parents' sake. But the language barrier, the different education system and disturbed concentration as a result of psychological problems all impede this. They experience failure in their studies as a failure to live up to parents' expectations, and the parents—at least if the refugee can keep in contact with them—are often unable to understand the reasons. This makes the process of emotional separation from the parents and the building of a future perspective which is better attuned to the new situation more complicated.

CHAPTER 10

Specific Issues in Working with Refugees

Burnout, Counter-transference and Vicarious Traumatization

Every mental health professional hears sad and unpleasant stories whatever the background of his clients. That is part of his job. Depending on the nature of the institution for which the clinician works, the type of assistance he provides and the background of his clients, he will hear more unpleasant stories or need to go into them more deeply. In the work with refugees and victims of trauma, the helping professional will certainly get his slice of the cake, and should be prepared for the psychological consequences of eating it.

Burnout

In the international literature (Van der Ploeg & Vis, 1989; Van der Ploeg, Van Leeuwen & Kwee, 1990; McCann & Pearlman, 1990) the psychological consequences of working with 'difficult populations' are often discussed under the heading *burnout*. This concept refers to the phenomenon that after a while some therapists become depressed, bored and discouraged. They show all kinds of somatic symptoms, and sympathy is replaced by a cynical and indolent attitude towards their clients. A first sign of burnout is dread of going to work, excessive boredom, feelings of tiredness or pessimism about the future in combination with fantasies about finding a new job that leads to a sense of being appreciated. Another important sign is neglect of activities or people that are unrelated to the job, including the family (Grosch & Olson, 1994).

On the one hand, this may partly be based on certain personality characteristics of the therapist, such as a tendency to perfectionism, a dedicated, idealistic attitude, the need to prove himself, difficulty in saying 'no', difficulty in delegating tasks and a tendency to have expectations about the results of care provision which are too high. On the other hand burnout may be related to factors which do not have anything to do with the personality of the therapist and on which he cannot exercise much influence, such as problems in the organization for which he works, professional isolation and lack of professional success because the clients cannot really get better.

The concept of burnout offers a number of interesting points of recognition. For the enthusiast there is even a burnout questionnaire (Maslach & Jackson, 1986). But the burnout concept offers few theoretical points of departure, and describes the most extreme and unfavourable consequences of working with difficult populations only in very general terms.

Counter-transference

Another group of publications which can be considered relevant have counter-transference as a key word. Counter-transference can be defined as the therapist's total emotional reaction *vis-à-vis* the client in the therapeutic situation (Kernberg, 1975, see Shapiro, 1984).

In the literature on counter-transference in the provision of care to people who have been traumatized a narrower definition of counter-transference is sometimes used. The concept of counter-transference is then reserved for the therapist's emotional reactions which can be seen as the result of an interaction between the stories which the client tells him and his own unresolved inner conflicts. The client's dreadful stories evoke impulses in the therapist which cannot be easily integrated, and against which all kinds of defence mechanisms, such as repression, splitting, projection and denial are brought to bear. This defence can result in various forms of dysfunction during the therapeutic interviews and in interaction with colleagues (Benedek, 1984; Blank, 1987; Bustos, 1988, 1990a,b; Chu, 1988; Danieli, 1980; Lindy, 1988; Shapiro, 1984; Schwartz, 1984a).

Working with refugees who have been seriously traumatized in the relatively recent past, but who did not previously have very serious mental problems, is somewhat different to working with people whose personal functioning has been coloured by traumatization from early childhood. As a result, certain forms of counter-transference which are encountered in the literature on incest victims, such as doubt on the part of the therapist about whether what the client describes really happened (Goodwin, 1985), are not relevant, or not relevant in the same way, in the case of refugees. However, the publications written from a psychodynamic perspective and relating to working with Vietnam veterans offer many points of recognition. For example, Haley (1974, 1978, see Schwartz, 1984a) writes that listening to stories of war crimes made her 'numbed and frightened', but that it also evoked all kinds of aggressive impulses.

The counter-transference concept is part of a complex theoretical framework. In particular, it directs attention to the inner life of the therapist as an individual, but thus limits itself to the drives and impulses within the therapeutic interview. It thereby offers few points of departure for explaining changes in the therapist's behaviour and attitudes outside the therapeutic situation. The attempts by Bustos (1988, 1990a) to explain conflicts in a care-providing institution in terms of counter-transference and the defence forms which it evokes make an interesting exception.

Vicarious Traumatization

The psychological effects of working with traumatized clients have been discussed under the title of 'vicarious traumatization' (McCann & Pearlman, 1990). The contribution of this approach consists mainly of descriptions of specific symptoms which the therapist may manifest (such as nightmares, intrusive memories and avoidance behaviour), the changes in thinking which can be the long-term consequence of listening to appalling stories, and the existential questions which they can place before the therapist.

The psychological consequences of working with refugees can, according to the author's clinical experience, be elucidated by dividing them into three main categories. These are: consequences for functioning during the therapeutic contact, temporary consequences shortly after the therapeutic contact, and long-term consequences.

During the Therapeutic Contact

Listening to a refugee who is trying to make clear how political repression and the violation of human rights have dislocated his life, can at first lead to unusual empathic reactions on the part of the therapist. These are reactions which are based on normal sympathy, but are somewhat unusual within a therapeutic situation. For example: the client tells a moving story so vividly that the therapist gets cold shivers, or feels tears welling up in his eyes.

According to Kernberg's (1975) definition of counter-transference, these unusual empathic reactions could also be considered as counter-transference. In any case, the line between an unusual empathic reaction and an emotional reaction which is strongly dependent on personal idiosyncrasies of the therapist cannot always be clearly drawn.

> A.V. told the therapist a very moving story, while he cried. As the therapist listened tears welled up in his eyes. The therapist empathized with his client's sadness, but also experienced a kind of euphoria because he had been able to feel so close to this client.

In addition, being confronted with all kinds of atrocity and injustice can lead to the kind of inadequate reaction which can, in psychodynamic terms, be referred to as counter-transference in a narrower sense, and which can be partly understood against the background of the therapist's own inner conflicts. A few examples: the therapist experiences an impulse to embrace the weeping client, although he considers this to be an inadequate reaction from a professional point of view. After a while the therapist may realize that he has avoided certain questions, questions which were obvious given the objective of the therapeutic contact. It is possible that he does not notice certain of the client's statements, for example statements which express aggression towards himself, or which evoke aggression in him. It may also chance that the therapist ignores remarks which, for him, refer to an emotionally loaded topic and adroitly (but not wholly consciously) changes the subject (cf. Benedek, 1984).

Something similar occurred in the contact with B.V., a refugee whom the therapist liked from the first moment he met him. In the course of ten interviews, during which B.V. talked about what had happened to him in prison, the therapist came to consider B.V. to be a very good-natured, sensitive person. During the eleventh interview B.V. told the therapist about his involvement in a horrible war crime. He described the event, but the therapist did not understand exactly what had happened. The therapist did not ask any questions which would have given him a clearer picture.

It could also happen that the therapist asks various explorative questions, but with a slightly reproachful, accusing, condemning or disapproving undertone, or that he is tempted to express an explicit moral judgement with regard to the client's behaviour.

The stories of traumatized clients can, as was mentioned, evoke strong emotions in those who listen to them. The therapist will generally attempt to keep his emotions under control to such an extent that he can keep his concentration on his client, or at least not burden the client with his own emotions. The behaviour which is aimed at keeping one's own emotions under control could be characterized as coping behaviour. For example: the therapist feels horror as a result of what the client has said, but puts this aside by consciously taking a few deep breaths. He then attempts to empathize with the client, and considers an intervention. Or, if he cannot manage that, he explains to the client that it has become too much for him for the moment and that he would prefer to break for a cup of coffee, or continue on another occasion.

Shortly after the Therapeutic Contact

During the discussion of traumatic experiences the therapist will sometimes succeed in setting aside the emotional meaning which the client's stories have for him by simply concentrating on the client's feelings (cf. Draijer, 1987). Shortly after the therapeutic contact the therapist will have to work through the emotions he set aside. As a result he may find it difficult to put the story out of his mind. He will not be able to concentrate on other matters for some time. Or he may feel temporarily incapable of social interaction, because he cannot open himself up to others, particularly when they make a demand on his capacity to empathize.

C.V had told the therapist a series of extraordinarily lugubrious stories about his experiences on the front in the war between Iran and Iraq. The interview lasted a quarter of an hour longer than expected. The next client, D.V., was in the waiting-room. He looked very unhappy. With the doorhandle still in his hand he told the therapist that his cat had died. Although the therapist knew from experience what it can mean to lose a pet, he nonetheless had difficulty suppressing a giggle.

It is also possible that the therapist feels a strong desire to share the story he has just heard with someone else. This may lead to an inner conflict: for example if he does not want to burden his colleagues, housemates or friends, while at the same time realizing that as long as it keeps bugging him he will not be very pleasant company. In the interaction with colleagues a sick joke sometimes has a liberating effect.

Furthermore, it is also possible that the therapist has difficulty in recognizing certain feelings which he experienced during the therapeutic interview, such as powerlessness, melancholic pessimism, bloodlust and sexual aggression, and as a result cannot dismiss them from his mind. He becomes tired, feels tense and cannot concentrate (cf. Mollica *et al.*, 1990). This may also be expressed in other ways, for example in reluctance to write a report after an interview, or in feeling great relief when a certain client cancels an appointment.

When the therapist recognizes such confusing impulses, emotions and alarming thoughts, this does not automatically mean that he can directly relate them to his contacts with clients. As a result he is not sure what to do about them.

Another source of confusing feelings is that the therapist is confronted with the client's feelings of powerlessness. These feelings are based on facts for which the therapist is himself responsible to a certain extent. For example: a seriously traumatized client on whom therapy has a positive effect, leading to a reduction of symptoms, regresses when his request for recognition of his refugee status is rejected. The therapist not only feels hindered in carrying out his work; being a voter he may also feel partly responsible for the government policy which has led to the rejection of his client's request for asylum (Van der Veer, 1989).

Therapists sometimes have intrusive memories, graphic impressions and/or disconcerting fantasies of the traumatic events described by the client.

The last client of the day, E.V., looked miserable and agitated. The therapist poured a cup of tea for him and said: 'you look as though you haven't slept well.'
'I haven't', E.V. answered. 'I've had some more terrible nightmares.'
*   'Do you want to say something about them?'*
*   'I can't remember very much about them. Except that I was back on the front. We drove into a village that had been attacked by enemy soldiers the pre-*

vious day. It was a terrible sight. The main street was full of bodies. The enemy had apparently rounded up all the villagers and killed them. It looked as though they had been slaughtered with bayonets. There were the bodies of old women, babies, mothers with a child in their arms. They were cleared away with bull-dozers. The gutters along the street had become rivers of blood.'

Two hours later the therapist was at home and supper was on the table. It tasted excellent. But during the washing up, when he saw the hot water run in crazy patterns over a plate, he imagined 'rivers of blood'.

A therapist can also have nightmares about the violent events which the client has described to him (McCann & Pearlman, 1990), or he can be unexpectedly confronted with intrusive memories of violent events which he himself has witnessed. He may also imagine that it is he himself who maltreats or rapes the client. All this is experienced as confusing, disturbing and burdensome. On the other hand such experiences can increase the therapist's capacity to react empathically.

The result of all this is often that job satisfaction declines and activities which were previously interesting or even relaxing are now experienced as burdensome because they remind the therapist of stories heard at work. For example: the therapist develops a loathing for war films, avoids watching television documentaries about starvation and other disasters or has less interest in sexual contact. Some therapists have sleep disturbances and somatic complaints (Benedek, 1984).

In the Long Term

Working with seriously traumatized clients can also have long-term consequences for the therapist. For example, there may be a change in the cognitive schemes, attitudes, expectations and assumptions which he has regarding himself and others (McCann & Pearlman, 1990). Put differently, being continually confronted with the blackest side of human evil, the most horrible forms of injustice and repression, all thinkable forms of cruelty, as well as the most fateful forms of accident can make a therapist very tired (Figley, 1995). It can alter the therapist's view of himself, the world and human nature. Moreover, his thoughts may be structured round images which are derived from the stories of his traumatized clients.

This may lead to a change in the therapist's attitude towards his work. He may either become more distant and less empathic, or become overinvolved and in some way dependent on his clients (cf. Wilson & Lindy, 1994; Lansen, 1996). Moreover, the therapist may become too careless with regard to professional norms. The temptation to become indolent, to not write reports, to become prejudiced against certain 'minorities' among the clients, to keep clients with serious problems or problems which are difficult to treat at a distance through rigid procedures or an uninviting attitude, and so on, is sometimes great (cf. Bustos, 1990a).

A similar phenomenon can be observed among therapists who receive refugees, whose request for political asylum is still pending, for consultation. They are sometimes overwhelmed by the helpless situation in which their clients find themselves as long as they have to live with the fear of being deported. The lowering of professional norms then becomes visible in the following manner: the therapist concludes that he is unable to help these refugees with the means at his disposal. He fails to make a detailed study of either the client's problems, capacities and problem-solving skills, or of the point of application for psychotherapeutic methods; even if there are descriptions of various psycho-social or psychotherapeutic forms of treatment in the professional literature which are suitable for asylum seekers. The therapist also does not get around to consulting a colleague who has more experience with the problems of asylum seekers.

The same thing might occur if the refugee adopts a theatrical, coercive or manipulating attitude in the eyes of the Western therapist. What the average European or American person considers to be theatrical can, given the cultural background of the client, be an adequate expression of emotions. Coercive, manipulating behaviour is often understandable and recognizable if one has an eye for the compelling circumstances in which the refugee may find himself. A lowering of professional norms has occurred when the therapist no longer takes the trouble to discover the background to the theatrical or coercive behaviour but, without the necessary diagnostic reflection, applies a label referring to a personality disorder, brands the client as unmotivated, or concludes, without trying even a single intervention, that he is not capable of profiting from psychotherapeutic techniques.

Changes may also occur in the way in which the therapist relates to himself and to others. This can include some dysfunction, for example in contacts with housemates and colleagues (Bustos, 1988). These changes will eventually lead to a personality change in which one may recognize positive and less positive aspects: the therapist loses a number of illusions but in a certain sense may possibly become milder.

Recommendations

In order to keep particular reactions during the therapeutic interview under control and to expand one's own repertoire of adequate coping behaviour, it is useful to carefully record how the interviews pass off. If the use of recording devices is not indicated then a standardized reporting procedure may be used (see Chapter 7). The material obtained in this way can be used to keep an eye on one's own functioning, but may also be used in consultation with colleagues or supervisors.

After some interviews with a seriously traumatized refugee the therapist needs some extra time to regain his breath. His diary and caseload should be adjusted to take this into account. It is often useful, and sometimes necessary, to discuss some of the emotions which have been evoked in the course of the job with fellow team members. This requires time, as well as effective leadership (Lansen, 1996). These emotions sometimes concern intimate matters which it is better to discuss with a colleague outside the team. Such collegial contacts must be anticipated beforehand and made possible by the therapist's employer.

In order to prevent the blurring of professional norms it may be useful to regularly question them explicitly, for example by considering, together with one or more colleagues, the diagnosis and the course of the assistance provided to each individual client. This seems rather obvious, but in practice this often does not happen for various very understandable reasons, such as the therapist being overloaded with work, or a lack of interest among colleagues for the specific problems of refugees.

Working with seriously traumatized clients has consequences for the personal functioning of the therapist, and some of these are not particularly pleasant. As a result the therapist may wonder why he has chosen to do this work. Continual reflection on the philosophy of life, but also on the unsolved inner conflicts or unassimilated traumatic experiences that underlie this choice can help the therapist to make working with seriously traumatized clients into a enriching experience.

References

Abend, S.M. (1986). Counter transference, empathy and the analytic ideal: the impact of life stresses on analytic capability. *Psychoanalytic Quarterly*, **55**, 563–575.

Agger, I. (1988). *Psychological Aspects of Torture with Special Emphasis on Sexual Torture: Sequels and Treatment Perspectives*. Copenhagen, Institute of Cultural Sociology.

Agger, I. (1989). Sexual torture of political prisoners: an overview. *Journal of Traumatic Stress*, **2**, 305–318.

Agger, I. & Jensen, S.B. (1990). Testimony as ritual and evidence in psychotherapy for political refugees. *Journal of Traumatic Stress*, **3**, 115–130.

Akhtar, S. (1995). A third individuation: immigration, identity and the psychoanalytic process. *Journal of the American Psychoanalytic Association*, **43**, 1051–1084.

Alexander, A.A., Klein, M.H., Workneh, F. & Miller, M.H. (1981). Psychotherapy and the foreign student. In: P.B. Pederson, J.G. Draguns, W.J. Lonner & J.E. Trimble (eds), *Counselling across Cultures*, revised and expanded edition. Honolulu, University Press of Hawaii, pp. 226–243.

Allodi, F. (1982). Psychiatric sequelae of torture and implications for treatment. *World Medical Journal*, **29**, 71–75.

Allodi, F. & Rojas, A. (1985). The health and adaptation of victims of political violence in Latin America (Psychiatric effects of torture and disappearance). In P. Pichot (ed.), *Psychiatry: The State of the Art*, New York, Plenum Press, pp. 243–248.

Amen, D.G. (1985). Post-Vietnam stress disorder: a metaphor for current and past life events. *American Journal of Psychotherapy*, **39**, 580–586.

Amnesty International (1991). *Geschonden rechten, geschonden levens*. Amnesty International, The Netherlands, Amsterdam.

APA (1994). *Diagnostic and Statistical Manual of Mental Disorders* (Fourth Edition). Washington DC, American Psychiatric Association.

Arcos, V. & Araya, P. (1982). Claustrofobia, paralización y participación. Psicoterápia de un militante político. Santiago, unpublished study.

Bailly, C., Jaffe, H. & Pagella, A. (1989). *Psychological sequelae of torture: PTSD with psychotic Features?* Paris, Association pour les victims de la repression en exil.

Bala. J. (1996). *Coping of Children and Families.* Amsterdam, Pharos Foundation for Refugee Health Care, Mental Health Care Department.

Baranger, M., Baranger, W. & Mom, J.M. (1988). The infantile psychic trauma from us to Freud: pure trauma, retroactivity and reconstruction. *International Journal of Psychoanalysis*, **69**, 113–128.

Bartels, A. & Heiner, H. (1994). De condities voor optimale ontwikkeling. Het belang van het kind in hulpverlening, preventie en beleid. *Jeugd en samenleving*, **24**, 282–295.

Barudy, J. (1981). *Self-help and Mutual Aid in a Mental Health Program for Political Exiles.* Leuven, Colat.

Basoglu, M. (1992). Behavioral and cognitive approach in the treatment of torture-related psychological problems. In M. Basoglu (ed), *Torture and its consequences.* Cambridge, Cambridge University Press.

Beck, A.T., Rush, A.J., Shaw, B.F. & Emery, G. (1979). *Cognitive Therapy of Depression.* New York, Guilford Press.

Becker, D. & Weinstein, E. (1986). La familia frente al miedo: aspetos psicodinámicos y psicoterapéuticos. *Revista Chilena de Psicologia*, **8**, 57–63.

Beets, N. (1974). *Persoonsvorming in de Adolescentie.* Utrecht, Bijleveld.

Begemann, F.A. (1991). *Het onvertelbare. Een verkennend onderzoek naar psychotherapie met oorlogsgetroffenen en hun kinderen.* Amsterdam, Swets & Zeitlinger.

Beiser, M. (1988). Influences of time, ethnicity, and attachment on depression in Southeast Asian refugees. *American Journal of Psychiatry*, **145**, 46–51.

Benedek, E.P. (1984). The silent scream: counter transference reactions to victims. *American Journal of Social Psychiatry*, **4**, 49–52.

Benson, D., McCubbin, H.I., Dahl, B.B. & Hunter, E.J. (1974). Waiting: the dilemma of the MIA wife. In H.I. McCubbin (ed.), *Family Separation and Reunion: Families of Prisoners of War and Servicemen Missing in Action.* Washington DC, Center for Prisoners of War Studies, Naval Health Research Center, pp. 57–169.

Bettelheim, B (1960). *The Informed Heart: Autonomy in a Mass-Age.* Glencoe, Ill., Free Press.

Blank, A.S. (1987). Irrational reactions to post traumatic stress disorder and Vietnam veterans. In S.M. Sonnenberg (ed.), *The Trauma of War: Stress and Recovery in Vietnam Veterans.* Washington, DC, American Psychiatric Association Press, pp. 66–99.

Bleich, A., Garb, R. & Kottler, M. (1986). Treatment of prolonged combat reaction. *British Journal of Psychiatry*, **148**, 493–496.

Blitz, R. & Greenberg, R. (1984). Nightmare of the traumatic neurosis. Implications for theory and treatment. In H.J. Schwartz (ed.), *Psychotherapy of the Combat Veteran.* Lancaster, UK, MTP Press, pp. 103–124.

Blos, P. (1962). *On Adolescence. A Psychoanalytic Interpretation.* New York, Free Press.

Boehnlein, J.K. (1987). Culture and society in post traumatic stress disorder: complications for psychotherapy. *American Journal of Psychotherapy,* **41,** 519–530.

Boekhoorn, P. (1987). *Omvang van de immateriele hulpvraag onder oorlogs en geweldsgetroffenen in Nederland.* Leiden, Stichting Research voor Beleid.

Boman, B. & Edwards, M. (1984). The Indochinese refugee: an overview. *Australian and New Zealand Journal of Psychiatry,* **18,** 40–52.

Boszormenyi-Nagy, I. & Spark, G.M. (1973). *Invisible Loyalties.* New York, Harper & Row.

Bot, H. (1996). Working with interpreters in psychotherapy. Paper presented at the first congress of the World Council for Psychotherapy. Wolfheze (The Netherlands), Psychiatric Hospital Wolfheze.

Brainin, E., Ligeti, V. & Teicher, S. (1990). De tijd heelt geen wonden. *ICODO-Info,* **7,** 5–25.

Brett, E.A. & Ostroff, R. (1985). Imagery and Posttraumatic Stress Disorder: An Overview. *American Journal of Psychiatry,* **142,** 417–424.

Brown, L.S. (1986). From alienation to connection: feminist therapy with posttraumatic stress disorder. *Women Therapy,* **5,** 101–106.

Bruers, J.J.M. (1985). *Vervreemding, geborgenheid en integratie.* Wolfheze (The Netherlands), Psychiatrisch Ziekenhuis Wolfheze.

Bustos, E. (1988). Psychopathological processes in the treatment of torture victims. Paper presented at the XXIV International Congress of Psychology. Sydney, Australia, 28 August – 2 September, 1988.

Bustos, E. (1990a). Dealing with the unbearable: Reactions of therapist and therapeutic institutions to victims of torture. In P. Suedfeld (ed.), *Psychology and Torture.* New York, Hemisphere Publications, pp. 143–163.

Bustos, E. (1990b). *The need of relatedness and the impact of introjective-projective processes in transferential and countertransferential reactions.* Paper presented to the symposium 'Assistance to victims of organized violence' organized by the Refugee Health Care Centre (CGV) and the Social Psychiatric Centre for Refugees (SPD-V). 28 September, Utrecht, The Netherlands.

Butcher, J.N., Egli, E.A., Shiota, N.K. & Ben-Porath, Y.S. (1988). *Psychological interventions with refugees.* Report prepared for the Refugee Assistance Program—Mental Health: Technical Assistance Center, Minnesota, University of Minnesota.

Cancelmo, J.A., Millán, F. & Vazquez, C.I. (1990). Culture and symptomato-logy—The role of personal meaning in diagnosis and treatment: a case study. *American Journal of Psychoanalysis,* **50,** 137–149.

Caplan, G. (1964). *Principles of Preventive Psychiatry.* New York, Basic Books.

Chu, J.A. (1988). Ten traps for therapists in the treatment of trauma survivors. *Dissociation,* **1,** 24–32.

Cienfuegos, A.J. (1982). 'Borra todas las huellas.' Psicoterapia de una mujer atrapada en el miedo. Santiago, unpublished study.

Cienfuegos, A.J. & Monelli, C. (1983). The testimony of political repression as a therapeutic instrument. *American Journal of Orthopsychiatry*, **53**, 41–53.

Coelho, G.V. (1982). The foreign students sojourn as a high risk situation: the 'culture-shock' phenomenon re-examined. In R.C. Nann, *Uprooting and Surviving*, Dordrecht, D.Reidel Publishing Company, pp. 101–107.

Comision de derechos humanos de El Salvador—CDHS (1986). *La tortura en El Salvador, Penal 'La Esperanza'*, San Salvador, Ayutuxtepeque.

Cox, A. & Rutter, M. (1985). Diagnostic appraisal and interviewing. In M. Rutter, & L. Hersov (eds), *Child and Adolescent Psychiatry, Modern Approaches* (second edition). Oxford, Blackwell, pp. 233–248.

Curtis Alley, J. (1982). Life-threatening indicators among Indochinese Refugees. *Suicide and Life-Threatening Behaviour*, **12**(1), 46–51.

Dahl, C. (1989). Some problems of cross-cultural psychotherapy with refugees seeking treatment. *The American Journal of Psychoanalysis*, **49**, 19–32.

Daly, R.J. (1985). Effects of imprisonment and isolation. In P. Pichot, P. Berner, R. Wolf & K. Thau *Psychiatry: The State of the Art, vol. 8*. New York, Plenum Press, pp. 249–254.

Danieli, Y. (1980). Counter transference in the treatment and study of Nazi holocaust survivors and their children. *Victimology*, **5**, 355–367.

Dare, C. (1980). Gezinsgeheimen. *Maandblad Geestelijke Volksgezondheid*, **36**, 1073–1083.

Davey, G.C.L. (1989). UCS revaluation and conditioning models of acquired fears. *Behaviour Research and Therapy*, **87**, 521–528.

Davidson, J., Swartz, M., Storck, M., Krishnan, R.R. & Hammet, E. (1985). A diagnostic and family study of posttraumatic stress disorder. *American Journal of Psychiatry*, **142**, 90–93.

De Anda, D. (1984). Bicultural socialization: factors affecting the minority experience. *Social Work*, **29**, 101–107.

Delany, G.M.V. (1979). *Living your Dreams*. San Francisco, Harper & Row.

Denley, J. (1987). Personal communication cited in J. Reid, & T. Strong, *Torture and Trauma*. Sydney, Cumberland College of Health Services, p. 96.

De Silva, P. (1985). Early Buddhist and modern behavioral strategies for the control of unwanted intrusive cognitions. *Psychological Record*, **35**, 437–443.

De Wind, E. (1969). Psychotherapie van vervolgden. *Inval*, 99–107.

De Wind, E. (1970). Psychotherapie van vervolgden (2). *Inval*, 127–138.

De Wit, J. (1987). Protectieve factoren: maatschappelijk en wetenschappelijk een uitdaging. In H.J. Groenendaal, R.W.J. Meijer, J.W. Veerman & J. deWit (eds), *Protectieve factoren in de ontwikkeling van kinderen en adolescenten*. Lisse, Swets & Zeitlinger, pp. 9–16.

De Wit, J. & Tak, J.A. (1996). Theoretische achtergronden van de klinische diagnostiek. In T. Kievit, J. De Wit, J.A.H. Groenendaal & J.A. Tak (eds), *Psychodiagnostiek voor de hulpverlening aan kinderen*. Utrecht, De Tijdstroom.

De Wit, J., Van der Veer, G. & Slot, N.W. (1995). *Psychologie van de adolescentie. Ontwikkeling en hulpverlening.* Baarn, Intro.

Diekstra, R.F.W. (1983). Suicidal behaviour among adolescents. In W. Everaerd, C.B. Hindley, A. Bot & J.J. van der Werff ten Bosch (eds), *Development in Adolescence,* Boston, Martinus Nijhoff Publishers, pp. 206–225.

Draijer, P.J. (1987). De omvang van sexueel misbruik van kinderen door verwanten. Kanttekeningen bij epidemiologisch surveyonderzoek naar pijnlijke gebeurtenissen. In *Seksuologie: Incest.* Leiden, Boerhaave Commissie voor Postacademisch Onderwijs in de Geneeskunde, Rijksuniversiteit, pp. 1–16.

Dweck, C.S. & Wortman, C.B. (1982). Learned helplessness, anxiety and achievement motivation. In H.W. Krohne & L. Laux (eds), *Achievement, Stress and Anxiety.* Washington DC, Hemisphere Publishing Company.

Eisenbruch, M. (1984). Cross-cultural aspects of bereavement. I: A conceptual framework for comparative analysis. *Culture, Medicine and Psychiatry,* **8,** 283–309.

Eisenbruch, M. (1989). The cultural bereavement interview: a new clinical and research approach with refugees. Melbourne, Royal Childrens Hospital.

Eisenbruch, M. & Handelman, L. (1989). Development of an explanatory model of illness schedule for Cambodian refugee patients. *Journal of Refugee Studies,* **2,** 243–256.

Eitinger, L. (1960). The symptomology of mental disease among refugees in Norway. *Journal of Mental Science,* **106,** 947–966.

Erikson, E.H. (1960). Identity and uprootedness in our time. In *Uprooting and Resettlement.* New York, World Federation for Mental Health.

Erikson, E.H. (1968). *Identity, Youth and Crisis.* New York, Norton.

Eth, S. (1986). Freud and traumatic neurosis. *American Journal of Psychiatry,* **142,** 1057.

Figley, C.R. (1985). The family as a victim; mental health implications. In P. Pichot, P. Berner, R. Wolf & K. Thau, *Psychiatry: The State of the Art, vol. 8.* New York, Plenum Press, pp. 283–291.

Figley, C.R. (1988). Post-traumatic family therapy. In Ochberg, F.M. (ed.), *Post-traumatic Therapy and Victims of Violence.* New York, Brunner/Mazel, pp. 83–109.

Figley, C.R. (ed.) (1995). *Compassion Fatigue.* New York, Brunner/Mazel.

Fischman, Y. & Ross, J. (1990). Group treatment of exiled survivors of torture. *American Journal of Orthopsychiatry,* **60,** 135–142.

Folkman, S. & Lazarus, R.S. (1988). The relationship between coping and emotion: implications for theory and research. *Social Science and Medicine,* **26,** 309–317.

Freud, S. (1955). Beyond the pleasure principle. *Complete Works,* vol. 18. London, Hogarth Press. *Jenseits des Lustprincips.* Wien, Internationaler Psychoanalitischer Verlag, 1920.

Furman, E. (1986). On Trauma. When is the death of a parent traumatic? *Psychoanalytic Study of the Child,* **41,** 191–208.

Galli, V.A. (1984). Terror, silencio y enajación. Buenos Aires, unpublished study.

Garmezy, N. (1985). Stress resistant children. In J.E. Stevenson (ed.), *Recent Research in Developmental Psychopathology*. New York, Plenum Press, pp. 213–233.

Garza-Guerrero, A.C. (1974). Culture shock: its morning and the vicissitudes of identity. *Journal of the American Psychoanalytic Association*, **22**, 408–429.

Genefke, I.K. (1984). *Rehabilitation of Torture Victims*. Copenhagen, International Rehabilitation and Research Centre for Torture Victims.

Giel, R. (1984). *Vreemde zielen. Een sociaalpsychiatrische verkenning in andere culturen*. Meppel, Boom.

Gielis, A. (1982). Geleerde hulpeloosheid all depressiemodel, een literatuurstudie. *Gedragstherapie*, **15**, 3–31.

Glassman, J.G. (1988). PTSD in Refugees. *American Journal of Psychiatry*, **145**, 1486–1487.

Glover, H. (1988). Four syndromes of post-traumatic stress disorder: stressors and conflicts of the traumatized with special focus on the Vietnam combat veteran. *Journal of Traumatic Stress*, **1**, 57–78.

Goodwin, J. (1985). Credibility problems in multiple personality disorder patients and abused children. In R.P. Kluft, *Childhood Antecedents of Multiple Personality*. Washington, American Psychiatric Press, pp. 2–19.

Greenson, R. (1967). *The Technique and Practice of Psychoanalysis*. New York, International Universities Press.

Grimberg, L. & Grimberg, R. (1984). *Psicoanálisis de la migración y del exílio*. Madrid, Alianza Editorial.

Grinker, R. & Spiegel, J. (1945). *Men under Stress*. Philadelphia, Blakiston.

Groenenberg, M. (1984). *Psicoterapia con refugiados Latinoamericanos*. Amsterdam, Social Psychiatric Centre for Refugees.

Groenenberg, M. (1991). Female refugees. Paper presented at the conference on Mental Health and multicultural societies in the Europe of the nineties. Rotterdam, September 15–18 1991.

Groenenberg, M. (1992). Female victims. In G. Van der Veer: *Counselling and Therapy with Refugees. Psychological Problems of Victims of War, Torture and Repression*. (With contributions from Victor Vladár Rivero and Mia Groenenberg). New York, Wiley.

Grosch, W.N. & Olson, P.C. (1994). *When Helping Starts to Hurt*. London, Norton.

Grosjean, F. (1982). *Living with Two Languages*. Cambridge, Cambridge University Press.

Haley, J. (1963). *Strategies of Psychotherapy*. New York, Grune & Stratton.

Haley, S.A. (1974). When the patient reports atrocities: specific treatment considerations in the Vietnam veteran. *Archives of General Psychiatry*, **30**, 191–196.

Haley, S.A. (1978). Treatment implications of post-combat stress response syndromes for mental health professionals. In C. Figley (ed.), *Stress Disorders among Vietnam Veterans*. New York, Brunner/Mazel, pp. 254–268.

Handelman, L. & Yeo, G. (1996). Explanatory models to understand chronic symptoms of Cambodian refugees. *Family Medicine*, **28**, 271–276.

Hartmann, E. (1984). *The Nightmare: the Psychology and Biology of Terrifying Dreams*. New York, Basic Books.

Helmreich, W.B. (1992). *Against All Odds. Holocaust survivors and the Successful Lives They Made in America*. New York, Simon & Schuster.

Hertz, D.G. (1987). Research on migrants and psychological effects of uprooting. Lecture as a visiting professor at the University of Amsterdam, 29 April 1987.

Hondius, A.J.K. & Van Willigen, L.H.M. (1992). *Vluchtelingen en gezondheid. Deel II*. Amsterdam, Swets & Zeitlinger.

Horowitz, M.J. (1976). *Stress Response Syndromes*. New York, Aronson.

Horowitz, M.J. (1986). Stress-response syndromes: a review of posttraumatic and adjustment disorders. *Hospital and Community Psychiatry*, **37**, 241–249.

Janoff-Bulman, R. (1989). The benefits of illusions, the threat of disillusionment, and the limitations of inaccuracy. *Journal of Social and Clinical Psychology*, **8**, 158–175.

Keilson, H. (1979). *Sequentielle Traumatisierung bei Kindern*. Stuttgart, Ferdinand Enke Verlag.

Kernberg, O. (1975). *Borderline Conditions and Pathogical Narcissism*. New York: Jason Aronson

Kinzie, J.D. (1978). Lessons from cross-cultural psychotherapy. *American Journal of Psychotherapy*, **32**, 110–120.

Kinzie, J.D., Frederickson, R.H., Ben, R., Fleck, J. & Karls, W. (1984). Post Traumatic Stress Disorders among survivors of Cambodian concentration camps. *American Journal of Psychiatry*, **141**, 645–650.

Kinzie, J.D. & Fleck, J. (1987). Psychotherapy with severely traumatized Refugees. *American Journal of Psychotherapy*, **41**, 82–94.

Kinzie, J.D. & Boehnlein, J.J. (1989). Post-traumatic psychosis among Cambodian refugees. *Journal of Traumatic Stress*, **2**, 185–198.

Knudsen, J.C. (1991) Therapeutic strategies and strategies for refugee coping. *Journal of Refugee studies*, **4**, 21–38.

Kordon, D.R. & Edelman, L.I. (1986). Efectos psicológicos de la represión política. II. In D.R. Kordon, L.I. Edelman & Equipo de Asistencia Psicológica de Madres de Plaza de Mayo, *Efectos psicológicos de la represión política*. Buenos Aires, Sudamericana Planeta, pp. 149–178.

Korrelboom, C.W., Kernkamp, J.H.B., Eelen, P., Hoogduin, C.A.L. & Duivenvorden, H.J. (1989). *Panic and UCS-revaluation*. Presentation held at the first European Congress of Psychology, Amsterdam.

Kortmann, F. (1986). *Problemen in transculturele communicatie*. Assen, Van Gorcum.

Kramer, M., Schoen, L.S. & Kinney, L. (1987). Nightmares in Vietnam veterans. *Journal of The American Academy of Psychoanalysis*, **15**, 67–81.

Krystal, H. (1984). Psychoanalytic views on human emotional damage. In B.A. van der Kolk (ed.), *Post-traumatic Stress Disorder: Psychological and Biological Sequelae*. Washington DC, American Psychiatric Press, pp. 2–28.

Krystal, H. (1987). Speech to the third annual meeting of the Society for Traumatic Studies, Baltimore, 25 October.

Lansen, J. (1996). *Was tus 'es' mit uns*. In S. Graessner, N. Gurris & C. Pross (eds), *Folter*. München, Verlag C.H. Beck.

Lansky, M.R. & Bley, C.R. (1995). *Posttraumatic nightmares: psychodynamic explorations*. Hillsdale, NJ: Analytic Press.

Laufer, R.S., Brett, E.A. & Gallops, M.S. (1985). Symptom patterns associated with posttraumatic stress disorders among Vietnam veterans exposed to war trauma. *American Journal of Psychiatry*, **142**, 1304–1311.

Lavelle, J. (1987). Contribution to a panel on 'The counter transference of torture and trauma' during the third annual meeting of the Society for Traumatic Studies, Baltimore, 25 October.

Lee, E. & Lu, F. (1989). Assessment and treatment of Asian-American survivors of mass violence. *Journal of Traumatic Stress*, **2**, 93–120.

L'Hoste, M. (1986). La desaparición: effectos psicosociales en Madres. In D.R. Kordon & L.I. Edelman, *Efectos psicológicos de la represión política*, Buenos Aires, Sudamericana Planeta, pp. 105–112.

Lin, K.M., Masuda, M, & Tazuma, L. (1982). Problems of Vietnamese refugees in the United States. In R.C. Nann (ed.), *Uprooting and surviving*, Dordrecht, D. Reidel Publishing, pp. 11–24.

Lindy, J.D. (1988). *Vietnam, a Casebook*. New York, Brunner/Mazel.

Lira, E. (1986). Personal communication.

Lira, E. & Weinstein, E. (1986). *La tortura sexual*. Ponencia para el seminario 'Consecuencias de la represión en el Cono Sur: sus efectos médicos, psicológicos y sociales'. Montevideo, Uruguay, 1986.

Littlewood, R. (1992). How universal is something we call therapy? In J. Kareem & R. Littlewood, *Intercultural Therapy*. London, Blackwell Science, pp. 38–56.

Lyons, J.A. & Keane, T.M. (1989). Implosive therapy for the treatment of combat-related PTSD. *Journal of Traumatic Stress*, **2**, 137–152.

Malan, D.H. (1979). *Individual Psychotherapy and the Science of Psychodynamics*. London, Butterworth.

Marx, E. (1990). The social world of refugees: a conceptual framework. *Journal of Refugee Studies*, **3**, 189–203.

Maslach, C. & Jackson, S.E. (1986). *Maslach Burnout Inventory: Manual* (2nd edition). Palo Alto, CA: Consulting Psychologists Press.

McCann, L. & Pearlman, L.A. (1990). Vicarious traumatization: a framework for understanding the psychological effects of working with victims. *Journal of Traumatic Stress*, **3**, 131–149.

McCormick, R.A., Taber, J.I., Kruedelbach, N. (1989). The relationship between attributional style and post traumatic stress disorder in addicted patients. *Journal of Traumatic Stress*, **2**, 477–487.

Meichenbaum, D. (1979). *Cognitive-Behaviour Modification—an integrative approach*. New York, Plenum Press.

Mernissi, F. (1985). *Achter de sluier. De islam en de strijd der sexen*. Amsterdam, Nijgh en van Ditmar.

Mikulas, W.L. (1978). For noble truth of Buddhism related to behaviour therapy. *Psychological Record*, **28**, 59–67.

Miller, P.M., Surtees, P.G., Kreitman, J.G., Ingham, J.G. & Sashidharan, S.P. (1985). Maladaptive coping reactions to stress; a study of illness inception. *Journal of Nervous and Mental Disease*, **173**, 707–716.

Minuchin, S. & Fishman, H.C. (1981). *Family Therapy Technics*. Cambridge, MA, Harvard.

Mollica, R.F. (1987). The trauma story: the psychiatric care of refugee survivors of torture. In F.M. Ochberg (ed.), *Post-traumatic Therapy and Victims of Violence*. New York, Brunner/Mazel.

Mollica, R. F. & Son, L. (1988). Cultural dimensions in the evaluation and treatment of sexual trauma: an overview. Unpublished study.

Mollica, R.F., Wyshak, G. & Lavell, I. (1987a). The psychosocial impact of the war trauma in Southeast Asian refugees. *American Journal of Psychiatry*, **144**, 1567–1572.

Mollica, R.F., Wyshak, G., De Marneffe, D. Khuon, F. & Lavelle, J. (1987b). Indochinese versions of the Hopkins Symptom Checklist -25: a screening instrument for the psychiatric care of refugees. *American Journal of Psychiatry*, **144**, 497–500.

Mollica, R.F., Wyshak, G., Lavelle, J., Truong, T., Tor, S. & Yang, T. (1990). Assessing symptom change in Southeast Asian refugee survivors of mass violence and torture. *American Journal of Psychiatry*, **147**, 83–88.

Monelli, C. (1982). Soledad y el vacío: un caso de psicoterapia con un familiar de ejecutado. Santiago, unpublished study.

Montessori, M.M. (1987). Problemen rond de indicatiestelling voor psychotherapie bij ernstig getraumatiseerden. *Icodo-info*, **4**, 30–39.

Mueser, K.T. & Butler, R.W. (1987). Auditory hallucinations in combat-related post traumatic stress disorder. *American Journal of Psychiatry*, **144**, 299–302.

Murdock, G.P. (1965). *Social Structure*. New York, Macmillan.

Ochberg, F.M. (1988). Post-traumatic therapy and victims of violence. In F.M. Ochberg (ed.), *Post-traumatic Therapy and Victims of Violence*. New York, Brunner/Mazel, pp. 3–19.

Oei, T.I. (1987). Psychisch dysfunctioneren en de rol van sociale steun. *Nederlands Tijdschrift voor de Psychologie*, **42**, 55–61.

Olness, K.N. (1986). On 'Reflections on caring for Indochinese children and youths'. *Developmental and Behavioural Pediatrics*, **7**, 129–130.

Op den Velde, W. (1989). Posttraumatische stress-stoornissen. *Nederlands Tijdschrift voor Geneeskunde*, **133**, 1586–1593.

Parry, G. & Shapiro, D.A. (1986). Social support and life events in working-class women. *Archives of General Psychiatry*, **43**, 315–323.

Pederson, P.B. (1981) The cultural inclusiveness of counselling. In P.B. Pederson, J.G. Draguns, W.J. Lonner & J.E. Trimble (eds), *Counselling across Cultures* (revised and expanded edition). Honolulu, University Press of Hawaii, 22–58.

Pellegrini, D. (1985). Training in social problem-solving. In M. Rutter & L. Hersov (eds), *Child and Adolescent Psychiatry: Modern Approaches* (2nd edition). Oxford, Blackwell, pp. 839–850.

Pennebaker, J.W. & Klihr Beall, S. (1986). Confronting a traumatic event: toward an understanding of inhibition and disease. *Journal of Abnormal Psychology*, **95**, 274–281.

Pentz-Moller, V., Hermansen,A., Bentsen, E. & Knudsen, I.H. (1988). *Interpretation in the Rehabilitation of Torture Victims at the RCT*. Copenhagen, The International Research and Rehabilitation Centre for Torture Victims.

Perelberg, R.J. (1992). Familiar and unfamiliar types of family structure: towards a conceptual framework. In J. Kareem & R. Littlewood *Intercultural Therapy*. London, Blackwell Science, pp. 112–132.

Perren-Klinger, G. (1991). Confrontation as a tool in the therapy of tortured clients. Paper presented at the XIth World Congress for Sexology. Amsterdam, 18–22 June 1991.

Peterson, C. & Seligman, M.E.P. (1984). Causal explanations as a risk factor for depression: theory and evidence. *Psychological Review*, **91**, 347–374.

Piaget, J. (1973). The affective unconscious and the cognitive unconscious. *Journal of the American Psychoanalytic Association*, **21**, 249–261.

Pincus, L. & Dare, C. (1978). *Secrets in the family*. London, Faber & Faber.

Pope, B. & Siegman, A.W. (1972). Relationship and verbal behaviour in the initial interview. In A.W. Siegman & B. Pope (eds), *Studies in Dyadic Communication*. New York, Pergamon Press, pp. 69–89.

Price, J. (1975). Foreign language interpreting in psychiatric practice. *Australian and New Zealand Journal of Psychiatry*, **9**, 263–267.

Puget, J. (1986). Psicoanalizar en estado de amenaza. Buenos Aires, unpublished study.

Putsch, R.W. (1985). Cross-cultural communication. The special case of interpreters in health care. *JAMA*, **254**, 3344–3348.

Rachman, S.J. (1979). The concept of required helpfulness. *Behaviour Research and Therapy*, **17**, 1–16.

Reinoso, D.G. (1985). El niño bajo el terror de estado. Buenos Aires, unpublished study.

Rohlof, H. & Jasperse, A. (1996). Gedwongen migratie, verlies en cultuur. *Medische Antropologie*, **8**, 78–86.

Rohlof, J.G.B.M. (1997). *Psychopharmacological Treatment of Traumatized Refugees.* Utrecht, Stichting Pharos.

Roth, S. & Lebowitz, L. (1988). The experience of sexual trauma. *Journal of Traumatic Stress,* **1,** 79–107.

Roth, S. & Newman, E. (1990). The process of coping with sexual trauma. *Journal of Traumatic Stress,* **4,** 279–297.

Runia, E. (1986). Ruth Cohen over tegenoverdracht. *Tijdschrift voor Psychotherapie,* **12,** 271–278.

Rutter, M. (1987). The role of cognition in child development and disorder. *British Journal of Medical Psychology,* **60,** 1–16.

Sabin, J.E. (1975). Translating despair. *American Journal of Psychiatry,* **132,** 197–199.

Santini, I. (1985a). *A propósito de la identidad en el exílio y el retorno.* Amsterdam, Social Psychiatric Centre for Refugees.

Santini, I. (1985b). *Experiencia de un grupo de jóvenes en el exílio.* Amsterdam, Social Psychiatric Centre for Refugees.

Santini, I. (1986a). *Retornar no solo es volver, sino también irse (análisis de la decisión).* Amsterdam, Social Psychiatric Centre for Refugees.

Santini, I. (1986b). *Post Traumatic Stress Disorder, Tratamiento corto.* Amsterdam, Social Psychiatric Centre for Refugees.

Santini, I. (1987). *Hasta puedo soñar lindo.* Amsterdam, Social Psychiatric Centre for Refugees.

Santini, I. (1989). *Trauma tratamiento y recuperación. Tratamiento de larga duración.* Amsterdam, Social Psychiatric Centre for Refugees.

Santini, I. & Escardo, M. (1981). *Onderdrukking en ballingschap van kinderen en adolescenten.* Amsterdam, Social Psychiatric Centre for Refugees.

Sarrel, P.M. & Masters, W.H. (1982) Sexual molestation of men by women. *Archives of Sexual Behavior,* **11,** 117–131.

Scaturo, J.D. & Hayman, P.M. (1992) The impact of trauma across the family life cycle: clinical observations. *Journal of Traumatic Stress,* **5,** 273–288.

Schoepf, J. (1981). Ungewohnliche Entzugssymptome nach Benzodiazepin-langzeitbehandlungen. *Der Nervenartz,* **15,** 282–292.

Schumacher, W. (1982). Ueber coping-Verhalten bei schwerer NS-Verfolgung (Ueberleben im Vernichtungslager). In R. Berna-Glanz & P. Dreyfuss (eds), *Trauma, Konflikt, Deckerinnerung.* Frankfurt, Fromann Holzboog Verlag, pp. 121–144.

Schwartz, H.J. (ed.) (1984a). *Psychotherapy of the Combat Veteran.* Lancaster, UK, MTP Press.

Schwartz, H.J. (1984b). Conscious guilt and unconscious guilt in patients with traumatic neurosis. *American Journal of Psychiatry,* **141,** 1638–1639.

Schwartz, L.S. (1990). A biopsychosocial treatment approach to post-traumatic stress disorder. *Journal of Traumatic Stress,* **3,** 221–238.

Seifert, K.L. & Hoffnung, R.J. (1987). *Child and Adolescent Development.* Boston, Houghton Mifflin.

Seligman, M. (1975). *Helplessness: on Depression, Development and Death.* San Francisco, Freeman.

Seligman, M.E.P., Maier, S.F. & Geer, J. (1968). The alleviation of learned helplessness in a dog. *Journal of Abnormal Psychology,* **73**, 256–262.

Shapiro, R.B. (1984). Transference, countertransference and the Vietnam veteran. In H.J. Schwartz (ed) *Psychotherapy of the Combat Veteran.* Lancaster, UK, MTP Press, pp. 85–102.

Silver, J.M., Sandberg, D.P. & Hales, R.E. (1990). New approaches in pharmacotherapy of Posttraumatic Stress Disorder. *Journal of Clinical Psychiatry,* **51**, 33–38.

Silver, R.L. & Wortman, C.B. (1980). Coping with undesirable life events. In J. Gorber & E.P. Seligman, *Human helplessness. Theory and application.* New York, Academic Press, pp. 279–340.

Simons, A.D., Murphy, G.E., Levine, J.L. & Wetzel, R.D. (1986). Cognitive therapy and pharmacotherapy for depression. Sustained improvement over a year. *Archives of General Psychiatry,* **43**, 43–48.

Sluzki, C.E. (1990). Semantic and somatic effects of political repression in a family seeking therapy. *Family Process,* **29**, 131–143.

Solursh, L.P. (1989). Combat Addiction: overview and implications in symptom maintenance and treatment planning. *Journal of Traumatic Stress,* **2**, 451–662

Somasundaran, D.J. (1993). Psychiatric morbidity due to war in Northern Sri Lanka. In J.P. Wilson & B. Raphael, *International Handbook of Traumatic Stress Syndromes.* New York, Plenum Press, pp. 333–348

Somnier, F.E. & Genefke, I.K. (1986). Psychotherapy for victims of torture. *British Journal of Psychiatry,* **141**, 1628–1639.

Southwick, S.M. & Yehuda, R. (1993). The interaction between pharmacotherapy and psychotherapy in the treatment of posttraumatic stress disorder. *American Journal of Psychotherapy,* **47**, 404–410.

Spiegel, D. (1981). Vietnam grief work using hypnosis. *American Journal of Clinical Hypnosis,* **24**, 33–40.

Spolyar, L. (1974). The grieving process in MIA wives. In H.I. McCubbin (ed.), *Family Separation and Reunion: Families of Prisoners of War and Servicemen Missing in Action.* Washington DC, Center for Prisoners of War Studies, Naval Health Research Center, pp. 77–85.

Srinivasa, D.K. & Trivedi, S. (1982). Knowledge and attitude of mental diseases in a rural community of South India. *Social Science and Medicine,* **16**, 1635–1639.

Stierlin, H., Ruecker-Embden, I., Wetzel, N. & Wirsching, M. (1980). *The First Interview with the Family.* New York, Brunner/Mazel.

Strunz, F. (1987). Ätiologie und Therapie der Alptraume. *Fortschritte der Neurologie Psychiatrie,* **55**, 306–321.

Sue, D. & Sue, S. (1987). Cultural factors in the clinical assessment of Asian Americans. *Journal of Consulting and Clinical Psychology,* **55**, 479–487.

Sundberg, N.D. (1981). Research and research hypotheses about effectiveness in intercultural counselling. In P.B. Pederson, J.G. Draguns, W.J. Lonner & J.E. Trimble (eds), *Counselling across Cultures, revised and expanded edition.* Honolulu, University Press of Hawaii, pp. 304–342.

Swartz, L. (1987). Transcultural psychiatry in South Africa. Part II. Cross cultural issues in mental health practice. *Transcultural Psychiatric Research Review*, **24**, 5–30.

Tailor, S.E., Wood, J.V. & Lichtman, R.R. (1983). It could be worse: selective evaluation as a response to victimization. *Journal of Social Issues*, **39**, 19–40.

Teter, H., Mauldin, D., Nhol, S., Conkin, D. & Sum, S. (1987). *Treatment through Training: a Cambodian Mental Health Workshop.* San Francisco, International Institute of San Francisco.

Thompson, J. (1989). Torture by tradition. *Nursing Times*, **885**, 16–17.

Tiedemann, J. (1987). Angst in de therapeutische relatie. *ICODO-info*, **4**(1), 27–35.

Truong, T. D. (1987). *Contribution to a panel on 'The countertransference of torture and trauma'.* The third annual meeting of the Society for Traumatic Studies, Baltimore, 25 October.

Tsui, A.M. (1985). Psychotherapeutic considerations in sexual counselling for Asian immigrants. *Psychotherapy*, **22**, 357–362.

Tsui, P. & Schultz, G.L. (1985). Failure of rapport: why psychotherapeutic engagement fails in the treatment of Asian clients. *American Journal of Orthopsychiatry*, **55**, 561–569.

Tuiavii (1985). *De Papalagi.* Weesp, Heureka.

Tuk, B. (1988). Vietnamese jongeren in Nederland. *Jeugd en samenleving*, **18**, 243–254.

Tyhurst, J.S. (1951). Individual reactions to community disaster. The natural history of psychiatric phenomena. *American Journal of Psychiatry*, **1071**, 764–769.

University Teachers for Human Rights (1989). *Report no. 3: January–August 1989.* Jaffna, Sri Lanka.

Van de Lande, J. (1980). Gezinsgeheimen, *Maandblad Geestelijke Volksgezondheid*, **36**, 1071–1072.

Van de Put, W. (1997). Self, time amd Buddhism in Cambodia: some clinical implications. Phnom Penh, IPSER Community Mental Health Program.

Van der Kolk, B. (1985). Adolescent vulnerability to posttraumatic stress disorder. *Psychiatry*, **48**, 365–370.

Van der Kolk, B. (1988). The traumaspectrum: the interaction of biological and social events in the genesis of the trauma response. *Journal of Traumatic Stress*, **1**, 273–290

Van der Kolk, B., Greenberg, M., Boyd, H. & Kristal, J. (1985a). Inescapable shock, neurotransmitters, and addiction to trauma: toward a psychobiology of post traumatic stress. *Biological Psychiatry*, **20**, 314–325.

Van der Kolk, B., Boyd, H., Krystal, J. & Greenberg, M. (1985b). Post traumatic stress disorder as a biologically based disorder: implications of the animal model of inescapable shock. In B.A. Van der Kolk (ed.), *Post Traumatic Stress Disorder: Psychological and Biological Sequelae*. Washington DC, American Psychiatric Press.

Van der Ploeg, H.M. & Vis, J. (eds) (1989). *Burnout en werkstress: ieders verantwoordelijkheid*. Amsterdam, Swets & Zeitlinger.

Van der Ploeg, H.M., Van Leeuwen, J.J. & Kwee, M.G.T. (1990). Burnout among Dutch psychotherapists. *Psychological Reports*, **67**, 107–112.

Van der Veer, G. (1989). *Dilemma's bij de hulpverlening aan suicidale asielzoekers*. *ICODO info*, **6**, 9–21.

Van Ree, F. (1987). De blinde vlekken van de therapeut en joodse oorlogsslachtoffers. In R. Beunderman & J. Dane (eds), *Kinderen van de oorlog*, Utrecht, ICODO, pp. 73–94.

Viñar, M. (1985). *Trauma psíquico, trauma social?* Santiago, FASIC.

Vladár Rivero, V.M. (1986). De Latijnsamerikaanse vluchtelingen. In R.E. Offerman (ed.), *Agressie, door psychiaters bezien*. Lisse, Swets & Zeitlinger, pp. 123–135.

Vladár Rivero, V.M. (1989). *Diagnostic Evaluation and Indications for Treatment with Victims of Organized Violence*. Amsterdam, Social Psychiatric Centre for Refugees.

Vladár Rivero, V.M. (1991). Sexual torture, consequences for psychological health. Paper presented at the 10th World Congress on Sexuology. Amsterdam, SPD for Refugees.

Vladár Rivero, V. M. (1992). The use of psychotropic medication. In G. Van Der Veer, *Counselling and Therapy with Refugees. Psychological Problems of Victims of War, Torture and Repression*. (With contributions of Victor Vladár Rivero and Mia Groenenberg). New York, Wiley.

Vontress, C. E. (1981). Racial and ethnic barriers in counselling. In P.B. Pederson, J.G. Draguns, W.J. Lonner & J.E. Trimble (eds), *Counselling across Cultures* (revised and expanded edition). Honolulu, University Press of Hawaii, pp. 87–107.

Walker, L.J. (1989). A longitudinal study of moral reasoning. *Child Development*, **55**, 677–691.

Watzlawick, P., Beauvin, A.B. & Jackson, D. (1967). *Pragmatics of Human Communication*. New York, Norton.

Weinstein, E. & Ortic, E. (1985). Estudio psicosocial de 25 familias retornadas. In *Escritos sobre exilio y retorno*, pp. 47–60. Santiago, FASIC.

Werner, E.E. (1989). High-risk children in young adulthood: a longitudinal study from birth to 32 years. *American Journal of Orthopsychiatry*, **59**, 72–81.

Westermeyer, J. (1989). Cross-cultural care for PTSD: research, training, and service needs for the future. *Journal of Traumatic Stress*, **2**, 515–536.

Wilson, J.P. & Lindy, J.D. (eds) (1994). Empathic strain and countertransference. In *Countertransference in the Treatment of PTSD*. New York, Guilford
Press, pp. 5–30.

Winston, A., Pinsker, H. & McCullough, L. (1986). A review of supportive psychotherapy. *Hospital and Community Psychiatry*, **337**, 1105–1113.

World Health Organization (1992). *International Statistical Classification of
Diseases and Related Health Problems: Tenth Revision*. Geneva, WHO.

Wortman, C.B. (1983). Coping and victimization: conclusions and implications for future research. *Journal of Social Issues*, **29**, 195–221.

Wren, C.S. (1986). Hulp aan slachtoffers van marteling. Opnieuw leren leven.
Intermediar, **43**, 19–27.

Yuksel, S. (1991). Therapy of sexual torture. Paper presented at the XI World
Sexology Congress, Amsterdam, 18–22 June 1991.

Author Index

Subject Index

Related titles of interest from Wiley...

Cross-Cultural Practice
Assessment, Treatment and Training
Sharon-Ann GoPaul McNicol and Janet Rochelle Brice-Baker

A hands-on guide to assessing and treatment immigrants and individuals
from different ethnic backgrounds using a "multicultural, multisystems,
multimodal" approach.

0-471-14849-0   228pp   1997   Hardback

The Influence of Race and Racial Identity in Psychotherapy
Towards a Racially Inclusive Model
Robert T. Carter

Presents a rigorous conceptual framework that affords clinicians a deeper
awareness of how racial issues affect their dealings with patients and a
means of integrating that knowledge into their practices.

0-471-24533-X   320pp   1998   Paperback

Communication and Culture
A Guide for Practice
Gynthia Gallois and Victor Callan

Introduces the basic principles of communication within and across
cultures and includes many everyday examples to aid the development of
knowledge and skills needed to interact with people of different cultures.

0-471-96622-3   184pp   1997   Paperback

Culture and Health
Malcolm MacLachlan

Explores the fascinating interplay between culture and health to help
students and clinicians think through the practical implications of working
with people from different cultures.

0-471-96626-6   332pp   1997   Paperback